KW-482-236

# THE INCORPORATED TRADES OF EDINBURGH

*f 1*

# The Incorporated Trades Of Edinburgh With An Introductory Chapter On The Rise And Progress Of Municipal Government In Scotland

## James Colston

**Nabu Public Domain Reprints:**

You are holding a reproduction of an original work published before 1923 that is in the public domain in the United States of America, and possibly other countries. You may freely copy and distribute this work as no entity (individual or corporate) has a copyright on the body of the work. This book may contain prior copyright references, and library stamps (as most of these works were scanned from library copies). These have been scanned and retained as part of the historical artifact.

This book may have occasional imperfections such as missing or blurred pages, poor pictures, errant marks, etc. that were either part of the original artifact, or were introduced by the scanning process. We believe this work is culturally important, and despite the imperfections, have elected to bring it back into print as part of our continuing commitment to the preservation of printed works worldwide. We appreciate your understanding of the imperfections in the preservation process, and hope you enjoy this valuable book.

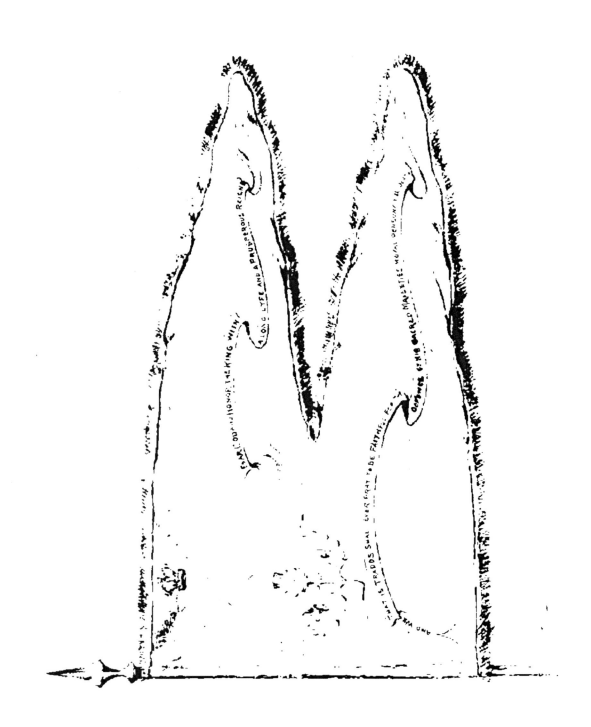

# The Incorporated Trades of Edinburgh

WITH

## AN INTRODUCTORY CHAPTER

ON

## *The Rise and Progress of Municipal Government in Scotland*

BY

## JAMES COLSTON

AUTHOR OF "THE GUILDRY OF EDINBURGH—IS IT AN INCORPORATION?" "THE
EDINBURGH AND DISTRICT WATER SUPPLY—A HISTORICAL SKETCH;"
"HISTORY OF THE SCOTT MONUMENT;" ETC., ETC.

Edinburgh

PRINTED BY COLSTON & COMPANY
AND SOLD BY
RICHARD CAMERON, WILLIAM BROWN, ANDREW ELLIOT
AND ALL BOOKSELLERS
MDCCCXCI.

HD
5462
.E3
C72

IMPRESSION:—

THREE HUNDRED COPIES.

*This Copy is No.* 210

1171528 - 176

TO THE

Right Hon. ARCHIBALD-PHILIP PRIMROSE,

LL.D., F.R.S.,

EARL OF ROSEBERY,

Lord-Lieutenant of the Counties of Mid-Lothian and Linlithgow,

ETC., ETC.,

This Volume

IS

BY PERMISSION MOST RESPECTFULLY

Dedicated.

# PREFACE.

EVERAL years ago, I was requested by various leading Members of the Convenery, to write a History of the Incorporated Trades of Edinburgh. I then told these gentlemen that my spare time was fully occupied; but that, when opportunity permitted, I would have pleasure in gathering up, so far as I was able, everything I could find interesting regarding these ancient Trades or Arts Combinations in the city. This I have made it my endeavour to do in the volume now submitted.

It cannot fail to be matter of great regret that the Minute-Books of most of these Incorporations have been either lost or destroyed. This fact will at once account for the comparative paucity of information observable in the notices of several of the Incorporations in comparison with others. An attempt has been made in the work to bring together all the various charters granted by the Town Council from time to time to these bodies; and a study of these is of itself interesting, as partly serving to illustrate the state of burgensic life, and of society generally, in the several periods to which they relate. This, however, would have been done in a much more interesting way, had many valuable relics of our civic history, which were contained in the Minute-Books, been still in preservation.

It may be worthy of note, that the Minutes of the Gild were originally written in mediæval Latin; and that important deeds of the Gild, as well as of the Town Council, were composed and extended in the same language. As an illustration of this, it may be observed, that a Deed of Appointment of a Town Clerk is extended in the Town's Minutes in Latin. Latin was at that time the language of the Church and the learned; and was more likely to be read and understood by the Members of other nationalities, than would have been the case had the Scottish or English language been made use of in these records or deeds.

Reference also may be made to the apparently quaint mode of spelling to be found in those charters, and the notable want of uniformity in the orthography of the period. The same words are sometimes spelt in a variety of ways in the same charters. This anomaly is not to be wondered at. Proficiency in spelling is regulated chiefly by what may be called the "Memory of the Eye." Mere scholarship, however exact, will not avail much in the art of spelling. It is further to be borne in mind that many of the charters were composed and written at a time when there was little or no opportunity for reading on the part of the general public. They had, indeed, nothing to read except the mottoes or short passages of Scripture which occasionally were placed as daily monitors over the doorways or on the fronts of some of the buildings of the period. Although the art of printing was introduced into England by Caxton in 1474, it was not until 1507 that the first printing press was established in Edinburgh, by Walter Chepman and Andro Myllar, who obtained from King James IV. a royal privilege for their work. Books, therefore, must have been rare for a long period after this. And it is chiefly by our daily practice of reading, that we are enabled to become familiar with the usual form in which words are presented to the eye, either in writing or in print.

In the "Introductory Chapter," an attempt has been made to give a brief account of the Rise and Progress of Municipal Government, chiefly with the view of showing the laudable desire which existed among the Crafts Incorporations, to take their own fair share in the civic management and control. Although they did not find much encouragement from either the Crown and Parliament on the one hand, or the Merchant Class on the other, they were always successful in re-asserting from time to time their right to be represented in the Common Council of the Burgh. They believed in popular election; and the list they sent up to the Town Council as recommended by them was always prepared on this principle. It was otherwise with the Merchant Burgesses. They had no voice in the choice of Town Councillors. The Merchant Councillors were appointed on the principle of self-election.

In the volume there appears a list of the various Conveners
of Trades from the institution of the office down to the present
time, as well as a Historic Account of the Trades Maiden Hospital,
instituted chiefly by the Crafts Incorporations; while in the Appendix will be found a notice of the two Incorporations which are
not represented in the Convenery, as well as a List of the Minor
Arts or Crafts.

It was deemed expedient to reproduce the "History of the
Blue Blanket, by Alexander Pennecuik." That work is now becoming very scarce; but it has always been looked upon by the
Craftsmen with considerable favour. Little is known regarding its
author, except what is told on the title page, that he was a
burgess and gild brother of the Town. In 1720, he published a
small volume of Poetry called "Streams from Helicon," and in 1726,
he produced another entitled "Flowers from Parnassus." He seems to
have been an ingenious writer, with small pecuniary resources; and
common report gives it forth that he led a somewhat "dissipated
and irregular" life. Claudero (Wilson) the Town's Rhymer, in his
Poem, "Farewell to the Muses and Auld Reikie," with a considerable amount of fellow-feeling thus describes Pennecuik's end :—

> To shew the fate of Pennecuik,
> Who starving died in turnpike neuk ;
> Though sweet he sang with wit and sense
> He like poor Claud was short of pence.

How very similar was the fate of poor Desagulier, the engineer who brought a supply of "sweet water" from the country into Edinburgh. He died at the Bedford Coffee House, Covent Garden, London, and was buried in the adjacent ground belonging to the Savoy.

> Can Britain still permit the weeping muse to tell
> How poor neglected *Desagulier* fell,
> How he who taught two gracious Kings to view,
> All Boyle ennobled, and all Bacon knew,
> Died in a cell, without a friend to save,
> Without a guinea, and without a grave.

Although Pennecuik wrote in a highly stilted style, and although many may be apt to discredit his account of the "Blue Blanket," and rather concur with Maitland as to its origin, I frankly confess that, whatever were the sources of the author's information otherwise, I have found his knowledge of his subject generally accurate.

The Right Hon. the Earl of Rosebery has kindly agreed to allow this volume to be dedicated to him. I consider it my duty here to record my obligations to His Lordship, whose ancestors in the Imperial Parliament always supported the Trades Incorporations in their demand for free and popular election in our Municipal Institutions.

I have to thank the editor of the *Scotsman* newspaper for his insertion in that most influential journal of the Papers regarding most of the Incorporations. By means of this, I have been enabled to correct some errors into which I fell, from not having had at the time sufficient information, or from the sources of my information being at fault.

I acknowledge my indebtedness to the various Deacons and Clerks of the Incorporations for their kindness in furnishing me with such information as was available for my purpose. The Works on which I had to depend chiefly were "Maitland's History of Edinburgh," 1753; "Report by the Royal Commissioners on Municipal Institutions," presented to both Houses of Parliament in 1835; and the volumes of Records of the City of Edinburgh, published by the Scottish Burgh Records Society, 1869–82.

Attached to each of the Chapters on the several Incorporations will be found the Seal or Coat of Arms of the various bodies.

Mr T. Lauder Sawers; artist, kindly contributes the engraving of the Blue Blanket, and of the buildings of the Trades Maiden Hospital, past and present.

J. C.

23 REGENT TERRACE,
EDINBURGH, *October* 12, 1891.

# CONTENTS.

———◆———

# *INTRODUCTORY CHAPTER.*

---

## CONCERNING MUNICIPAL GOVERNMENT IN SCOTLAND, AND THE INCORPORATED TRADES.

BEFORE the establishment of a firm and vigorous Government in Scotland, the inhabitants of populous places, villages, or hamlets were usually under the protection of some royal or baronial castle. The country was a feudal kingdom, split up into many small principalities, almost independent, and held together by a feeble and nearly imperceptible bond of union. The Monarch was not only stripped of a great part of his authority, but his revenues must have suffered considerably by the grasping nature of the nobles. The want of great cities contributed largely to increase the power of the baronial sway and weaken the Throne. The division of the country into clans conduced to a similar end. The general bulk of the people, in those times, might be said to be in a state of absolute villanage or serfdom, having no property of their own, and they were entirely dependent upon the will and caprice of the Lord of the Soil. Even the greatest amount of industry on their part, and the comparatively little traffic in the way of business which they were able to conduct, by barter or otherwise, was frequently subjected to heavy burdens, either on the part of the Crown on the one hand, or the overlord on the other. This state of matters, however, was not destined

c

to endure. In fact, the very rigorous nature of the exactions which were imposed tended ultimately to work out the cure. The Crown, as well as many of those local magnates, began, even from a purely selfish point of view, to take a greater interest in the growing prosperity of their vassals; and, strange to say, the school of political economy which seemed to prevail—the rectifier of all their wrongs—was what may be termed the exercise of Exclusive Privilege.

The late Professor Cosmo Innes, in a preface which he wrote for one of the volumes of the Scottish Burgh Records Society, entitled,—"Ancient Laws and Customs of the Burghs of Scotland," p. xxxii., thus writes:—"With the twelfth century rose the general desire, through France and over Europe, to shake off the oppression of the feudal lords, and to restore or establish some municipal rights and freedom in towns,—a share at least in the choice of their own magistrates, and in administering their property and affairs. The people of the cities entered vehemently into the struggle for independence; swore mutual support and alliance; and within each town established for their common affairs, *guilds, communes, conjurations*, which drew upon them the censure of the early monkish writers, who were mostly good Tories,—*communis, novum ac pessimum nomen*, says Abbot Guibert de Nogent, writing in the twelfth century."

In Scotland, in the formation of these associations, or gilds, for protecting trade, the towns belonging to the Crown seem to have taken the foremost part. These associations of traders were eventually recognised by, and received the direct sanction of, the Crown, who fostered them by granting them protection from outside injury and oppression. They were recognised as alone having the right to trade within a certain territorial area, subject to such regulations, and the imposition of such tolls, duties, maills, or customs, as might be mutually agreed upon.

These associations of traders were, therefore, a privileged class of dealers within the area of their respective communities, and became known under the name of *hanses* and *gilds*. They were, no doubt, somewhat analogous to the hanses and gilds which existed in those days in most of the continental countries of Europe. They were the first beginning or development of that important system of municipal control and power, in the larger and more comprehensive organisation, which the Gilds or Gildry of large cities and towns so long exercised for the good of the people of Scotland. Indeed they may be said to have been the first development of what is now known as "the Third Estate of the Realm."

To what period, in the history of Scotland, the first erection of Royal Burghs can be traced, it is impossible now to prove. Their institution has not in general been dated prior to the beginning of the twelfth century. The generally accepted idea is that David I., who reigned between 1123 and 1153, was their chief promoter, if not their first originator. It is right, however, to state that, down to the present time, there has not been produced any direct charter of erection granted by that Monarch in favour of any royal burgh; nevertheless, there are to be found frequent references to particular burghs in the chartularies of religious houses granted by him. His great weakness seemed to consist in a desire to endow Religious Houses, which led to the observation that he was "a sair Saunct for a crown."

Maitland, in his History of Edinburgh (p. 7), says that King David styles Edinburgh *meo burgo*. He also adds, "David made laws at his town of New-castle-upon-Tyne, and his charters are still extant in several Scottish burghs. In all probability he erected Edinburgh into a Royal Burgh." Of such erection, however, he adduces no direct evidence. He merely asserts the fact unsupported by any proof. On the other hand, if the ancient capitulary, styled *Leges et Consuetudines Burgorum Scotiæ*, or any considerable portion of it be, as has been supposed, the work of King David I., then there must have existed, even prior to his reign, and contrary to the generally accepted opinion, Royal Burghs, somewhat similar in constitution and privileges to those which were afterwards established.

Referring to these grants to religious houses, and the allusion to Royal Burghs in the charters, the following examples may be cited, viz. :—

To the Abbot and Friars of Dunfermline, David I. granted "unum plenarium toftum in burgo meo de Hadingtun—libere et quiete ab omni consuetudine et servicio sicut predictus Abbas tenet aliquod toftum melius et liberius per burga mea." To the same monastery he gave, by an instrument addressed "Prepositis de Perth,"—"unum toftum in meo burgo de Perth quietum de omnibus rebus;" and by another document,—"unam mansuram in burgo meo de Dunfermelin liberam et quietam, et aliam, in burgo meo in Strivelin, et aliam in burgo meo de Perth, et aliam in burgo meo de Edenesburgh." And to the priory of Urquhart, a cell of Dunfermline,— "viginti solidos singulis annis ad vestimenta eorum de firma burgi mei et aquarum de Elgin."

Again, when David I. founded the Abbey of Holyrood, he granted by charter in favour of its Canons, "the power to erect the burgh of Canongate between the Church and the Toune." It is the oldest existing charter in the Edinburgh repositories, in favour of the Abbot and Convent of Holy Rood, and runs thus :—Quadraginta solidos de *meo burgo de Edwynesburgh* singulis annis et redditum centum solidorum singulis annis ad indumenta canonicorum de cano meo de Perth, et hoc de primis navibus que negociationis causa veniunt ad Perth ; et si forte non venerint, concedo prefate ecclesie de *meo redditu de Edwynesburg* quadraginta solidos," etc., "Et unum toftum in *burgo meo de Edwynesburg* liberum et quietum ab omni consuetudine et exactione." "Concedo etiam eis herbergare quoddam burgum inter eandem ecclesiam *et meum burgum;* et concedo ut burgenses eorum habeant communem (libertatem) vendendi et emendi res suas venales in *foro meo* libere et absque calumnia et consuetudine, sicut *mei proprii burgenses,*" etc.

It will be apparent that the language of this charter seems not quite clear. By several writers it has been supposed to indicate the existence of Edinburgh at that time as a burgh in demesne rather than as a royal burgh. The distinction, it must be confessed, is not very easily traced. It appears evident, however, that although not incorporated, the burgesses of the King had at least certain privileges of traffic and merchandise within the burgh, and that certain tolls and customs were exacted—besides maills for their several *tofts* or possessions holden off the Crown. The erection of the burgh of Canongate was one of regality. It was thus one of the earliest examples of these local authorities which were afterwards so well known in Scotland.

The difference between a Royal and other Burghs in Scotland seemed to consist in the former possessing or occupying property, for the good of the community, and which property belonged to the Crown. The late Lord Kames thus describes a Royal Burgh in Scotland:—

"By a Royal Borough is in Scotland understooood, an incorporation that hold their lands off the Crown, and are governed by magistrates of their own naming. The administration of the annual revenues of a Royal Borough termed the *common good,* is trusted to the Magistrates, but not without control. It was originally subjected to the review of the Great Chamberlain, and accordingly the chapter 39, sec. 45 of *Iter Camerarii* contains the following articles, recommended to the Chamberlain to enquire into— 'Giff there be an good assedation and uptaking of the common good of the burgh, and giff faithful compt. be made thereof to the community of the burgh; and giff no compt. is made, he whom and in quhaes hands it is come, and how it passes by the community.' In pursuance of these instructions, the Chamberlain's precepts for holding the Ayr or circuit is directed to the provost and bailies, enjoining them to 'call all those who have received any of the town's revenues, or used any office within the burgh since the last Chamberlain-ayr, to answer such things as shall be laid to their charge.' And in the third chapter, which contains the forms of the Chamberlain-ayr, the first thing to be done, after fencing the Court, is to call the bailies and serjeants to be challenged and accused from the time of the last Ayr."

It will be observed that the references which have been made to various chartularies, during the reign of David I., would not serve to prove the absolute existence of Royal Burghs, but rather that of burghs which belonged in property to the Crown. The inhabitants of such, or at least many of them, may have been in the enjoyment of certain privileges and immunities consisting in exemption from restrictions which tended to fetter trade and commerce; but there is no proof existing of their erection at that time into a general gild, or municipal community, or corporation, which would fulfil the description of Lord Kames — wherein property was held by the municipal authority for the good of the community, under a permanent feudal tenure or title, in return to the Crown for certain fixed rents or *maills*, and the performance of certain services to the State in the preservation of the public peace in the various burghs.

William the Lion, the second in succession to David I., is said to have given to Edinburgh the dignity of a Royal Burgh, to have assembled within it the Estates of the realm, and to have converted it into a place of mintage for the King's currency; while Alexander III. constituted Edinburgh as the depository of the insignia of royalty and the records of the Kingdom.

William the Lion in 1197 built a castle on the river Ayr, and encouraged the settlement of a town or burgh, where probably a village or hamlet had previously existed. In the language of the Chronicle of Melrose, the fact is thus stated:—"Anno 1197—Factum est novum oppidum inter Don et Ar." In the charter of the King which he granted about ten years thereafter, he declares that at his new castle upon Ayr, he had made a burgh (*burgum fecisse*) and that he had granted to *his burgesses* resident therein (*burgensibus meis in eo manentibus*) all the liberties and free customs throughout the kingdom enjoyed by his other burghs and resident burgesses, together with a weekly market; and to the burgesses who shall come and inhabit his said burgh, and shall there settle and remain, he grants an exemption from all tolls and customs on their own proper goods (*dominicis catallis suis*), the exaction of which he strictly prohibits. To the burgh, or general community thereof, including the resident burgesses, he gives an adjacent territory, under certain conditions, and for a rent payable to the Crown by each burgess; and certain stations are specified for the collection of tolls and customs by the burgh officers.

In this charter, there are no words of *incorporation*. It would, therefore appear that the mere denomination of *burgum* in a royal grant was held to imply a duty upon the community to set about, of itself, the creation of a corporate existence, or representative body, for the purpose of looking after the property so freely granted to them by the King. The erection of such corporate bodies was, therefore, the natural result of the growth of circumstances and situation; rather than the obeying an edict of the Throne. In fact, the original rents exigible by the Crown, were collected by the *ballivi*, who were first appointed to discharge this duty by the Lord High Chamberlain, the chief officer of the Crown.

So far as can be traced, the Gild was the first constituted authority in Scotland. The Town of Berwick upon Tweed was in the days of David I. regarded as part of his dominion. Subsequently, it seemed to be an independent place of residence, being connected with neither England nor Scotland. In many Acts of the British Parliament this independence was rigidly maintained. Laws were enacted for the benefit of England, Scotland, and our good Town of Berwick. The town of Berwick was the frequent resort in former times of outlaws—fugitives from justice in England or Scotland. The town by somewhat recent legislation, though situate north of the Tweed, forms part of the English territory.

The object of the General Gild of Berwick was, as stated in its constitution, to suppress all the smaller gilds or associations which existed at the time, so that by good fellowship, and a brotherly feeling one towards another, the interests of all might be protected, no one being allowed to aggrandise, or deprive his neighbour of his due. The three prevailing sentiments in the establishment of the Gild were Peace, Goodwill, and Fair-play. It was essentially the first attempt to form a system of burgh police, and the Statutes of the Gild of Berwick, or the Leges quatuor Burgorum (whichever is the older of the two) were the first known codification of Municipal law in Scotland. There is no doubt that burgh government by the Gild preceded that of Town Councils in Scotland. In fact, it would appear from the earliest records we possess of Town Councils, that the representatives to the corporate body were elected at a Meeting of the Gildry of the Town. The former was therefore a further development of municipal rule and control.

This may be readily taken for granted from the fact that the *Leges Burgorum* do not contain any reference to a body called a town or burgh council; while on the other hand the *Statuta Gildæ* clearly lay down that there shall be, besides the Alderman (Provost) and four bailies, twenty-four "probi homines de melioribus et discretioribus et fide dignioribus ejusdem burgi ad hoc electi;" and on this body is conferred the power of declaring who should be the Magistrates, in the event of there being any controversy

as to their election by the community. The original idea of municipal representation and control in Scotland was conceived, and for a considerable time conducted, on a most popular basis. Indeed it remained so, until the statute of King James III. in 1469 (Act. Parl. Scot. c. 5), when the system of the Council electing their successors began, and which proved to be for nearly four centuries so great a scandal in regard to our Municipal Institutions. After this Act became law, the Town Council dominated the Gildry; the latter becoming practically *effete* as an independent Civic body.

But as was the case in the various Continental Towns, the Gild in Edinburgh, though no doubt consisting originally of the Merchant class, had in course of time introduced into its numbers members of the Craftsmen class, provided they possessed the full right of citizenship by holding estates of a certain recognised value within the liberties of the Town. In all probability the line of demarcation, which was latterly drawn between Merchants and Craftsmen was (as Wilda, one of the most accomplished writers on Gilds says) one of municipal and business development. It soon became apparent in the contest for municipal control, and in regulating the affairs of the Town, that the Merchant class and the various Arts or Trades became as distinct from each other as was the *Collegia Sodalitia* which represented the Patricians, and the *Collegium Opificum* which embraced the Plebian union, in the days of ancient Rome. They not only differed in opinion, but frequently came into hostile collision with each other. The kingdom of Scotland was not alone in the development of these civic turmoils. They were also found in England and all over the Continent of Europe.

Emancipation from the baronial control having been attained, the ancient and honourable spirit of Freedom seemed quickly to disappear. The municipal rulers soon became proud, avaricious, and overbearing. The exclusion of the Craftsmen from the brethren of the Gild was one of the first steps in this

*d*

direction. This led to a system of oppression on the part of the latter towards the former, the Gild being the local governing power. They began to regard the Craftsmen in the same light as the οἱ πολλοί of ancient Athens; and the Craftsmen had no Solon to act as "mediator and archon."* As might be expected when merchants began to amass wealth, they became more exclusive in their association, an early development of what is now known as *caste.* Professor Lujo Brentano, of Bavaria, a well-known writer on the subject of Gilds, referring to this question, states that "an ordinance was repeated in Danish, German, and Belgian Gild statutes, that no one 'with dirty hands,' or with 'blue nails,' or 'who hawked his wares on the streets,' should become a member of the Gild, and that Craftsmen, before being admitted, must have foresworn their trade for a year and a day." Eventually, however, as a rule, the Craftsmen were excluded from the Gild, and this led to frequent civic disputes and turmoils in these countries. Indeed, in the German and Belgian towns, the oppression of the Gild was regarded as more general and severe than in the various towns of Great Britain and Denmark. There was in the latter a stronger executive power in existence, which had a beneficial effect on the community. In the former the towns soon became something like independent constitutions, governed by an exclusive aristocracy. This Patriciate it was the object of the Craftsmen to overturn, and great was the party spirit, and numerous were the conflicts which took place during the thirteenth and fourteenth centuries.

For instance, at Magdeburg, in the year 1301, ten aldermen of the Crafts-Gilds were burnt alive in the market-place; while in Cologne, on 21st November 1371, thirty-three weavers were executed; and, on the following day, a search was made among the houses, monasteries, and churches: all

---

* *Vide*—Aristotle's Constitution of Athens, by Thomas J. Dymes, B.A., London. Seeley & Co. Page 9.

that were found were murdered. The exiled found a refuge at Aix-la-Chapelle, where they afterwards greatly flourished in trade. Bruges, Brussels, Frankfort-on-Main, Strasburg, Halle, and other towns witnessed similar civic broils. Towards the close of the fourteenth century, however, the Trade-Gilds prevailed. They were ultimately successful in obtaining a share in the civic administration.

It will thus be seen that the origin of Trade or Craft-Gilds was occasioned by the necessities of the period. Combination was the only means by which they could successfully resist the oppression of the Mercantile Gild. Foremost among the Trade-Gilds were the weavers, who were a kind of middle-class between Patrician and Plebeian. It is interesting to observe in this relation, that in the Royal Charter granted by King Alexander II. to the burgesses of Aberdeen to have their *Gilda Mercatoria*, the dyers (fullers or litsters) and the weavers are specially excepted, *ut habeant gildam suam merchatricem, exceptis fullonibus et tellariis*. The weavers and waulkers were also specially excepted in King James VI.'s charter to Perth, which was rescinded in 1770.

The Craft-Gilds on the Continent, at an early date after their institution, began to see that it was indispensable to have a responsible elected chief. This official they called "the Warden," whose duty was to regulate the trade and manage the Gild. He had the right to examine all manufactures, and to search for all unlawful tools and products. No member of the Gild was allowed to use tools "unless the same was testified to be good and honest." To insure good workmanship the use of the midnight oil had to be condemned, because the Gild statutes provided that "no one shall work longer than from the beginning of the day until curfew, nor at night by candlelight." While the ostensible objects of these Craft-Gilds was self-defence and mutual help, yet, in general, they resembled all the other Gilds in their attention to religious offices and ordinances. They also tried to maintain a high standard of good and substantial workmanship,—a merit much to be desiderated in many of the products of modern times.

In England, also, the Craftsmen were eventually successful in obtaining an enormous share in town government. During the time of Edward II., no person could be admitted to the freedom of the city of London unless he was " a member of one of the trades or mysteries." Again, during the reign of his successor, an enactment was passed by the whole assembled commonalty of the city, by which the right to elect the Members of Parliament, as well as all the other city dignitaries and officials, was transferred from the ward representatives to the trading companies. The number of these companies who took part in the elections of the following year was increased from thirty-two to forty-eight. The burghers, however, ultimately obtained the supremacy by getting enrolled in the Craft-Gilds, from which no doubt sprang up what is known in later days as " the Twelve great Livery Companies " of the city of London.

While Trade-Gilds or Craft-Gilds became prevalent in the Towns of England, as they were also on the Continent, there seems no evidence whatever of their existence in Scotland. Indeed there is no trace of the original development of the Gild—the social and religious one—which existed in other countries. The Gild seems in Scotland to have been confined solely to the Merchant or Burgensic class. Nevertheless, there were early appearances of organisations among the Crafts for mutual help and defence. In the days of James I. (1424) a Statute was passed empowering handicraftsmen, in their different branches, to elect a preses, who was called a " Deakon or Kirkmaister," which would serve to prove that they were somewhat numerous at the time. The words of the Act are as follow :—" That in every towne of the realme, of ilk sindry Craft usyt tharin, thar be chosyn a wise man of thar Craft be the layff of the Craft, and be the counsel of the officiaris of the towne, the quhilk sall be haldyn Dekyn or Maister-man owre the layff, for the tyme till hym assignyt, till assay and govern all werkis that beis made be the werkmen of his Craft, sua that the Kingis lieges be nocht defraudyt and scathyt in tyme to cum, as thai have bene in tyme bygane through untrew men of craftis."

The original constitution of these Trade-Societies, or as they became afterwards better known by Trade Incorporations, seems to have flowed out of a desire for union, self-protection, and self-government among the members. They also, in pre-reformation times, had religious duties strictly to fulfil. The members were bound to pay, in addition to other benefactions, the "ouklie penny" (weekly payment) for the maintenance of the altar, and sustenance of the priest attached thereto. Each of these art or trade organisations had a patron saint to whom they dedicated an Altar in St Giles' Church. Their charter of incorporation consisted in a "Seal of Cause" (*sigillum ad causas*), granted by the Lord Provost, Magistrates and Town Council on the requisition of the body; and in the earlier charters there were strict rules laid down for the observance by the Members of their religious duties. It is a singular fact that although the Craftsmen, in civic turmoil, never failed to give a most hearty allegiance to the Crown, they did not receive much support or countenance from the legislature. In many of the earliest charters to Royal Burghs, there is an express provision in favour of the *Gilda Mercatoria*, and for the protection of their privileges the interpositions of Parliament were frequent. In the Golden Charter to Edinburgh (James VI.) there is the following clause:— "We are forever to have, enjoy, and possess, in the aforesaid town and liberties, a Mercantile Gild, with its courts, councils, members, jurisdictions, liberties, and privileges belonging to the same, and in all things as freely as is granted by us and our predecessors to the aforesaid town, or to any other royal free burgh within our Kingdom." Nevertheless, it has not been found that the original incorporation of the Crafts or Trades in Scotland can be directly traced either to the Crown or to the authority of Parliament. In charters of a comparatively later date, there may be traced a power to the Superior or to Municipal Authorities authorising them to erect subordinate corporations; but, as a rule, the power seems to have been chiefly assumed by the Town Councils themselves, as a matter of internal regulation, and to promote a policy of civic harmony and peace. At what time any of the Companies or Crafts first obtained the patronage of the Civic Magistrates, it is impossible now to determine. The muniments of Edinburgh are far from being complete. The earliest trace of the Town Council, which was chiefly composed of the Merchant Class, receiving into their civic counsels the trades, was in 1469, when it was enacted that two of the Craftsmen should have a voice in the "chusing" of the Magistrates; and in 1475 they began to grant Charters of Incorporation. The Wrights, Masons, and Weavers received a Charter during that year, the Hammermen in 1483, the Butchers in 1488, and the Cordiners in 1489. These Seals of Cause practically re-enact the regulations which the self-constituted bodies had previously passed among themselves for their own government; and some of them bear unmistakable evidence that some of these organisations had a previous existence for a long period of years.

It has already been shown that the first recognition by the Crown of the Trades or Crafts was in 1425, James I., c. 39, wherein handicraftsmen in their various arts in every town in Scotland, were empowered to elect one of the members to preside over the others, to be designated " Deakon or Maister-man over the laife for the time," so that his Majesty's lieges should not be defrauded in any way in time to come, as they had been in by-past times through unfremen who were not connected with any of the arts or crafts. On the following year, the Statute c. 27 provides that "Deakons of ilk Craft be elected"; while c. 86 of the same year ordains that the office of Deakon being of general prejudice to the Kingdom, the same should be rescinded, all licence to elect Deakons recalled, and the former Meetings of the various Arts with their Deakons, be condemned as "Assemblies of Conspirators."

The power of electing a Preses was, however, restored to the Goldsmiths' Craft by James II. in 1457, c. 83. They were required to appoint a Deacon to inspect their work, so that it be of good workmanship and the metal of standard fineness; and by a statute of James III., 1483, c. 96, the office of Deacon once more became general among the trades.

A few years later the Statute (James III., Parlt. 2, c. 12) first makes a distinction between Merchants and Craftsmen, wherein tradesmen using merchandise are required to renounce their Craft, and it is further ordained (1487) that this Act be put into execution by "escheit" of the merchandise to be accounted for to His Majesty's Exchequer.

That Statute contains the following :—

BECAUS it is cleirly understandin to the Kingis Hienes and his Thre Estates, that the using of deyknnis of men of craft in burrowis is rycht dangerous, and, as thay use the samin, may be the caus of greit troubill in burrowis, and convocatioun and rysing of the Kingis liegis, be statutes making contrair the commoun proffet, and for their singular proffet and avale, quhilk [de] servis greit punytioun; And als belangand masonis and uther men of craft, that convenis togidder and makis reule of thair craft, sic as masonis, and wrichtis, and utheris, that thay sall have thair feis als weill on the haly dais as for wark dais, or els they sall nocht laubour nor wirk; And als, quhat personis of thame that wald begin ane uther mannis werk, and he at his plesour will leif tae said werk, and than nan of the said craft dar nocht compleit nor fulfill the samin wark: It is heirfoir avisit, statute and ordanit, that all sic dekynnis sall ceiss for ane yeir, and have na uther power, bot allanerly to examyne the fynace of the stuffe and werk that beis wrocht with the remanent of his craft: And als belangand masonis, wrichtis, and uther men of craft, that statutis that they sall have fee alswele for the haly day as for the werk day, that all the makaris and usaris of the said statutes sall be indictit as commoun oppressouris of the Kingis liegis be thir statutis, and that the clerk of the Justiciary sall tak dittay thairupoun, and thai to be punist as oppressouris; and in likewise of the makaris of the statutis, that quhair ony begynnis ane mannis werk, ane uther sall nocht end it, that all the makaris and usaris thairof sal be punyst as oppressouris of the Kingis liegis, and dittay to be taken thairupon as is abone written.

Troublous times were again in store for the Trades. In 1493, the office of Deacon was again considered by Statute of James IV., c. 43, as highly dangerous, and the cause of great trouble in burghs; and it was ordained "that all Deakons shall cease for a year at least [especially masons and wrights] except to examine works." By a subsequent statute, passed during the regency of Mary of Guise in 1555, the office of Deacon was condemned and abolished, as being the frequent cause of civic commotion, by the unlawful combination among the members of the various Arts, and betwixt burgh and burgh,—such as was deserving of severe punishment.

The Trades or Crafts of Edinburgh were no exception to the general rule. As frequent disputations occurred between the Merchant Gild and the Crafts in other towns, there was a similar state of matters from time to time found in Edinburgh. Notably was this the case in the year 1543. The Town Council of the day was self-elected, and consisted almost exclusively of the Merchant Class. They for some time had taken it upon themselves, without consulting the Arts, to elect whom they pleased as Magistrates. On the 12th of August of that year, the Town Council had passed a law infringing on the rights of the Craftsmen. The Deacons of Trades were greatly incensed; and, in the Council Chamber they drew their swords to manifest that they considered themselves greatly injured, and that they were determined to have redress. The poor Deacons were soon overcome. They were seized by an armed force, and placed in prison. When the general body of Craftsmen heard this, they assembled as one united band, and determined to rescue their Deacons from the hands of the authorities. When matters began to wear so serious an aspect, the Regent Arran interposed, and was the means of effecting a reconciliation between the contending parties, and the release of the Deacons.

The effect of this action against the Craftsmen did not die away. It was rather the means of making them more persistent as to their rights, and more hostile to the constitution of the civic administration. Fresh disturbances arose, the result of which was, that a statute was passed in 1555, to which more direct reference shall be afterwards made, and which law was applicable not only to the Town of Edinburgh, but also to all the other Burghs in Scotland.

The step taken at this time seems to have soon become a subject of regret, because, during the following year, viz., 16th April 1556, by the advice of the Queen Regent, Her Majesty (Mary Queen of Scots) granted the following Charter in favour of all the Craftsmen of the Burghs of Scotland, amply restoring to them their former rights and privileges, which was issued and published by a royal proclamation to the following effect:— "Restoris and repones them to use and have Deacons of all Craftis, togidder with all and sundry privileges, faculties, freedoms, consuetudes and uses, granted to them be our maist noble progenitors, and alsua the use and possession of the saidis liberties, bruikit and joisit by them in tymes bygane, notwithstanding the said Act of Parliament, etc., ratifying and approving all their former privileges given in tyme bygane," etc.

A communication received from Mary of Lorraine * by the Town Council

---

* The minutes of the Town Council in this matter are so complete, that they are printed at length. They are as follows :—

20 *September* 1559.— . . . . In presens foirsaid, Robert Fynder dekin of the wrychtis, Thomas Jaksone of the masonis, Robert Meid of the wobstaris, Johne Auldinstoun of the bakstaris, Peter

of Edinburgh in regard to the Burgh elections of 1559 refers to the above Statute of Queen Mary's. Nevertheless, the Trades having gained their former position, it was not long until civic broils again broke out. Eventually both parties agreed to refer their differences to King James VI. By the decreet-arbitral pronounced by the King it is provided that "nather the Merchants among themselves, nor the Crafts, and their Deacons and Visitors, should hold particular or general 'Conventions,' except and always that the Dean of Gild

Turnett of the skynneris, Hew Canney of the furrouris, Richart Henrisone of the fleschouris, James Stirk of the walkeris, James Lausoun for Johne Welche dekin of the bonat makeris, James Cranstoun of the hammermen, Alexander Sauchie of the talyouris, Robert Huntrodis of the cordineris, and Patrik Lyndsay of the barbouris presentit the Quenis grace writing efter following, and alledgit that be vertew thairof, and of the gift of the restitutioun of thair craftis to thair priuelegis vnder the Quenis grace greitt seill producit with the said writting, thai aucht to voit particularlie in electioun of the said counsaill, and thairfoir protestit that nane wer chosin without thair votis tane thairintill, at the leist that thai wer nocht hald to obey the statutis and ordenances to be sett furthe be thame, of the quhilk writing the tenour followis :—

Oure Soueranis Lord and Lady, vnderstanding that the craftismen of burrowis within thair realme of Scotland ar reponit to all priuilegeis fredomes and jurisdictioun vait and occupyit be thame within burgh in thair maist noble progenitouris dayis, and in speciall to the cheaing of thair dekynnis yeirlie at the tymes limite thairto for conseruatioun of guid ordour amang thameselfis, quhilkis dekynnis aucht and suld haue priuilege als weill in voting, particularlie in electing and cheaing of all lytis quhilkis ar to be chosin to bruke offices within burgh at the feist of Michaelmes, sic as provest ballies counsale dene of gild thesaurer seriandis and all kynd of officeris within the samin, as in voting cheaing and electing vpone the principall officeriis foirsaid ; and albeit the saidis dekynnis of Edinburgh, sen thair restitutioun to the saidis liberteis be the space of thre yeiris syne or thairby, hes yeirlie the tyme of the electing of the new counsale offerit thame in reddines to vote in electing thairof, newirtheles the provest baillies and coun-sale of the said burgh refusit to ressawe thair wote thairunto nochtwithstanding the liberteis grantit to thame thairvpone, in hie contemptioun of thair auctoritie and expres aganis justice ; chargeing heirfoir the saidis provest baillies and counsale foirsaid, now present and to cum, to suffir the saidis dekynnis and euirilkane of thame particularlie be thameselfis to woit in electing and cheaing of the counsale lytis and all vther officeris abone specifiit in all tymes cuming, conforme to the priuilegeis grantit to thame may assemble his brethers and counsel in their Gild Courts, conform to the antient laws of the Gildry and privileges thairof." Further, "It is agried and concludit that nather the Merchants among themselves, nather the Crafts and their Deacons or Visitors sall have or make any particular or general 'Conventions,' as deakens with deakens, deakens with their crafts, or crafts among themselves, far less to make privat laws or statutes, poind or distrenzie

thairvpoun, quhilkis priuilegeis be thir presentis we ratifie apprewis and amplefiis in all poyntis, and speciallie in the chesing of the counsall and lytis foirsaid, vnder the pane of dissobedience of our auctorite and all charge and punisment that may follow thairvpone. Subscriuit be our said Soueranis darrest moder, at Halyruidhous the [*blank*] day of September 1559. *Sic subscribitur:* MARIE R. The saidis dekynnis being removit and incallit agane, and the saidis ballies and counsale with thair assessouris foirsaidis being ryple awysit vpone the said writting and priuelegis mentionat therein, findis that the saidis dekynnis suld haue na wote in the electioun of the new counsall in respect of the said writting as the samin is consavit, becaus it is relative to the said gift quhilk contenis allanerlie the restitutioun and repositioun of the saidis dekynnis to thair priuilegis fredomis and liberteis quhairof thai wer denudit by the act of parliament maid in the moneth of [June] the yeir of God j$^m$ v$^c$ l and [v] yeirs, and that thai wer in vse of befoir the making of the said act, and that it is of veritie that the dekynnis of craftis hes hade in na tymes bypast vote in electioun of the new counsale nor electioun of lytis but onlie in electioun of officeris; and thairvpone maister James Lyndesay theasurer askit instrumentis.

The baillies and counsale commandit and chargit [the deacons of crafts] and ilk ane of thame to remove thameselfis incontinent forth of the counsalehous, and to suffer the electioun of the counsaill for this yeir to cum to tack effect eftir the consuetude continewalle obseruit in tymis past, vnder the pane of dissobedience; and the saidis personis and euerilk ane of thame being seuerale requyrit gif thai wald obey the said charge or nocht ansuerit euerie ane seueralie that thai wald nocht remove thameselfis nor suffir the said electioun to tak effect without thai wotit particularlie thairintill, and maister James Lyndesay theasurer protestit for the townis actioun aganis the saidis disobeyariss.

[The deacons of crafts] protestit that insafer as thai hade power grantit to thame be the Quenis grace to wote in electioun of the new counsale, and be vertew thairof remanit in the counsall hous nochtwithstanding that thai were commandit be the baillies and counsale to remove thame furth thairof, that thai incurit na panis of dissobedience thairfoir.

22 *September* 1559.— . . . . . The quhilk day in presens of the prouest ballies and counsaill.

(distrain) at their awen hands for transgressions, except by the advice and consent of the Provost, Baillies, and Counsel."

Regarding the holding of "Conventions," Maitland in his *History of Edinburgh* throws considerable light. He says,—"It having till this time been a custom whenever any of the Craftsmen of Edinburgh were summoned to appear to answer for an offence committed, he was accompanied by the several Corporations of Arts to assist him in his defence; which frequently

---

being convenit for electioun of the lyttis to bruke offices within this burgh this yeir to cum, compeirit [the deacons of crafts] and desyrit to be admittit to voit in the said electioun in respect of the priuilegis grantit to thame be the Quenis grace thairvpone, and producit the xx day of September instant, and desyrit the saidis provest, ballies and counsaill answer thairvpone. The saidis dekynnis being furthe of courte removit and incallit agane, and the saidis provest, ballies and counsaill being with thair assessouris riplie awisit vpone the said allegiance fyndis that the saidis dekyunis aucht to haue na voit in the said electioun in respect of the Quenis grace writing producit be thame and registrat in thir bukis the said xx day of September instant, as the samyn is consauit, in respect of the answer gevin thairto the said day and for the cussis contenit thairin, and the saidis dekynnis askit instrumentis that the provest, ballies and counsaill disobeyit the charge contenit in the said writing as thai alledgit, and protestit that thair disobedince wer nocht prejudiciall to thair priuleges and liberteis contenit in the said charge, and declarit that thai wald obey na officeris to be chosin for this yeir to cum in cais thai be nocht present at the electioun of thame, and thairvpone askit instrumentis.

Followis the tennour of the Quenis grace writting direct to the provest baillies and counsaill of this burgh for electing and chesing of officeris :—REGINA. Prouest baillies and counsall of Edinburgh, we greit you weill : Forsamekle as we for certain caussis moving vs hes thocht neidfull that ye at this present feist of Michaelmes elect and cheis sic personis, honest merchandmen of your awin burgh, to be vpoun your counsale and beir other hiear offices aboue you for this yeir intocum, quhais names we sall send to yow be sum speciall seruand of our awin or other wyis declair to sum of yow be our awin mouthe, quhilkis personis we pray yow effectuouslie, as ye will do vs singulair plesour and report our speciall thankis, that ye elect and admit to be vpoun your counsale and beir your other offices for this yeir intocum as said is, promitting be this present that the samin sall nocht be hurtfull preparatiwe nor preiudiciall to your priuillegiis nor auld liberteis in tymes cuming be this present. Subscriuit with our hand at our palyce of Halyruidhous, the xxij day of September 1559. *Sic subscribitur :* MARIE R.

occasioning great commotions, for preventing of which in all time coming, it was by the Council enacted, that no such Convention shall assemble anytime hereafter, under the penalty of the loss of their freedom, and otherwise to be fined at the discretion of the Magistrates."

The ostensible object of the decreet-arbitral of the King in regard to these Conventions, and to the power of assembling of the Corporations, was to connect the Members of the Guildry and the Craftsmen more closely with the Magistrates of the Burgh; or, as might be said in the language of the present day, to bring them more *in touch* with the Magistracy, and to destroy their powers of acting independently.

The erection of the Crafts into separate Incorporations was not understood as depriving the Magistrates of the Burghs of their right of complete and absolute control over the whole individual Members of such Incorporations in the exercise of their privileges. In various statutes that right was recognised and enforced, and in their capacity of *nobile officium*, the Town Council did not fail to recall the charters they had previously given, and to renew these on fitting occasions. They very often exercised the power of regulating the prices of bread, fish, flesh, and other requisite commodities. They also from time to time appointed markets, and fixed the hours of sale. The recognition on the part of the Scottish Parliament as to the Magistrates' right of control is clearly set forth in an Act passed in 1535, c. 43, during the reign of King James V., wherein it narrates the great wrong that is daily done to our Sovereign Lord's lieges by cordiners, smiths, baxters, browsters, and all other Craftsmen, sellers of victuals and salt, compelling them to pay for their stuff and for their workmanship exorbitant prices to the great hurt (scaith) of all our Sovereign Lord's lieges, bringing on such dearth in the country "that the samyn may nocht be sustenit." To remedy this state of affairs, it was provided that certain Commissioners should be appointed, of whom the Provost of Edin-

burgh should be one, to enact such statutes and ordinances as they should deem
most expedient for the good of the community ; to cause all Craftsmen within
the precincts of the town of Edinburgh, as well as others of the realm, to
manufacture good and sufficient stuff, and sell " the samyn of ane competent
price. And the saidis Commissaris to do justice upoun the brekaris of thir
ordinancis als oft as thai here murmur or complant thairof."

By another Act of King James V., passed in 1607, c. 8, regarding the conduct of Craftsmen, which proceeded upon the narration of " its being hevily
murmuret " that all Craftsmen within this realm, and especially within Burghs,
make use of " sic extortiounis upoun uthers Oure Soverane Lordis liegis," by
reason of their crafts and of private acts and constitutions made among themselves, contrary to the good of the community, and to the great hurt, damage,
prejudice and scaith to all the lieges of this realm,—certain enactments are made
against combinations, particularly among artificers employed by those that " hes
ony biggingis or reparationis to be maid for making of policy in this realme," of
which the most remarkable is, that they may choose " guid craftismen, freemen
or utheris, as they may think most expedient for ordouring, bigging and ending
of all sic warkis." This Act was passed and put into execution, " notwithstanding whatsumever Act or Statute made to the contrare." The introduction
of Craftsmen within the liberties of a burgh to which they did not belong, was
secured against any impediment by others of the Craft, by a declaration that,
besides other penalties, it would infer a forfeiture of their freedom ; and the
" Provost and Baillies of all Burrows were enjoined to tak inquisitioun hereupon, and putt this Act to execution in all punctis." Nevertheless, it would
appear from Sir George Mackenzie's Observations (p. 146) that, by a case in
1675, the Act received a most liberal construction from the Town Council of
Edinburgh, by finding " that, where a freeman either deserted or delayed, the
owner of the work might employ any, even unfreemen ; though it was alleged

it was not just to punish all the freemen for the part of one; nor was it convenient for the commonwealth that unfreemen should be admitted, for whose work none can be answerable."

In the Acts of the Scottish Parliament of 1551, there are strong complaints made against the gross negligence of the Provosts and Bailies, as well the inefficiency of the Deacons, in consequence of the alleged extortions practised by the Craftsmen; and an injunction is given that steps be immediately taken for attaching a reasonable price to all articles, and the same to be reported to the next Parliament. This injunction seemed to have been of no avail. Four years thereafter (1555) another Act was passed, in which it is stated that it is clearly understood that the choosing of Deacons and Men of Crafts within burghs has been "Rycht dangerous, and as they have usit thame selfis in tymes bygone, hes causit greit troublill in burrows, commotion, and rysing of the Quenis liegis in diverss partis; and be making of leggis and bandit amangis thame selfis, and betwixt burgh and burgh, quhilk deserves greit punishment," etc., it is statute and ordained that "NA DEAKONS" be chosen; but that the Provost, Bailies, and Town Council should "cheis the maist honest man of Craft of gude conscience, ane of everie craft" to visit their own Craft, and see that they do their work properly, and the same be of sufficient quality and workmanship; and that such persons "be callit visitouris of thair Craft;" but withdrawing all power to have gatherings or assemblies of their number to any private conventions, or of making any acts or regulations of their own; but that in all time coming they should be under the control of the Provost, Bailies, and Town Council. It would thus appear that their alleged extortions had highly incensed the Government of the day, which led to this drastic measure being passed. The law enacted was not only applicable to Edinburgh, but to all the other Scottish Burghs, where similar conditions seemed to prevail. The statute, however, proved ineffective.

The policy of Exclusive Privilege so much resorted to in former times was a decidedly conservative or protective measure. It was in entire antagonism to Free trade. It restricted enterprise on the part both of merchants and tradesmen, while it had a most injurious effect on the community at large. It caused high prices to prevail, and put down the least approach to rivalry. It is amazing that the Legislature of the day did not take speedy measures for obtaining a better state of matters.

King James VI., on ascending the throne of England, and obtaining the experience of the much larger area of London, soon discovered how a system of greater freedom would become of considerable public utility. Dealing with this very question in the ΒΑΣΙΛΙΚΟΝ ΔΩΡΟ or "Instructions to his son Prince Henry," he says :—" The Craftes-men think we should be content with their worke, how bad and dear soever it be, and if they in anything be controlled, up goeth the *blew blanket.* But for their part take example of England, how it hath flourished both in wealth and policie since the strangers Craftesmen came in among them. Therefore, not only permit, but allure strangers to come here also ; taking as straite order for repressing the mutining of ours at them, as was done in England at their first in-bringing there."

The system of Exclusive Privilege continued for many generations after this, as it had done for centuries preceding. The Convention of Royal Burghs was the means to a great extent of preventing any change upon the system. That body is a very old organisation, instituted in the reign of King James III., and was appointed to be held annually at Inverkeithing. By an Act of James VI., however, it was appointed to meet four times a-year, at any Burgh it thought proper ; and to avoid confusion it was ordained that only one Commissioner should appear for every Burgh except Edinburgh, which should have two. The Convention took the place of the Four Burghs—Edinburgh, Roxburgh, Berwick and Stirling—which previously had been a Court of Consultation, in which the Great Chamberlain of the Kingdom presided, and where he was assisted in the adjudication of disputes by Commissioners from the four burghs referred to. On the suppression of the office of the Great Chamberlain, the power of controlling the Magistrates' accounts was vested in the Exchequer; that of reviewing their sentences was transferred to the ordinary Courts of Law; while the power of the Chamberlain himself, in regulating matters concerning the common welfare of the State, was transferred to the Convention of Royal Burghs.

The influence of these Royal Burghs on the Scottish Parliament was undoubtedly great, and a system of mild modification in reference to trade was the most that could be resorted to with any hope of success. This was made apparent by an Act passed in 1661, in the first Parliament after the Restoration of Charles II. It contained powers for "establishing companies and societies for making linen cloth, stuffs," &c.

And that manufacturies may be promoved, and for the encouraging of skilful artisans to come from abroad, for training up the persons foresaid, and working for the use of the said companies, it is hereby declared, that all such as shall be brought home and employed for the said companies, shall be free to set up and work in burghs and landwart where the companies shall think fit, without paying any thing whatsoever to any person or persons, under whatsoever pretext, for their freedom, and shall be free of taxes, public burdens or exactions, during their lifetime; notwithstanding of any law, statute, privilege or indulgence made or granted in the contrair by His Majesty or any of his predecessors, in favors of any committee or incorporation whatsoever, which are all hereby cassed, rescinded and declared void and null, in so far as they may be conceived to derogate from the privileges and immunities granted by this present Act in favors of tradesmen, natives or strangers belonging to or brought home by the said companies for working in the said manufactures.

As a counter-blast to this, there is another Act of the same Parliament which inhibits and discharges all tradesmen and mechanics from importing from any foreign parts, any made work belonging to that trade or calling

*f*

whereof they are freemen, or to sell the same, or any such ware brought home by merchants, in their shops or otherwise, under the pain of confiscation. While, therefore, the former Act indicated a desire to have liberal and advanced views, the latter contained in its very essence the old traditional exclusiveness.

Of course this system of privilege existed only within prescribed limits. As cities and towns got enlarged and the original area extended, there was the utmost freedom in the outside districts in regard to the matter of trade. This fact could not fail to help most materially the bringing about of larger views in the conducting of business; and latterly the privileged classes, as they were supposed to be, began to realise the fact that there was greater scope for them in the exercise of their calling, if they were left quite unfettered in the development of their business. Nevertheless, no doubt owing to the old feuds between the Merchant class and the Crafts in regard to their respective municipal rights, frequent cases occurred in the Courts of Law which were bitterly fought by both parties. For example:—

At so comparatively recent a date as the 2d of March 1802, a question of this kind was decided. An action was raised in the Law Courts against the Guildry, to have it found and declared that, as they were not members of the Goldsmiths' Incorporation, they had no right to sell gold or silver ware within the precincts of the city. It was urged on the part of the defenders that, as members of the Guildry, they had the privilege of importing and selling goods within the precincts of the city; and that from time immemorial, goods of all sorts had been so imported into the city and sold by members of the Guildry, in their shops and warehouses, without the slightest desire to infringe the rights of the craftsmen. The Court of Session declared that the defenders were entitled to import made articles of gold and silver work, and to sell and retail the same in the shops kept by them; but they reserved the question as to their right to manufacture the gold and silver work; which seemed to imply that this was a breach of good faith with the craftsmen—at least they had difficulty in deciding against the latter in this department. There were other cases came before the Courts from Aberdeen, Inverness, Perth, and Dunfermline. While reference has been made to these cases as illustrative of the manner in which these two great bodies of burgesses strove sedulously to protect their respective rights and privileges as against each other, even down to the present century, their differences were far more frequently as well as conspicuously apparent in connection with the great struggles of both for municipal rule.

In many of the Burghs, there existed a central body among the Trades, called the Convenery, or Convener's Court. Its functions were to consult regarding the general interests of the various Incorporations, to protect their rights and privileges, to determine all differences that might arise between them, and in some cases to frame bye-laws relative to the various arts. The Convenery had no judicative power; its powers, when tested in the Law Courts, were not sustained. The Convenery existed in Edinburgh, Glasgow (there denominated the Trades' House), Aberdeen, Dundee, Banff, Perth, Inverness, and several other Burghs. The constitution of the Convenery varied in the different towns. As a rule the body consisted of the Deacons of the various Incorporations, who elected out of their number a preses, who used to be called the Deacon-Warden, but is now designated the Deacon-Convener or rather Convener of Trades. Strange to say, there has never been a similar Court instituted in any of the Continental Towns.

It is not known at what time this Court was first instituted. It could not have been before the year 1424, when Parliament, for the better government of the respective Crafts throughout Scotland, conferred upon them the right to elect from among themselves a prudent and judicious man for their Deacon.

The election of a preses would necessarily become part of the organisation after it was established. Maitland, with a considerable amount of plausibility, attributes the institution of the office to about the year 1556, during the reign of Queen Mary, when civic disputes ran so high between the Merchants and Trades of Edinburgh. It has been since ascertained, that 1578 was the proper time, when Robert Abercromby, deacon of the Hammermen, was elected the first Deacon-Convener.

An incident which occurred on the 17th day of December 1596 will serve to illustrate the high civic position of the Convener of Trades at the time referred to. It was on occasion of a scare having been given to the King while he was in the Tolbooth Church, which resulted in His Majesty temporarily withdrawing from the City, and taking up his abode in Linlithgow Palace. An account of this occurrence is fully narrated in Spottiswood's History of the Church of Scotland; but the quaint manner in which it is refered to by Birrel, in his Diary of the Remarkable Events of that period, may be more interesting to the reader. It is as follows :—

"The 17th day of December 1596, being Fryday, hes Maiestie being in the tolbuith sitting in session, and ane convention of Ministers being in the new Kirke, and some noblemen being convenient yame, as in special Blantyre and Lindesay, ther came in some divilish officious persone, and said that the Ministers were coming to tak hes lyfe ; upone the qlk. the tolbuith dores wer shut and steikit ; and yair araise sic ane crying, God and the King—and uther some crying, God and the Kirk, that the haill commons of Ed^r. raise in armes, and knew not quher for. Yair (There) wes ane honest man quha was *Deiken of Deikens*, hes name wes Johne Watt, Symth. This Johne Watt raist the haill craftis in armes, and came to the Tolbuith quher the entrie is to the checker hous, and yair cried for a sight of his Maiestie, or ellis he sould ding up the zet (break up the gate) wt. foir hammers ; sua that nevir ane wt. in the tolbuith sould come out wt. yair lyfe. At length, hes M. lookit out the window, and spake to the commonis, quha offerit to die and live with him; quhilk commonis of Ed$^r$· offerit to die all in ane moment far hes Maiestie; weill far hes Maiestie came doun after the tounsmen were commandit of the gait, and was convoyit be the Craftismen to the abbay of Holyruid-house quhair he stayit that night, and, upon the morne he rode out of the toune, and sent back the chairges, as ze sall heir heirafter. This tumult bred grate troubell betwixt hes M. and the toune of Ed$^r$· "

The King fled to Linlithgow; and a deputation of four citizens was despatched to that Town to induce him to return. The well-known George Heriot was one of the number selected to go and remonstrate with His Majesty to return to Edinburgh. The King complied with their request.

The Convenery were in the habit of meeting at *Michaelmas* term, for the purpose of considering who of all the persons on the list or in nomination for the office of Magistrates were the best men to be elected. In a matter of this kind they were generally unanimous. The very fact of their unanimity could not fail to have exercised considerable influence on elections, as well as on the general affairs treated upon by the Civic body. This led to great jealousy on the part of the Merchant class in the Town Council. They strenuously tried many stratagems to get the Trades representation and the Convenery abolished. The Convenery, however, as rigorously maintained its rights. This was specially the case in 1684, when the Convenery obtained a Decree in the Court of Session, in favour of its retaining many of its most valuable privileges, particularly that of meeting and discussing the merits of those proposed as Magistrates. This decision of the Court was confirmed by the Scottish Parliament on the 13th day of June, of the same year.

In 1721 the Incorporated Trades made another effort for extension of their power. On this occasion they demanded that the Convener of Trades ought to be received into the Town Council in his official capacity. To this the Corporation replied, "That he was already qualified as Deacon, and there was no mention of Convener in the Sett of the Burgh." They further desired that the extraordinary Deacons should be allowed to vote in the choosing of all proxies, and insisted that no Committee could be legally appointed by the Town Council, without the concurrence of the extraordinary Deacons, and that the Convener was officially a Member of all Committees. These demands alarmed the Provost and Magistrates, who brought an action before the Court of Session to set aside King James' Decree-Arbitral of 1684. The Trades on the other hand brought a counter action, to have the decree-arbitral confirmed, and the various privileges which they sought given effect to.

The long period of ten years had elapsed, and no settlement had been come to, when both parties agreed to refer their differences to the award of Archibald, Earl of Islay, afterwards Duke of Argyle, who in 1730 pronounced his decree-arbitral, which as explanatory of that of King James, in conjunction with the Acts of Council of 1658 and 1673, formed the established Municipal Constitution of Edinburgh down to the year 1833.

The decree of Lord Islay gave universal satisfaction at the time. Nevertheless thirty-three years thereafter (1763), the Trades having conceived an ill-will against the Town Council in regard to their exercise of patronage of some of the city churches, which was not by popular call, procured an Act of Council the object of which was that the Corporation should apply to the Convention of Royal Burghs for their authority to put an end to the Craftsmen sending up leets to the Town Council, but to give the Trades an uncontrolled power of electing their own representatives. Several Members of the Town Council presented a Bill of Suspension to the Court of Session to prevent the application to the Convention. The Court granted a temporary interdict; and as the Trades declined to take any further proceedings in the meantime, the same proposal was revived in

1776, when Lord Provost Dalrymple and a majority of the Council appealed to the Court of Session. The question was ably and keenly argued, with the result that the Court unanimously granted a perpetual interdict.

The following is the decree of Lord Islay, in regard to the Town Council's objecting to receive the Convener in his official capacity as a constituent member of the Town Council:—

And touching the office of Convener, and the Meeting of Deacons and Craftsmen among themselves:—" FINDS the office of Convener has the authority of too long usage, and has been too much admitted by the Magistrates and Council, to be at this time called in question, and that the Meeting of the Deacons has been also long practised; but that, by the Sett of the Town, neither the Merchants among themselves, nor the Crafts and their Deacons or Visitors, can have, or make any particular or general conventions, as Deacons with Deacons, Deacons with their Crafts, or Crafts among themselves, without the advice and consent of the Provost and Council, excepting the cases in the said Sett particularly accepted; and that the Meeting said to be frequently held the first Tuesday after Michaelmas, in the manner, and with the circumstances the same is particularly set forth in the Declarator of the Merchants, can in no ways be contained in the said expectations."—ISLAY.

The Convener of Trades is the last of the Ten Chains worn by the holders of office in the Town Council. He is, in virtue of his office, a J.P. of the county of the city, and is a representative at the boards of several of the public charities. To his care has been entrusted the *Blue Blanket* already referred to. Maitland thus writes:—"To him is committed the custody of the Flag, falsely called *The Banner of the Holy Ghost*, but commonly called the *Blue Blanket*; which is delivered from Convener to Convener with great ceremony, as a valuable jewel; the origin of which, according to an idle tradition, is that a number of *Scotish* Tradesmen, chiefly *Edinburghers*, having amongst other great feats performed in the Holy

War, were the first who fixed their Banner on the Wall of Jerusalem; and that such of them as returned being called *Knights of the Holy Ghost* had many privileges granted them, and their Banner hung up at *St Eloi's* Altar, in *St Giles'* Church *in Edinburgh.* But this deserves not the least credit; for the present Flag, properly called the *Tradesmen's Banner*, but vulgarly the *Blue Blanket*, so denominated from its colour, was granted to the Crafts of *Edinburgh* by King James III., in return for the great service done him in freeing him from Duress in the Castle of Edinburgh, in the year 1482, after a confinement by his rebellious subjects, for the space of nine months; and impowered them to display the said Banner, in defence of their King and Country and their own Rights. At the appearance of this Banner, attended by the Deacon-Convener, 'tis said that not only the several artificers in Edinburgh are obliged to repair to it, but all the Artisans or Craftsmen throughout *Scotland* are to resort to it, and to fight under the command of the said Convener. Besides the aforesaid Banner, the said Convener has in his custody the Trades-Youths' Banner. These were the Ensigns of Edinburgh, when its military force consisted of only two companies."

When a Royal Parliamentary Commission was appointed to inquire into the position and affairs of the Municipal Institutions in Scotland, who presented their Report to both Houses of Parliament in 1835, the Members of the Commission had to give their attention to the subject of the Incorporated Trades. At that time, there were connected with the Ancient and Extended Royalties of Edinburgh fourteen different Incorporations:—viz., the Surgeons, Waulkers, Skinners, Furriers, Goldsmiths, Hammermen, Wrights, Masons, Tailors, Baxters, Fleshers, Cordiners, Websters, and Bonnetmakers. There was also an Incorporation of Candlemakers, and one of Barbers; but neither of these were represented in the Convenery.

The main object of the enquiry was to ascertain the actual state of each

Incorporation, with reference to Exclusive Privilege, and the amount of money that had been expended in the Law Courts in defence of their rights. The Commissioners were also charged with reporting upon the various Incorporations as to any injury that would be done, if trade privileges were abolished, while the members of the Incorporation retained all their funds, hospitals, and patronage.

Evidence was also led on the part of non-incorporated tradesmen as to abuses which existed among the privileged classes, and the partial and arbitrary manner in which the rights of the latter were exercised.

The Commissioners reported adversely to the continuance of the system of Exclusive Privilege, more especially as its abolition was not likely in general to endanger the funds of the Incorporations, although a strong representation was made to them on the other side. The Incorporations as a rule were in favour of a continuance of the old system, although several held otherwise, more especially the Goldsmiths. The evidence led outside the various Incorporations was decidedly hostile to a continuance of the old practices, which was the means of causing the Commissioners to report as follows:—" We have ascertained that the general opinion of well-informed persons acquainted with the state of the trade and manufactures within the city was, that the time had arrived when the Exclusive Privileges might safely be taken away, leaving the various Incorporations in possession of their funds as benefit societies, with any other advantages of which they might be possessed." While, therefore, the Royal Commissioners reported to Parliament the desirableness of a change to the above effect in 1835, it was not until 14th May 1846 that the right of Exclusive Privilege was finally and for ever abolished.

When the Municipal Reform Act of 1834 became law, the whole state of matters in regard to municipal administration and representation was changed. The Town Council was made to consist of thirty-three members, thirty-one of whom were elected by the direct votes of their fellow citizens, while the Dean of Guild was appointed by the Members of the Guildry, and the Convener of Trades was elected by the Deacons of the various Incorporations. In consequence of the extension of. the city boundaries, the. number of Town Councillors was, in 1856, increased to forty-one. Although recently there has been a still further extension, there has been no change in that number down to the present day.

The Incorporated Trades are, no doubt, an institution of the past, intimately connected with our citizen struggles for municipal independence. Though they are now merely benefit societies, they still retain the right to send, from among their Deacons, a representative to the Town Council, in the person of the Convener of Trades, who in open Council has a seat opposite to that of the Lord Provost, as being practically Vice-Preses of the Meeting. Apart from the care and attention which in early times they bestowed on the productions of their respective crafts, to fulfil a high standard of workmanship, they will be remembered still more for their noble struggles, during many generations, on behalf of free and popular election in our Municipal Institutions.

THE

# INCORPORATED TRADES

OF THE

# CITY OF EDINBURGH.

# THE
# INCORPORATED TRADES
### OF THE
# CITY OF EDINBURGH.

———◆———

## THE INCORPORATION OF CHIRURGEONS (AND BARBOURIS).

N conformity with the custom of the Continental nations of Europe, the chirurgeons, or surgeons, were, in Edinburgh, originally united with the barbers. Their charter, or seal of cause, granted by the Town Council, is dated the 1st day of July 1505, being about eight years previous to the battle of Flodden. It is to the following effect :—

To all and sindrie, to quhais knawledge thir present Letters sall cum, the Provest, Baillies and Counsall of the Burgh of *Edinburgh*, greeting in God evirlesting.

With zoure Universities, that the Day of the Dait of thir Presentia, compeirit before us sittand in Jugement, in the Tulbuith of the said Burgh, the Kirk-maister and Brether of the Surgeanis and Barbouris within the samyn, and presentit till us thair Bill and Supplication, desyring us, for the Love of God, Honour of oure Sovirane Lord and all his Liegis, and for Worscheip and Polecy of this Burgh, and for the gude Reull and Ordour had and maid amongis the saids Craftis in Tym to cum ; that we wald grant and consent to thame the Privileges, Reullis and Statutis contenit in thair said Bill and Supplication, quhilk efter followis.

To zow, my Lord Provest, Baillies, and worthy Counsall of this gude Toune richt humblie meinis and schawis zoure daylie Servitors, the Kirk-maister and Brether of the

A

Chirurgeonis and Barbouris within this Burgh, at all Tymes, as uther Nichtbouris and Craftis dois within the samyn.

We desyre at zoure Lordship and Wisdomes, to give and grant to us and our Successours, thir Reullis, Statutis, and Preveligis underwrittin, quhilkis ar consonant to Resoun, Honure till oure Sovirane Lord, and all his Liegis, perfect and loveabill to this gude Toune.

The following regulations, set forth in the language of the present day, were the rules enacted for the government of the body :—.

1. That there shall be yearly chosen from among us, one "kirk-maister and overisman," to whom the whole brethren of the craft shall give obedience for that year.

2. That no person occupy or use "ony poyntis of oure saidis craftis of Suergerie or Barbourie craft" within this burgh, unless he be first made freeman and burgess of the same; and that he be tried and expert in all the points that the craft should know, and he should be carefully and advisedly examined and admitted by the "maisters" of the said craft for the honourable service of our sovereign Lord, his lieges, and the neighbours of this burgh. Also, that every man that is to be made a master and freeman of the craft shall be examined on the following points and his knowledge thereof tested. That is to say, he must know the anatomy of the human frame and the nature and complexion of every member of the human body; he must also know the veins of the same that he may "mak Flewbothomea (blood-letting) in dew tyme"; also, that he know in which member the sign has domination for the time, because every man "aucht to knaw the nature and substance of everie thing that he wiekis, or ellis he is negligent." Also, that we may have once in the year that one man has been condemned, to make anatomy of after he is dead; by means of which we may gain experience—one teaching others, and "we sall do suffrage for

the soule." That no master-barber within this burgh, nor any of his servants, do exercise the craft of surgery unless he be expert, and know perfectly the things before written. That any person on his admission to the craft as freeman or master, or on his practising any point of the same, shall pay, on entry for his "Upsett," five pounds sterling money of the realm of Scotland, for the purpose of repairing and upholding our said Altar of *St Mungo*, for divine service to be done thereat, with one dinner to the masters of the said craft, on his being admitted and entered among us—with the exception of one lawfully-begotten son of a master and freeman, who, after he has been examined and admitted, shall pay for the dinner, but have no other fees to pay.

3. That no master of the said craft shall take any apprentice or "feit-man" (fee'd man or servant) in future to use the surgery craft unless he can both write and read. Any master who takes an apprentice shall pay, on his entrance, twenty shillings for the keeping up of the altar. All masters were prohibited from resetting or receiving any other master's apprentices or servants until he had served his proper term. Neglect of this law subjected him on every occasion to the payment of twenty shillings for the repair of the altar.

4. That every master who is made a freeman by the craft shall pay his "ouklie" (weekly) pennie with the "Spistes Meill, as he sall happin to cum about"; and each fee'd servant shall pay "ilk oulk" (each week) one halfpenny to the said altar; so that no one had power to complain to do divine service daily at our said altar in time to come. They were also to choose an officer for the ingathering of the quarterly payments, as well as the weekly pennies, who should always precede us on *Corpus Christi* day and the *Octavis* thereof, and all other general processions and gatherings, "sicklyke as the uther Craftis hes within this Burgh." Also, that one of the masters of the

foresaid craft, with the chaplain and officer of the same, " pas at all Tymes neidful," collect the said quarters' payments from every one who owes the same ; and if any be disobedient, his goods to be poinded and distrained, and at all times they must have a town's officer with them.

5. That no master or freeman of the said craft shall purchase any lordship contrary to the statutes and rules above written, in hindering or " skaithing" of the craft foresaid, or common good thereof, under the pain of " tynsall" (losing) of their freedom.

6. That all the masters, freemen, and brethren of the said craft must readily obey and come to their kirk-master at all times when they shall be required by the officer, for the purpose of hearing the quarterly accounts, and for advising concerning any matters affecting the "commonweill" of the craft; and that he who disobeys shall pay twenty shillings to the reparation of the said altar. Also that no person, either man or woman, within this burgh, shall make or sell any *aqua vitæ* within the same, except the said Masters, Brethren, and Freemen of the said craft, "under the payne of escheit of the samyn but favour."

The Town Council's Seal of Cause then proceeds thus :—

Beseking thairfor your Lordschippis and wisdomcs, at the Reverence of God, that ze will avyse with thir our sempill Desyris, Statutis, Reullis, and Prevelegis above writtin, and grant us the samyn ratefeit and apprevit be zou under zour Seill of Cause. And, with the Grace of God, we sall do sic service and plesure to the King's Grace, and gude Toune, that ze sall be contente thairof, and zoure Delyverance heirintill humblis we beseik.

The quhilk Bill of Supplicatioun, with the Reullis, Statutis, and Preveligis contenit thairintill, being red (*sic*) befoir us in Judgement, and we therewith beand ryplie and distinctlie avysit, thinks the samyn consonant to reason, and nathurt to oure Soverane Lord's Hienes, us, nor nane utheris his Lieges thairintil; and thairfoir, we consent and grants the samyn to the foresaids Craftis of Suergeirie and Barbouris, and to thair sucessours, and in swa far as we may or hes powar, confirmis, ratefeis, and approis the saids Statutis, and Reullis, and Prevelegis in all Poynts and Articlis contenit in the Supplicatioun above writtin. And this to all and sundrie quhome it efferis, or may effere, we mak it knawin be thir oure Letters; and for the mair verificatioun and strenth of the samyn, we haif hung to oure Common Seill of Cause; at *Edinburgh* the first day of the moneth of July, the zeir of God ane thousand five hundred and five zeires.

During the following year, on 13th October 1506, the above charter was ratified by King James IV. Again, on the 11th May 1567, the surgeons were exempted from serving on juries, and from watching and warding within the city and liberties thereof. These privileges were conferred upon them by letters patent by Queen Mary, in consideration of their arduous duties in connection with their studies and their attendance on their respective patients. They were subsequently confirmed by James VI. on 6th June 1613, and eventually received the sanction of the Scottish Parliament on 17th November 1641.

The healing art must at all times and in all circumstances be regarded as the outcome of one of the most humane impulses of human nature. In all ages and in all climes, injuries by external violence implied that wounds had to be dressed, bleeding had to be stanched, and blood had occasionally to be drawn, each as the case might be; while injured limbs had sometimes to be taken off, and dislocated joints had to be put right. Where any accident occurred to the frame, there was need of the surgeon. The surgeon's functions imply a knowledge more or less of medicine, as the physician's functions, on the other hand, presuppose an acquaintance with the anatomy of the body and of the surgeon's sphere of operation. In fact, a knowledge of both is requisite, whether the science of healing by instruments is the one to be employed, or the administration of drugs or of other substances supposed to be of a sanative tendency is to be made use of. Surgery cannot now be altogether dissociated from medicine. They are twin brothers, and must always remain so. In the early history of the Incorporation, the culture now required of practitioners could not be possessed by them.

As has been already shown, the barbers formed an integral part of the craft. The barbers, however, have fallen very much from this high degree ; while the surgeons have advanced to so great an extent as to place them second to none of the professional classes in a civilised community. The symbol of the barber, which still takes its place at the door of those who practise the trade, usually exhibits a pole with a ribbon painted around it, and a brass plate at the end of the pole, thereby indicating bleeding and bandaging or binding up. Many, very many years afterwards, a separate profession appeared for this purpose—namely, the " cupper." He, too, is a practitioner of the past ; while the barber of the present day is restricted, notwithstanding of his ancient symbol, to the duty of hairdressing and manipulating the beards of Her Majesty's lieges, the latter of which is an occupation which, in these hirsute days, is likely to become " smaller by degrees and beautifully less." Bleeding, also, is now not often resorted to. The antiseptic mode of treatment of wounds by Sir Joseph Lister, Bart., is now the popular method among surgeons ; while accupressure—the invention of the late Sir James Simpson, Bart. (which he regarded as his greatest discovery, greater even than the use of chloroform)—is an unknown, because forgotten, agency.

A century or so after the Seal of Cause was granted to the chirurgeons, a marked line of demarcation began to exist between them and the barbers, as will appear from the following entries :—

On the 31st March 1585, Alexander Rattray, a " barbour," having offended the deacon and brethren, had to " humell him self to the deakin and brethiring, and ask thame forgevness on his kneis, and of his awin consent bindis and oblissis him, that gif evir he fall in the lyk offence to tyne his fredome of the craft."

5 March 1589.—Mark Libertoun admitted a barbour " to wit, to cow, clip, schaife, and wesche." He was likewise enjoined to practise "na point of chirurgie vnder the pane of tynsall of his fredome." He was strictly ordered to "haif na signe of chirurgie in his bught nor hous, oppynlie or privatlie, sic as pigis, buistis, or chirurgane caiss or box pertening to the chirurganis."

30 March 1603.—Williame Lawsoun admitted to the freedom and liberty of " ane barbour "—viz., " to kow, schave, wasche, and to mak *aqua vitæ* allanerlie : Lykeas the said Williame binds and oblissis him that he sall nowayis vse the art of chirurgie within the liberty of this burght, vnder the pane of tuentie pundis to be payit be him *toties quoties* in cais he contraveine, and sall act him in the tounes bukis heirto vnder the pane foirsaid.

Although the surgeons and the barbers eventually began to pursue entirely different vocations, the line of separation between them getting wider and wider as years progressed, it was not until the 23d of February 1722 that all connection ceased. This was the result of a process before the Court of Session. The barbers by the decree then pronounced were declared to be a separate society to govern themselves; and they formed certain constitutions and rules for their better government, and they applied to the Magistrates and Town Council to ratify the same, which the Town Council eventually did. But as the new body had no electoral privileges, it was not accounted as one of the incorporated crafts, and it is not requisite that its rules or future history should be here treated of.

Other crafts came in course of time to be associated with the surgeons. On an application by the body on 25th February 1657, the Town Council enacted that the surgeons and the apothecaries should belong to one community. This was confirmed by Charles II., and ratified by Parliament on the 22d August 1670. Pharmacy also, at a later period, was conjoined to surgery.

In 1694, by letters patent from William and Mary of date

28th February, liberty was granted to the body to practise in the counties of East, West, and Mid Lothians, and the shires of Fife, Peebles, Selkirk, Roxburgh, and Berwick. This arrangement received the sanction of the Scottish Parliament on the 17th July 1695.

During the first century and a half of the Incorporation's existence the members were in the habit of meeting in the house of the Deacon. On the 15th July 1647, they hired premises in "Diksone Close for £40 yearly." Twenty-two years thereafter—viz., 18th May 1669—they resolved to build a house of meeting for themselves, which was improved in 1697, when their anatomical theatre was completed. In 1705, a Professorship of Anatomy was constituted which received the favour of the Town Council, who connected the Professor with the University of Edinburgh, of which institution the civic body had control.

The erection of the Surgeons' Incorporation into a Royal College in 1778 was one of the most important steps in the history of the body. It gave them a national position, while their old relations with the civic Corporation continued. The same state of matters, which the other members of Incorporations laboured under, during the times when Town Councillors were not popularly elected, obtained in that of the Surgeons. They had their Deacon as an integral member of the Council, and they had to submit their leet to the Corporation, who chose the Deacon or President. They tried to shake off this thraldom; but they were for the time unsuccessful. It is right, however, to say that the Town Council very rarely disappointed them in their elections. The Reform Bill of 1833 made it no longer necessary that the President should be a member of the Town Council. It placed the Incorporation of Surgeons on the same platform as the other Trades Incorporations—viz., it vested in the

President or Deacon a vote in the election of the Convener of Trades. The Act and Charter of the Royal College of Surgeons of 1851 put an end to the civic connection; and thus terminated the ancient relations which existed between them and the Town Council of Edinburgh.

It may still be a subject of debate whether the old civic relationship did not materially help the surgeons in reaching to the high position to which they have now attained. That there was a kindly feeling at all times shown by the Town Council towards the Royal College of Surgeons is undeniable. Their thorough support of the extra-academical or out-door school, against the extreme nonsense urged by ravings of the University Professors of the period, is abundant evidence of this fact. What would the Medical School of Edinburgh now have been without its out-door competitors?

There are many of its members who supposed, and still suppose, that the civic connection was a drawback to the surgeons. That was not the opinion of the University Professors, as will be seen from the evidence of the late Sir Robert Christison, Bart., when he appeared before the Commissioners on Municipal Corporations, on 21st October 1833, in regard to the Town Council's control of University affairs. He said (page 364) :—

"Another serious objection I have is, that the Town Council has been, and will continue to be, open to the admission of men who may, and often indeed must, be prejudiced against the University at large, and also in regard to individual Professors. This took place under the present *régime*, in one department, the medical. The President of the Royal College of Surgeons is a member of the Town Council, and the only medical man there. It seems plain that the governing body of the University should not be so constituted that it may run the risk of falling into the hands of a medical man, and that medical man the head of a rival establishment."

It is pleasing to know that all the bickerings, animosities, and rivalries of those days are now at an end ; that the Professors of the University recognise the necessity and the value of the out-door schools which the Town Council and the Royal College of Surgeons did so much to foster, and that the Medical and Surgical Colleges, fully recognising their respective positions and value, are in entire accord with each other.

The handsome building in Nicolson Street, which is now the headquarters of the Royal College of Surgeons, was finished and inaugurated in 1832. It contains, in addition to the common hall, a fine museum, which it obtained partly by acquisition and partly by purchase. The former was the donation of the late Dr John Barclay, and the latter was bought from the trustees of the late Sir Charles Bell.

# THE INCORPORATION OF HAMMERMEN.

THE Incorporation of Hammermen is a very old civic Corporation in Edinburgh. Although its records go no further back than 1582, it is nevertheless true that the hammermen were at first created into a Society or Incorporation by a "seal of cause" or charter from the Town Council of Edinburgh, on the 2d day of May 1483.

The following is a quotation from the seal of cause :—

"Till all and sindrie quhais knawledge thir present lettres sal cum, Sir Patrick Baroun of Spittalfield, Knycht and Provest of Edinburgh, Patrick Balbyrnie of that ilk, Dauid Craufuird of St Gely Grange, and Archibald Todrik, baillies of the said burgh, with the consent and advyse of the counsall of the samyn, greting: Forsamekill as the hedismen and maisteris of the Hammermen craft, bayth blacksmythis, goldsmiths, lorymeris, saidlaris, cutlaris, buclar makaris, armoreris, and all vtharis, within the said burgh of Edinburgh, the day of the daitt of thir present lettres, presentit thair bill of supplicatioun till ws beseikand reformatioun and remeid of the greitt iniuris and skaythis done to thame, as was contenit in thair said bill, of the quhilkis thair follows a pairt, that thairthrow the said iniuris and vtharis may be eschewit in tyme to cum, sen they depend thairvpoun, and in lyikwis vpoun the honor and worschip of the said burgh, als weill as vpoun thair singular availl and profitt: In the first thair complaint buir and specifyit that thay war rycht havely hurt and put to greit poverty throw the doun cumming of the blak money, walking, warding, and in the payment of zeldis and extentis quhilkis thay war compellit to be vse, and to be compellit thairto be our Lordis authoritie mandimentis and chargis, and in lyik wyis that they wer havely hurt be the dayly mercat maid through the Hie Streitt in Cramis, and on the backsyde the toun in bachling of hammermenis werk pertening to them of thair craft, in greit dishonour to the burgh, and in braking of the auld gude rule and statutes of thair craft, and vpoun vther skathis that sustenit in default of reformatioun. We heirfoir, havand, etc., till equitie and iustice of remeid, considering weill thair supplicatioun and iust petitioun according to the gud reule of the burgh have statute and ordanit ; &c. &c."

The following may be popularly stated as the regulations for the protection of the members of the Incorporation in the exercise of their trade, and for the proper government of the body :—

1. That no hammerman, either master or servant, presume to practise more arts than one, to prevent damage or hurt to other trades.

2. That no person presume to expose to sale any sort of goods in the street at any other time than on the market day.

3. That certain of the best qualified persons of the said crafts be empowered to search and inspect the goods made by members ; and if found insufficient in material and workmanship, the same should be sold under " the pane of escheitt," or forfeiture.

4. That all hammermen be examined by the deacons and masters of their several crafts, in respect to their several qualifications ; and all that are found to be masters of their respective trades, to be admitted into the freedom of the Corporation ; and such as are not, to be rejected till by an industrious application he become a master of his business.

5. That no person harbour or employ the apprentice or servant of another without his master's consent, who shall receive his wages or money he may earn.

6. That no person not of the foresaid craft shall take upon him to sell or vend any sort of work made by any of the said hammermen.

7. That all persons guilty of a breach of the above specified articles, to pay eight shillings Scottish towards the support of the Corporation's altar of St Eloy, in the Church of St Giles, and maintenance of the priest officiating thereat.

The " armourers " were among the first of the hammermen, and, as the term will easily imply, were trained to the making of armour, which was much made use of in those warlike times ; but when that species of defence ceased to exist, they could no doubt take up the manufacture of sword-blades, which formerly existed as a separate trade. It is recorded in 1582 that " Hew Vans, dalmascar," was ordained not to buy " sword-blades to sell again," because the business of a dalmascar was solely confined to the gilding of iron and steel. The fashioning of sword handles was the business of the gairdmakers, and in the following year it is recorded that Robert Lyal, being admitted to the trade, had prescribed to him as his task or "essay" "ane pair of clain skellit gairds and ane pair ribbit gairds." Nevertheless, on the 5th of August 1581, there was an applicant admitted from the fact of his having produced "a pair gairdes, dalmash'd and gilt with lief gold."

These tasks or "essays," as they were termed at the time, constituted what we would now designate the "entrance examinations" for admission to the Corporation; and they were very varied—*e.g.*, in 1584 the cutlers' essay was "a plain-finished quhanzear." The saddlers' essay was "ane man's sadil (saddle) of the French fashion covered, ane woman's sadil ready for covering, ane man's sadil of the Scots fashion covered." The blacksmiths' essay was "ane door cruick and door band, ane iron spaid, ane iron schoile, and horse shoe and fix nails thereto." In 1586 the beltmakers' essay was "ane sword belt and ane belton belt," the use of the latter being to keep the body firm and to provide for the side pistols. The locksmiths' essay was "with consent of the blacksmiths, two kist (chest or trunk) locks." It would appear, therefore, that at this time the locksmiths and the blacksmiths formed two branches of the fraternity. The lorimers' (saddlers' ironmonger, who usually came from Sanquhar) essay was "ane bit of small ribbit sword gairds, and ane bridle bit, ane pair stirrip irons, and ane pair of spurs—these all to be of French fashion." In the year 1595 the manufacture of scissors appears on the record. The sheirmakers are called upon to submit "ane pair of skinners' sheirs and ane pair of taylors' sheirs." In 1600 the armourers had to produce "ane mounted braid sword, sufficiently wrought," and the cutlers "ane finished guinzeir." The "essays" proposed from time to time did not remain perpetual. Hence we find that on the 2d September 1609 the locksmiths' essay was ordained to consist of "ane kist lock, ane hing, ane bois lock, and ane double plate lock." Following out the same rule during the year 1614, a great addition was made to the beltmakers' essay, which was in future to consist of "ane bridle, ane headstill, and ane pair of stirrup leathers." In like manner the armourer was called upon to produce "ane mounted sword and scabbard." The essay of the pewtherers in 1620 was "a quart flaggon," while in 1621, with the special consent of the lorimers, a dagmaker was admitted on production of "a brazen buckle and an arrow head." In 1641 a coppersmith was admitted on account of his having manufactured "a stoving pair and a scovit"; while in 1644 the gairdmakers' essay was made to consist of "ane double scheith and pair of scheiths, ane single scheith, and ane pair of hulsters." During 1644, also, a "key and sprent band" were added to the locksmiths' essay. Up to the year 1647 each member of the Corporation was confined to the practice of his own particular branch of manufacture. This was, however, superseded on the 6th of December 1647, when a person, qualified as a locksmith and knockmaker (clockmaker) produced "a lock with the key and sprent hand, and knock and minutes and dyall." He was admitted with consent of the locksmiths and knockmakers, and the record of his admission bears he was "the first who was permitted to exercise these trades jointly." In 1648 the braziers' essay consisted of "ane little bell, ane hand bell, and ane mortar with ane pestil."

In 1649 and 1653 several changes were made in the future essays of the hammermen. For instance, the saddlers had to produce "ane French sadel and hunting sadel"; the braziers had to exhibit "three several sorts of buckles, three several sorts of nails, with ane sadel head"; the coppersmiths were obliged to submit "ane stewen pan and skeilit," while the armourers' essay was altered to the manufacture of "ane mounted sword, with a new scabbard, and ane Highland guard."

In 1659 and 1660 the saddlers' essay was again changed to "a great sadle, an woman's sadle, a small sadle, a side sadle, and a hunting sadle." Four years thereafter (1664) what we now know as a tinsmith appears on the scene. He is designated in the records "a white ironman." He produced as his credentials for admission "a lantern, a sugar box, a lamp, and a candlestick." In the records of 1688, the white ironmen got prescribed for their essay "a stoven pan, a lantern, a watering-pot for the gardening, and a chandler." During this year, although a "dagmaker" was admitted, eight years thereafter (1676) this particular branch of trade ceased to be recognised, the manufacture of the buckle and arrow head having been added to the gunsmith's essay, which also consisted of "a mounted pistol and a carriban."

The coppersmiths' essay at this time consisted of "a skellit of brass, a stoving pan of copper, and ane standing chandler of beaten brass"; while in 1677 the clockmakers' essay was "the movement of a watch." In 1686 a hookmaker was admitted to the Corporation on his production of "a dozen of hooks and a dozen of clasps." In 1689 the clockmakers' essay was changed to the production of "a house clock, with a watch alarum, and locks upon the doors." During this year a brassfounder was first admitted on his producing "a suit of oval buckles with the pertinents, a bullion-nail, a coach-nail, and a chair-nail." In March 1691 a distressed French Protestant of the name of Paul Martin was admitted as a member of the Corporation, for the purpose of manufacturing lancets, razors, and all manner of chirurgical instruments. His essay consisted of "a dismembering saw for the leg, a trepan, a razor, and a lancet."

Other changes took place upon the membership and their pre-scribed essays, which were originally few and simple; but, as time advanced and civilisation increased, the necessaries of life naturally extended, and the arts and manufactures combined to meet the popular demand. In illustration of this, we may mention the fol-lowing :—In 1728, for the safety of the lieges, the locksmiths' essay was ordained to consist of "a cruick and cruickband, a pass lock with a round filled bridge not cut or broke in the back side, with nobs and jamb bound." In 1733 the white ironsmiths were required to produce "a box with three cannisters in it, of beaten work, a struck globe lanthorn with sixteen horns, and a syphon with a brass bow or curtee"; while the pewtherers' essay was to consist of "a basin, a pint flaggon, and a decanter with a lid and stroup to it." In 1764 the first edge tool maker was admitted on producing "a set of boring bits and a plain iron"; while, during the same year, a fish-hook maker was received into the Corporation on his submitting "a fish-hook and a clasp and eye."

These changes are indicative of the progress of society; and although the various essays which we have enumerated may appear to the reader somewhat tedious and too detailed, nevertheless they not unfrequently serve to show in a very marked degree the manners and customs of the period. For example, in Wodrow's "Church History" it will be found that, in the latter part of the 17th century, no period of the country's history was more celebrated for the use of "handcuffs, gallow-stocks, spikes, chains, axes, cleavers, thumbkins, boots, and other engines of torture, death, and demembration." In fact, the period was remarkable for inventive genius of this sort, as will appear from the following Act of the Privy Council, of date 23d July 1684 :—"Whereas the *boots* were the ordinary way to expiscate matters relating to the Government; and that there is now a new invention called the *Thumbkins*, which will be very effectual to the purpose and intent foresaid; the Lords of His Majesty's Privy Council do, therefore, ordain, that when any person shall, *by their order*, be put to the torture, the said boots and thumbkins both be applied to them, as it shall be found fit and convenient."

Although the Incorporation of Hammermen existed essentially for the purposes of making freemen of the burgh and protecting trade within the limits of the same, it nevertheless does appear from the records that occasionally amateur tradesmen were admitted into the fraternity. For example, on the 21st of March 1657, Mr Charles Smith, advocate (a son of Sir John Smith of Grattle, Knight, who was Lord Provost of Edinburgh during the years 1643-5), was admitted as a blacksmith, on his submitting "the portrait of an horse's leg, shoed with a silver shoe, fixed with three nails, with a silver staple at the other end thereof; which was found to be a *qualified* and well-wrought essay."

Sir George Mackenzie of Rosehaugh was, on the 11th January 1697, also received into the body, at a meeting of the hammermen held in the presence of Sir James Dalrymple of Stair, who was the Lord President of the Court of Session, the Lord Arniston, and "several other persons of quality." He had taken great interest in the Incorporation, and, although at the time he produced no evidence of his practical skill, his services otherwise and goodwill to the body were regarded as a sufficient essay.

Again, it is minuted that on the 25th of March 1746, William, Duke of Cumberland, was admitted to the freedom of the Corporation of Hammermen. He was also admitted to the freedom of all Incorporations within the city; and the various acts of admission were transmitted to him by the then Lord Justice-Clerk (Lord Miltoun)

C

in a gold box, the expense of which amounted to £1212 Scots, equal to £101 sterling. The reason of his having received this signal honour was his victory at Culloden, which was regarded as a sufficient essay.

At a later period (19th July 1784) there is the following entry :— "The Corporation of Hammermen of Edinburgh unanimously resolved to transmit their sincere thanks and acknowledgments to Sir Thomas Dundas, Baronet, chairman, and the other nineteen members of Parliament from this part of the kingdom, who met at London on the 5th current, for their attention to the good of the country, and their resolution to oppose the proposed tax on coals. The meeting, as a testimony of their gratitude, did at the same time unanimously admit Sir Thomas Dundas, Baronet, to the freedom of the Incorporation in all its branches. Ordered this minute to be published in the newspapers."

It is recorded in the books of the Incorporation that on the 6th of October 1695 James Aitchison, engraver, was admitted into the Incorporation, as a proficient in the art of engraving and clasp-making. His essay was a "pair of lock brass clasps, and a cut seal bearing the Hammermen's arms." It would thus appear that at this early period the art of engraving, which has latterly been ranked among the fine arts, was at that time confined chiefly to the cutting of letters and seals. The comparatively recent productions of the late William Miller and William Forrest, as reproduced on plate paper, throw a flood of light on the great development of the engraver's art.

When Maitland wrote his "History of Edinburgh" in 1753, it would appear that the Corporation of Hammermen consisted of blacksmiths, cutlers, saddlers, locksmiths, lorimers, armourers, pewterers, and sheersmiths. To several of these, other trades were united. To the locksmiths were added the watchmakers, pin-makers, hookmakers, and gunsmiths. To the lorimers were added the beltmakers, founders, braziers, and coppersmiths. To the pewterers were added the white ironsmiths or tinmen. The Companies of Arts belonging to the Incorporation were seventeen in number. The meetings of the deacons, masters, and members of the Incorporation were held usually in the beautiful little chapel of St Mary Magdalen, in the Cowgate, almost opposite where the new Free Library now stands. At these meetings the affairs of the Hammermen's Incorporation were thoroughly discussed. The Incorporation of Hammermen were at that time patrons of the hammermen of Portsburgh and Potterrow, as they formerly were of the hammermen of the adjoining town of Leith.

It is right to state that in respect of the meetings of the Incorporation, these did not supersede separate meetings of the several arts, who transacted their business and jealously protected their own interests. The arts elected two officers, the eldest and the youngest master, who respectively presided over these gatherings.

The meetings of the Incorporations were always constituted by prayer. The form of prayer which was made use of was one inscribed on one of the blank pages of an old copy of "The Breeches Bible," of date "anno 1612." The prayer is said to have been composed for the hammermen by John Knox. It is to the following effect:— "Most Holy and Blessed Lord, make us Thy servants, met together before Thee at this time, mindful that all things are naked and open before Thy Majesty, with whom we have to do: Give us, we beseech Thee, to perceive Thee in everything we undertake, and help; and lead us through every difficulty and strait we meet with! Keep our hearts near Thyself! Remove from us all partiality, corrupt affections, and division; and grant us Thy grace to go about everything we, by Thy providence, shall happen to meet with; and that, with upright-

ness of heart, and singleness of eye, as in Thy all-seeing sight and
presence, so that the whole fruits of our labours, by Thy special grace
and assistance, may tend to Thy praise, and the glory of Thy dread-
ful and blessed name, the well-being of every one, and the comfort
and good of us, who are before Thee, and that for Christ, Thy Son's
sake, blessed for ever! AMEN." The prayer was always read by
the clerk; and the same practice continues even to the present
time.

The members who were admitted into the Incorporation had, as a
rule, to be sworn in, and the following entry, of 12th September 1751,
may be interesting, as illustrative of the social customs of the period :—
" One of the honble. the magistrates of the city came to the Chaple,
and qualified such of the members of the house as inclined, and that by
tendering to them the oath of allegiance, together with the assurance
conform to the respective subscriptions *adhibitate* to the said oath and
assurance, in order to such members being entitled to vote in the
election of a Deacon, in the terms of the laws on that behalf made and
provided. Thereafter the Deacon, with some of the senior brethren
who had qualified, went to entertain the Magistrate in a tavern, the
expense whereof ordered, as use is, to be defrayed by the house, and
given out by the Theasurer." This appears from the minute book to
have been a quarterly occurrence.

The oath was occasionally dispensed with—*e.g.*, on the petition of
John Kelly, white ironsmith, whose essay was approved of upon the 5th
of May 1770, and who had paid the last moiety of his entry money,
but was never received as a member of the Incorporation, because of his
refusing to take the oath of admission, as inconsistent with his present
profession of religion. The hammermen, at a meeting held on the
29th January 1774, resolved, out of their high regard for his con-
scientious scruples, to admit him to all the privileges of a freeman

white ironsmith and member of the Incorporation on his subscribing a declaration to the following effect :—

"I do solemnly Declare and Ingage that I shall serve my Customers in my vocation without fraud or guile, that I shall behave myself respectfully to the Deacon and quarter-masters, that I shall bear publick charges, and perform honest services with my brethren according to my ability, and that I shall according to my station maintain and defend the just libertys of the crafts, that I shall be subject to all the regulations of the crafts, which shall be for the just utility and welfare thereof, that I shall not colour unfreemen nor use any collusions with them, that I shall not take any of the brethren's houses, works, or booths over their heads, and I shall not seduce any of their apprentices or servants, nor employ them before they have a proper clearance from their masters."

Although the hammermen as a body were decidedly liberal in their views of civic government and control, and appeared to be liberal in their views of Parliamentary politics, and although the fact recorded above was indicative of a certain amount of religious toleration, there was one question on which their idea of religious liberty was found wanting, and that was the movement which led eventually to the passing of the Catholic Emancipation Act. An entry on 12th January 1779 is to the following effect :—"The Deacon informed the meeting that a petition had been presented to the Lord Provost, Magistrates, and Town Council by a great number of the citizens of Edinburgh, showing that 'they were afraid that a Bill was soon to be brought into Parliament for repealing the statutes that were enacted against Papists, similar to the late Act of Parliament regarding England, which they intended to oppose by every means in their power, and requesting that the Magistrates and Council, in the name of the community and as their guardians, would oppose such intended Bill'—a copy of which petition having been read, &c.—the Incorporation, after serious consideration, were unanimously of opinion that a repeal of the present laws against Papists would endanger their civil as well as their religious rights and liberties." They directed their Deacon to report their views to the Town Council, and to co-operate with and support the petitioners against any attempt for repealing said law.

The state of feeling at the time in reference to the question of religious liberty will be read at present with some interest. The following extract from the records of the hammermen will make this plain :—

"1st February 1779.—The Deacon informed that he had called the meeting at the desire of the Lord Provost and one of the Magistrates, who told him that different copies of an inflammatory letter had been drop'd and found by several persons. A copy of one of them he produces, and was read of the following tenor:—

"MEN AND BRETHREN—

"Whoever shall find this Letter will take a warning to meet at Lieth (*sic*) Wynd, on Wednesday next in the evening to pull down that pillar of Popery lately erected there.                                           "A PROTESTAN.

"Edin. Jany. 29, 1779.

"P.S.—Please to read this carefully, and keep it clean, and drop it somewhere else.

"To every Protestan into
"whose hand this letter
"shall come.            "GREETING.

"The members of the Incorporation present unanimously expressed their detestation of any tumultuous meetings whatever, and agreed to use every means in their power to prevent any such meetings of mobs, and in the meantime would endeavour to prevent their servants from being connected therein."

It is proper to explain that at that period there was no system of police established in the city other than the old Town Guard, for whom the public generally, and the unruly in particular, had a special detestation. While the dropping of the letter was in all probability one of the practical jokes or tricks which the youth of the day were fain to indulge in, it was nevertheless thought expedient to devise measures of defence, as mobs in those days, on mischief bent, were of too frequent occurrence. As an example of this, at a meeting of the Incorporation held on the 1st of February 1783 the Deacon intimated that he had called a meeting of the Couvenery this morning, and that the Lord Provost was present. That meeting recommended a proposal made by the Sheriff, and agreed to by the county, to the following effect:—"That, upon any appearance of a mob, the whole inhabitants should turn out and attend the Magistrates, and do their utmost endeavour to prevent mischief; and that members do keep their servants and apprentices at home, excepting such able-bodied persons as may choose to attend their masters." This was agreed to. The matter, however, again came up on 9th June 1784, thus:—"The meeting having taken into consideration the mobs and alarming riots in the neighbourhood of this city, they unanimously declare their abhorrence of such proceedings, and agree to talk with their servants and apprentices in a serious way, to behave in a decent and orderly manner; and to show them the bad consequences of a contrary behaviour, both to such rioters themselves and to the community; and particularly, that if any of the apprentices should appear among such rioters, they will forfeit their freedom agreeable to their indenture." It will be abundantly evident, therefore, that the hammermen, as well as the other Incorporations, were most helpful to the Magistrates and Town Council in their efforts to preserve the peace of the town.

The Incorporation took a lively interest in many civic matters. When the Town Council proposed to lay or cess upon the inhabitants in 1749, for the maintenance of the Charity Workhouse, a resolution was passed, as the minutes bear, *nemine contradicente* opposing the measure, in respect that they (the hammermen) provided for their poorer brethren. Their interest in their own poor may be illustrated by the following entry:—"2d February 1754.—Ordered that the masters of the several arts, between and the next quarter visit the poor on the roll of their several arts, and report the state of each person and their opinion of the same, under the penalty of half-a-crown each master." They also showed a kindly feeling towards the poverty-stricken clerical denomination of the day—"the poor Episcopal clergy." On 10th April 1751 the minute bears—"Ordered that the Theasurer (*sic*) pay to the poor Episcopal clergy one pound ten shillings sterling for the year to come, from Candlemas 1751 to Candlemas 1752, and so forth yearly in time coming, during the pleasure of the House, and the measure be recalled."

For some reason or other they opposed the South Bridge Act of 1776. They were greatly mistaken in this action. The South Bridge was an extension of the city southwards, and the necessity for it was so evident that the price obtained for the feus discharged the whole costs of the bill and the operations under it—a result not often attained.

They frequently agitated for being relieved from the thraldom of the Town Council in the election of their Deacon. They wished to be free handed, and not hampered by the Town Council selecting three members, out of whom they had to choose their Deacon or representative at the Council Board. The other Incorporations concurred with them in all these measures before the Council, the Convention of Royal Burghs, and the Imperial Parliament. The Reform Bill, however, set this matter right, and the various Incorporations, including the hammermen, were zealous supporters of, and advocates for, the passing of the Reform Bill. The minutes contain the terms of many petitions on this subject, as well as votes of money to help the good cause.

Reference might be made to many other public questions, such as the injudicious patronage of the Town Council in the appointment of a minister, the proposed Coal Tax, the placing of toll bars, the Mortmain Bill, the abolition of the Corn Laws, the First Police Bill, and other public matters. But these are only incidental to a notice of an Incorporation whose chief aim was to protect trade within the district, and to see that there was no *scamping* of work. That they were strict in their oversight of the members will be shown from the following entry :—" 28th January 1769.—A copper backet (bucket) having been seized as insufficient, and James Aberdour having claimed the backet as every way sufficient, the coppersmiths were desired to give their opinion, which they declined to do, in respect of the law process depending between the Incorporation and James Aberdour, but proposed that the Coppersmiths in Cannongate should be desired to inspect the backet, and report their oppinion ; however, the Coppersmiths and J. Aberdour having retired, communed, and returned—reported that they had agreed upon James Aberdour's putting new handles to the backet, at the sight of one of the coppersmiths, and paying the officer two shillings and sixpence for his trouble ; that the same should be returned, which agreement was ratified by the Incorporation, and the 2s. 6d. was instantly paid to the officer."

The passing of the Reform Bill in 1833 led eventually to the abolition of exclusive privilege of trading in Burghs in Scotland, by an Act passed on 14th May 1846. This was disastrous to the continued prosperity of the various Trades Incorporations. No one was likely to become a member of these unless he had a hereditary privilege. The result was that the various Incorporations became weakened as a rule, and took steps to have their funds adjusted, so that the utmost fairness should be shown to all who had a claim upon them. In regard to the hammermen, a scheme was prepared at the time, which took the form of a " contract of annuity," and the deed bears the signatures of the members. The Hammermen's Incorporation still

D

exists for the twofold purpose—(1) of paying the various sums of money to the remaining annuitants, and (2) of electing a Deacon, who has, in virtue of his office, a right to vote in the election of the Convener of Trades, who is a constituent member of the Town Council of Edinburgh. Mr John James Moir is at present Deacon-Convener of the Hammermen, and Mr Alfred Bryson, W.S., is the Treasurer and Clerk.

# THE INCORPORATION OF GOLDSMYTHIS.

THE Goldsmiths were originally included in the Incorporation of Hammermen. At what time they became separated from that body is not now known, as there seems to be no authentic record of the occurrence. It is likely, however, to have been a short time before they obtained from the Town Council a Seal of Cause in their own favour, on the 20th day of August 1581. The Seal of Cause granted to the Hammermen, was at so early a period as 1483, being ninety-eight years previous to that of the Goldsmiths.

The minute-books of the Incorporation, which are still extant, date back to 1525. The names of all the Goldsmiths are therein recorded. But, as many of the special crafts had meetings of their own, and would in all probability have a record of the proceedings of such meetings, it does not necessarily follow that at this time the Goldsmiths had seceded from the Incorporation of Hammermen. On the other hand, the presumption is, that they continued as members of that Incorporation, until they sought a separate and distinct charter from the Town Council in 1581.

Previous even to the existence of the Incorporation of the Hammermen, statutes had been passed by the Scottish Parliament, regarding the "Goldsmythis" of Scotland. During the reign of James II. in 1457, the following statute was enacted :—

"As anent the reformacione of golde and siluer wro$^t$ be goldsmythis ande to eschewe the desaving done to the kingis liegis thair salbe ordaynt in ilk burghe quhair goldsmythis wirkis ane vnderstandande and cunnande man of gude conscience, quhilk sall be dean of the craft. And quen the werk is brot to the goldsmyt and it be golde quhat golde that ever it beis brot till him, he sall gif it furt agane in werk na wer than xx granys. And of siluer quhat ever be brot him he sall gif it furt agane na wer na xj granys. And the said goldsmyt sall tak his werk or he gif it furthe and pass to the dene of the craft, and ger examyn that it be sa fyne as is before wrettyn. And the said dene of the craft sall set his merk and takyn thairto togidder wt the said goldsmytis. And gif faute be fundyne thairin efterwartis the dene foresaide and goldesmytis gudis salbe in eschet to the king and thair liffis at the kingis will. Ande the said dene sall haif to his fee of ilk vnce wrot jd. And quhair ther is na goldsmyt bot ane in a towne, he sall schawe that werk takin it wt his awne merk to the hede officiaris of the towne quhilkis sall haif a merk in like manner ordanyt thairfor and salbe set to the said werk. And quhat goldesmyt that giffis furth his werk vtherwayis thane is before wrettyne, his gudis salbe confyskyt to the king and his life at the kingis will."

In 1483, it was enacted that as " throw the negligence and avarice of the wirkaris and golde smithis the said siluer gevin to thaim is mynging with laye and uther stuife that is put in the said werk that fra the siluer cum agane fra the werkmen. It is sa fer scaithit of the avale fra the fyne siluer that the pupill is ouer gretly scaithit and dissauit therthrow. And thairfor the lordis avis and think speidfull that in ilka towne quhair that golde smiths ar and thair crafts exersit and vsit that thair be deput and ordanit a wardane and a decane of the craft that sall be suorne thairto and examyn all the werkmanschip that cummys fra thair handis. And quhair thai fynd it sufficient set thair merkis thairto. And quhair thai fynd it vnsufficient thai sall Refusit and Punice the wyrkar efter his demeritis. And quhair ony werkman walde culour or stele away his werk w$^t$out examinacioun it sall be eschetit quhaireuer it may be fundin. And the dampnage thairof fall in the werk manis hand."

By the Act of 1485, " a dekin and a sercho$^r$ of the craft " were to be duly appointed, and it was further enacted " that al goldsmytis werk be markit w$^t$ his avn mark, the dekynis mark, and the mark of the towne of the finace of vjd fyne."

It is understood that those enactments, although applicable to the various towns in Scotland, were more strictly carried out in Edinburgh, where the great majority of the Goldsmiths of the country at that time carried on business. Nevertheless, there were frequent complaints of the quality of silver in those days. In the Act of 1555, it is mentioned that the quality was found so low as "six and seven deniers." Pure silver at that time was reckoned as = 12 deniers. The denier was divided into twenty-four grains. The standard was in those days fixed at eleven deniers.

The Seal of Cause originally granted by the Town Council (20th August 1581) is to the following effect :—

1. That na Unfreeman of the said Craft ressave an Prenteis for ane schorter Tyme nor sevin Zeires, in respect of the Difficultie of the said Craft ; and that it sall nocht be lesum to ony Maister of the said Craft, that hes ony Prenteis for the Tyme, to tak or haif ane new Prenteis quhill thrie Zeires be expyrit of the Tyme of his last Prenteis, that he may help and learne the young Prenteis, under the Paine of Threttie Pundis to the Maister that sall faille in ony of the Premissis. And for the better Tryall and Confirmation heirof, that all Indentouris be subscryvit be the Dekin of the Craft, or ane Notair for him. And that nane be buikit in the Tounis Prenteis Buik, but quhair the Indentouris is subscryvit as said is.

2. Anent the ressaving of Fremen and Maisters, be resoun of the Excellence of the said Craft, and Difficultie thairof, and thairby subject to the gryter Fraude and Abusis that may be hurtfull to our Soverane Lordis Lieges, and caus an evil Brute and Dishonour to the Craft and Fremen thairof, that thair, in all Tymes cuming, nane be

ressavit or admittit Maister nor Fremen of the said Craft, bot upoun the Conditionis and Maner following, to witt :—

> (1.) That thay haif bene ane Prenteis of the said Craft, with ane Freman thairof, Burgess of the said Burgh, for the space of sevin Zeires; and haif and servit compleitlie the Zeires of their Indentouris. (2.) That the said Prenteis beand ane Burgess Sone, haif servit ane Freman of the Craft for ane Zeir, and ane Straynger for twa Zeires, efter the outrunning of thair Prenteischip, afoir thay be admittit Fremen and Maisteris of the Craft, according to the Set betwixt the Merchants and the Craftismen, and Actis of Counsall maid heiranent. (3.) That he be of gude Life and Conversation. (4.) That he be valiabill in Gudis and Landis, to the soume of Fyve hundret Pundis, to the Intent he may be mair responsall to answer to all Parties for thair Stufe ressavit, or ellis, that he find sufficient Caution before his Admissioun, to be answerabill to all Men for his Admission and Fidelitie. (*Lastly.*) That he, in haifing gevin ane sufficient Assay, Pruf, and Tryall to the said Deykin and Maisteris of the said Craft, for his cunnyng and Experience, bay thair Workmanschip and Knowledge of the Fynnes of the Metallis, be fund qualifiet thairinto. And gif ony sall be ressavit heirefter, bot in Maner foresaid; the Deykins and Maisteris, and ilk ane of thame Receiveris and Admitteris of the same Persoun to pay an Unlaw of Fortie Pundis.

3. To inhibite and discharge all Goldsmythis quhatsumevir, nocht beand admittit be the Deykin and Maister, is, as said is, to work, melt, or braik doun, or sell any Gold or Silver Work, within his Buith, under the Payne of Twentie Pundis; and gif ony beis fund doand the samyn, that Officiars of this Burgh pas with the Deykin, and Maisteris of the said Craft, serche and braik doun thair Hairthes and Rowmes maid for doing of the samyn, and put thair persouns in Waird, quhill the said Unlaw be payit, and forder Ordour fane with theme.

4. To inhibite and discharge, that na Maister sall ressave ane uther Maisteris feit Servand induring the Term of his Service agreit upoun with his Maister, without his Leive and gude Will of his Maister, so that he be knawin be the Deykin and Brether of the Craft, that he is cum from his Maister with his Leive, under the Payne of Ten Pundis.

5. That na Maister ressave ane Servand and cullour him under his Fredome, in gevin him Libertie to work at his Pleasure, to quhome he pleisis, in Defraude of the

Libertie of the Bretheren; bot, all Servandis sall work for Meitt and Fie, under the Payne of Fortie Pundis, to be tane of the Maister that sall cullour the said Unfreeman.

6. That nane of the said Craft melt any brokin or haill Work, without it be schawin to the Deykin, that it may be knawin quhidder it be stollin or nocht, under the Payne of Twentie Pundis.

7. That na Maister tak on him to work ony Wark in Lattoun or Copper, or gilt the samyn, in Defraude of the Lieges, under the Payne of his Fredome and Payment of Twentie Pundis.

8. That na Maister of the said Craft sall hald ony in a oppin Wark Buithis, bot ane, under the Payne of Twentie Pundis, and wairdin of his Persoun.

9. The uplifting and ressaving of the said Unlawis, to pertein to the Townis Collectouris, and Officiaris at the Command of the Magistrates; and the twa Pairts theirof to be imployit be the Toun to the Use of the Pure (poor); and the third Pairt thairof to be delyverit to the Craft for thair Travell in searching and delating of the Transgressouris. And to this Effect, that ane of the Tounis Officiaris pas with the said Collectouris, and Deykin and Brether of the said Craft, and arrest, waird, and poynd for the said Unlawis swa oft as Neid requyres.

By the Crown Charter of 1586, granted by King James VI. on the third day of January of that year, the Incorporation of Goldsmiths of Edinburgh would appear, as has been already shown, to have possessed for a long period anterior to that time, many rights, privileges, liberties, and immunities. By the terms of the charter referred to, not only all Unfreemen are discharged from exercising the business of a Goldsmith, within the City of Edinburgh and liberties thereof, but the Incorporation is further invested with the power to inspect, try, and regulate all gold and silver wares in all other parts of Scotland, with the right to punish offenders, in cases where they were convicted of working with adulterated gold or silver. The Incorporation also obtained powers to make bye-laws for the better government of the body.

By a charter of King James VII., on 14th December 1687, the Incorporation got all its ancient rights, immunities, and privileges reserved, but it also received the additional privilege of having power granted to the Incorporation to search, inspect, and try all jewels set in gold or silver, in all parts of the Kingdom; to destroy all those that are pronounced false or counterfeit; and to punish Transgressors according to their deserts either by Imprisonments or Fines; in which case they were to be assisted by the Magistrates of the several places where such searches were made, so that they might be able to bring to justice all offenders. There was also a power given to them to seize all the working tools of unfreemen (goldsmiths) that should presume to work within the city or suburbs of Edinburgh, and to detain the same in their custody, until satisfaction should be made to the Corporation of Goldsmiths, by the payment of such fines as were imposed by the Deacons and Masters of the said Incorporation.

The trial of the precious metals on the part of the Goldsmiths' Incorporation—to test their accurate value—was entrusted to the Wardens and the Assay Master, who made use of what is now known as "the ancient Pyx." For information regarding the Pyx, the writer is indebted to his friend Mr CHANEY, of the Imperial Standards Department, Old Palace Yard, Westminster.

It would appear that the first clear evidence that exists of the Trial of the Pyx was in the time of Edward I., about the year 1279, at the period when the Royal Mints were consolidated under one Mint Master, and when the Assay was ordered to be made at the Exchequer, at Westminster, by the King's Assayer. It is right to say that the trial of the justness of the coinage of this country is of still more ancient origin, dating back probably to the time of the Saxons, to whom, in all likelihood, may be ascribed the introduction of the old Standard of Silver in Britain, as regards its quality of fineness and weight. The word Pyx is derived from the Greek, and is of Roman origin, signifying a box. [In church rituals, the Pyx is a little chest or box wherein the consecrated host is kept.] The Master of the Mint was required to place in a box specimens of all gold and silver coins issued by him. This box is opened annually, even to the present day, and the several coins are tested by a Jury of Goldsmiths, both as to the weight and fineness of the metal. The Jury is formed of independent members of the Gold-smiths' Company of London, acting under the judicial authority of the Queen's Remembrancer. They are sworn to test the coins produced by the Deputy-Master of the Mint, by comparison with the standard trial plates of gold and silver, and the standard weights which are then produced from the Standard Department of the Board of Trade. Much interesting information on this subject may be obtained by the perusal of an Official Report made to the Imperial Parliament in 1866, by Mr H. W. Chisholm, the predecessor of Mr Chaney. The present King's Assay Master is Professor Roberts Austin, of the Royal Mint.

The Pyx Chapel at Westminster takes its name from the fact that it contained the Pyx-Box, or Mint Box, and that it has been used as a depository for the standards of the realm since the Norman period. It is now, and always has been, in the direct custody of the Crown. The ecclesiastical authorities, or Dean and Chapter of Westminster, have, therefore, no care of it. It does not appear that the Wardens of the Incorporation of Goldsmiths of the City of Edinburgh ever took part officially in the trials of the Pyx in London, although the Goldsmiths of Edinburgh were entrusted with the trial of the justness of the ancient coinage of Scotland, and took the oath *de fideli administratione* for the proper discharge of their duties.

By the Act 6 and 7 William IV., cap. 69 (1836), which fixes the standard qualities of gold and silver in Scotland, and provides for the arranging and marking thereof, the same gold and silver standards are adopted as in England, the Assayer's "diets" being required to consist of not more than eight grains per pound troy, one half for

E

"diet box," and one half of assay. That is to say, the Edinburgh Assayer or Assay Master was not allowed to take a scrape more than eight grains in the pound from the gold and silver ware sent to him to be assayed. The Act also provides that the "diet box" should be examined annually by such person or persons as the Treasury shall direct—a somewhat analogous procedure to that of the trial of the Pyx.

The duties of the Assay Office in Edinburgh, although quite distinct from the Goldsmiths' Incorporation, have been carried on for many generations under the direction of a Committee of the Incorporation. The Offices consist of two small rooms connected with the Goldsmiths' Hall. The "diet box," punches, assay-books, etc., are to be found there. The Office of Assay Master used to be a life appointment, and was latterly held by the late Mr A. H. Watt, and Mr Cross (of the late firm of Cross & Carruthers) respectively. The holder received a salary, and no other emoluments. Now Mr John Pollock occupies the position. His election is from year to year, and he is paid by fixed salary.

The last trial of the Pyx was on the first day of October last. It took place in the presence of the Deacon and Wardens. The meeting consisted of Mr John Crichton, *Deacon*; Mr John Crichton, *secundus*, *Treasurer*; Mr Archibald Pollock, *Assaymaster*; and Messrs R. B. Kirkwood and Keir. It is recorded that the standard was found to be correct, and the letter for the year then begun was changed to I Gothic. The punches for the previous year were destroyed.

On the 28th May 1890 the duties of 1s. 6d. per oz. on silver and 17s. per oz. on gold were abolished, but that in no way interfered with the obligation to have gold and silver articles hall-marked. It was only reverting to a state of affairs which existed for more than three hundred years before duties were imposed.

In former times the standard of silver was 12 ounces Troy. In the days when Hall-marking was obligatory, silver to the extent of 11 ounces and 2 dwt. required to be found in the 12 ounces—18 dwt. being therefore allowed for alloy. The standard of silver remains the same at the present day.

Gold articles are stamped according to carat. They are stamped with a figure indicating the carat, so that the intrinsic value of the article may be verified. Twenty-four carat constitutes pure or virgin gold. Twenty-two carat is the standard of sterling gold. The ordinary quality of gold for superior jewellery is from fifteen to eighteen carat. The currency is of sterling gold,—viz., twenty-two carat.

In 1588, George Heriot (the great Benefactor to the City of Edin burgh) was admitted a Member of the Goldsmiths' Craft. He occupied the position of Dean or Deacon of the Incorporation about ten years thereafter. He was in great favour with the King, and would no doubt be very popular with the Town Council of the period. It would be no great stretch of imagination to suppose that it was chiefly owing to George Heriot's influence that the Incorporation of Goldsmiths was indebted for its independent Seal of Cause three years after Heriot's entering the craft. The following extracts from the Town Council records of the period will show that George Heriot had other important public parts to play. In 1587, on the 21st day of April, there is the following minute :—" The sam day at efter none it wes proponit be my Lord Prouest that the King's Majestie had send for his Lordschip, and the baillies, qua exponet and declaret unto him that his Graice wes to direct embassadouris to Denmark for intreating of mariage, and thairfore desyret the Guid Town and burrowis to mak the charges and expensis of the schipping to the said Imbassadouris," etc. Again, regarding the expense of the marriage of the King's daughter, the following entry occurs on 17th June 1592 :—" The same day names and constitutes my Lord Prouost and George Hereott eldare commissioners for the Guid Toun to the Parliament of Estaitts, to be halden within this burch."

It may be interesting here to quote the description of George Heriot's attire as recorded by Sir Walter Scott in the "Fortunes of Nigel." "His hose were of black velvet, lined with purple silk, which garniture appeared at the slashes. His doublet was of purple cloth, and his short cloak of black velvet to correspond with his hose; and both were adorned with a great number of small silver buttons richly wrought in filigree. A triple chain of gold hung round his neck, and in place of a sword or dagger he wore at his belt an ordinary knife for the purpose of the table, with a small silver case, which appeared to contain writing materials."

George Heriot was appointed by His Majesty King James VI., under a writ of the Privy Seal, dated at Dunfermline, July 27, 1597, goldsmith to his Queen. He was soon after that event constituted jeweller and goldsmith to the King, with a right to all the profits and emoluments of that lucrative office. In the Diary of Robert Birrel, p. 44, there is the following entry:—"1597. The 27 of Julii, George Heriot maid the Quein's goldsmythe; and was intimat at the Crosse, be opin proclamatione and sound of trumpet; *and ane Clei, the French man*, dischargit, quha was the Quein's goldsmythe befor."

In ancient times the status of the Edinburgh Goldsmiths was a very high one, far superior to that of their brethren in Glasgow. The Edinburgh Goldsmiths, in addition to their ordinary avocations, traded as Bankers, Money Lenders, and Speculators. The business was a very popular one in the city; hence it is recorded that, in 1687, there were twenty-five goldsmiths in Edinburgh, whereas there were only 5 in Glasgow, 3 in Aberdeen, 1 in Perth, 1 in Inverness, 1 in Ayr, 1 in Banff, and 1 in Montrose. It is proper to state that the number of goldsmiths in the city did not include those of Canongate or Portsburgh. These were distinct municipalities—having separate Trades Incorporations of their own, with various privileges conferred upon them both by charters obtained from the Crown, and granted by the Lords Superior of the respective burghs. In most of the burghs, however, the goldsmiths had no separate incorporation; but they were included in the Hammermen.

From the institution of the Incorporation down to the present time, the meetings have been invariably opened with prayer. The following are the words of the original prayer :—

"*Ane prayer to be said alwayes att oure Meatingis.*"

"O Gratious God and loving Fathair, we humblie beseik Thy holy magestie, for Thy awin Chrystis saik, to be present in mercie withe us, in giving and blyssing to all our affairis; and, seeing Thou art only wyse, be Thou oure Wisdome in all oure adoes, and grant that partialitie and all corrupt affectiounes being sett asyide, we may deall in all materis presentit to us withe upricht hairtis and single eyis, as in Thy presence : Sha that the fruitis of owre travellis by thy speall grace may allwayes tend to the glorie of Thy holy name, the weillfair of this oure native toun, and comfort of everie faithfull member of the same, throw Jesus Chryst oure Blyssid Lord and Saviour. So be it."

In later years, the form of prayer was altered, so as to be more in conformity with the times. The following are the words now made use of :—

"O Most Gracious God and Loving Father ! We most humbly beseech Thy Holy Majesty for Thine own Christ's sake to be present in mercy with us in giving a blessing to all our affairs ; and seeing that Thou only

art wise, be Thou our wisdom in all our adoes; and grant that all
partiality and all corrupt affections whatsoever being set aside, we may
deal in matters presented to us with upright hearts and single eyes as
in Thy presence, so that the fruit of our travel by Thy special Grace,
may always tend to the glory of Thy Holy name, the welfare of this
our native Town, and comfort of every Member of the same, through
Jesus Christ, our Lord and only Saviour.   Amen."

The original Members were required to take an oath on their
being made freemen, as Members of the craft of Goldsmiths.   The
following is the original oath :—

*" Followes the forme of the aithe to be givin be these that ar maid
friemen to the craft of Goldsmythis."*

"Heir I protest befoir God and in zour prens and as I sall
ansuar to God that I profess and allow wt my hairt the trew
religioun prstlie professit within this kingdome, and sall abyde
thairat to my lyfe's end.   I sall be leill and trew to the Kingis
magestie and his leigeis.   I sall be leill and trew to my calling,
mantein and defend the liberteis wt my bodie and guidis.   I sall
work na gold nor silver bot that qlk is sufficient of the fyness
following, viz. :—All gold tuentie tua carrottis fyne, and the silver
ellevin dennier fyne, conforme to the Act of Parliament, and sall
not conceill nor cullour na unfriemen's guidis, nayair sall pack nor
peill withe thaime, and allowe and approve all ye actis made of before be my predicessouris Brethrine of the Goldsmythis to ye weill
of my caling, and sua oft as I brek any poynt of this my aithe I
obleid me to pay to ye use of my calling tuentie pundis for everie
fall *toties quoties,* but defalcatioun to be socht be me yairof, and sall
schift nor seik na meains to eschen the samyn at na oyr judge nor

judges bot in this realme, but before ye Deacone and Brethrine of
my calling. Sua help me God, and be God himselff.

"Be yir pntis sub' w' my hand."

In 1805, the form of oath, like the prayer, was, during the month
of September, altered to the following :—

" *Oath to be administered to each Member at his admission.*

"Here I protest before God, and in your presence, and as I shall
answer to God, that I profess and allow with my heart the True Religion
presently professed within this Kingdom, and shall abide therein to my
life's end. I shall be leal and true to the King's Majesty, and His
Heirs ; I shall be leal and true to my calling, maintain and defend the
liberties thereof with my Body and Goods. I shall work no gold or
silver but which is sufficient of the fineness allowed by law, and shall
not conceal nor cover any Unfreeman's goods, neither shall pack nor
peil with them ; and allow and approve of all the Acts made of before
by my predecessors, Brethren of the Goldsmiths, to the weil of my calling, and so oft as I break any part of this my Oath, I oblige myself to
pay to the use of my calling, Forty Pounds for my fault, *toties quoties*,
but defalcation to be sought by me thereof ; and shall shift nor seek no
means to screen the same at no other Judge nor Judges within this
realm, but before the Deacon and Brethren of my calling. So help me
God, and by God himself."

At the present time, there is no oath taken by entrants, a simple
declaration to the following effect being held as sufficient :—

" I hereby declare that I shall be true and faithful to the Incorporation of which I have now been admitted a Member."

The Deacon, also, when he is elected has to make a declaration of fidelity to his office; and the Members on the other hand have to declare that they will be true and faithful to the Deacon, and stand to all the Acts of the Incorporation.

Oaths *de fideli* are still administered to the Treasurer, Quarter-Masters, Wardens, Assay-Master, and Collector and Treasurer.

The Hall of the Incorporation was originally situate in Parliament Close. There, for several generations, the meetings used to be held. The present premises in 98 South Bridge Street were purchased by the body in August 1809, and from that time to the present day, these premises have continued to be their headquarters. There is mention in the Records of the north-west corner of South Bridge Street having been purchased and used as a hall. This, however, must have been only for temporary use. There is evidence in the minutes of these premises having been afterwards let, and finally disposed of prior to 1823.

The Great Fire in Parliament Square, which was the means of destroying so much valuable property, occurred on 15th November 1824. The old Hall in Parliament Close must by that time have passed into other hands, as there is no mention in the records of any loss having been sustained by the Goldsmiths. On the other hand, there is the following entry in the Minute-Book of date 22d November 1824 :—"The Deacon moved that Twenty Guineas be granted to the poor sufferers by the late calamitous fires; which motion was seconded by Mr Craig. Mr Francis Howden moved as an Amendment that the consideration of the subject be delayed until the state of the funds already received and their application shall have been published; which amendment was seconded by Mr Nasymth. The names of the members present were then called, and the vote taken, the state of the question being Amendment or Motion, when the following members voted for the Amendment, viz. :—Messrs Adam

Elder, William Marshall, Francis Howden, James Nasmyth, Andrew Wilkie, William Cunningham, Daniel Walker, William Edmonstone, Alexander Ramage, and Simon Cunningham ; and for the Motion, Messrs Deacon Cunningham and James Craig. The Amendment was therefore declared to be carried."

It is proper to state that the Goldsmiths' Incorporation has, as a rule, been most liberal in their benefactions to public charities ; and several of the charitable institutions of the city receive at the present time an annual contribution from their funds.

The following entry from the Minute Book will serve as an illustration of Burghal life at the period referred to :—" 15 July 1794.— . . . Mr P. Cuningham then represented to the meeting that Mr Ochiltree, a member of their body, had been last night cruelly beat and bruised, and otherwise very ill used by the soldiers of the City Guard, when he was returning home in a peaceable and orderly manner, and requested that an investigation should be made into the affair, and a note written to the Lord Provost, soliciting him to take it under his cognisance."

From time to time the Incorporation has passed Laws for the regulation of its affairs. On the 12th of August 1766, certain Rules were made for the establishment and management of a Widows' Fund. Again, on 29th June 1813, Regulations were enacted regarding the providing of Annuities to Members of the Incorporation on their attaining a certain age and complying with certain conditions. During the years 1823, 1825 and 1826, certain modifications took place on these. The last and existing code of Laws was agreed to, so recently as 10th November 1886.

In terms of the Charter by King James VII. in favour of the Incorporation, apprentices are required to be indentured for seven years, and the office-bearers must be present at the signing of the

F

Indenture, which has to be entered in the Minute Books. A note is also recorded when the Indenture is discharged. Applicants for admission into the Incorporation are admitted at 21 years of age, provided that three years have elapsed from the date of the completion of their apprenticeship. They must produce, along with their Indenture, a Burgess Ticket. If the Meeting of the Incorporation agree to the application, an Assay Piece is resolved upon, to be made by the applicant, at the sight of two of the Members, as Assay Masters, in any workshop the Incorporation may direct. Four months thereafter, the report regarding the Assay is presented; and, if favourable, the applicant is admitted to the body, on his paying to the Treasurer the requisite fees.

There are quarterly Meetings for the passing and auditing of all accounts, and the office-bearers are elected annually. Mr John Crichton is the present Deacon; Mr John Crichton, *secundus*, is the Treasurer; and Mr John P. Wright, W.S., is clerk and law agent of the Incorporation.

# THE INCORPORATION OF BAXTERS.

CONCERNING the origin and history of the Incorporation of Baxters, or Bakers, very little is known in the present day. Maitland, when he published his History of Edinburgh, thus wrote:—" Although the Company of Baxters, or Bakers, be one of the chief Incorporations in Edinburgh, I cannot learn the time when it was first erected into a fraternity; though for that end I not only applied to their clerk, but likewise to the chief men of the Company, but without success. However, it must have been before the year 1522, when by a grant from the Common Council of this city to this Corporation, of the 21st March in the said year, concerning grinding their corn at the town's mills, they then appear to have had both a deacon and master, which shows them to have been a Society before that period. And to transact their affairs in, they have a convenient hall in James' Court."

The writer cannot well understand where Maitland sought for his information. He seems, like Moses of old, to have been in sight of the promised land, and yet was not permitted to enter. On the day previous to the said Act of Council to which Maitland refers—viz., 20th March 1522,—the records of the Corporation bear that the Provost, Magistrates and Town Council had granted the Baxters a seal of cause, which is to the following effect :—

To all and sundrie quhaise knawledge thir present letteris sall to come, the provest, bailies, and council of the brugh of Edinburgh, greeting in God everlasting. Witt your universities that ther compearit before us counsally gatherit within the Towbuith of the said brugh, our lovite neighboures and toune burgesses—viz., George Foulis, Walter Scott, George Gibson, David Gillaspie, William Wilkieson, Robert Rodger, Johne Maider, Henry Scot, Alexander Heriot, Andrew Simson, Michael Gibson, James Baird, James Scot, John Fallsyde, Johne Black, Archibald Bartillmo, Johne Bartillmo, James Gillaspy, Edward Thomson, Andrew Bovss, Arther Mowbray, and Michael Lochmyll, Kirkmaisteries, and the laif of the maisteries of the Baxter Craft within the brugh, and present thair supplicautione till us, makand mentione that the facultie and power they had of before upon the guid guyding and reule of thair said craft was destroyit and our seal of cause tane thairfra be negligent in time of troubill, and thairfore desyrit the samyne newlinges againe to be granted for the honour and lovage of Godis service at thair altar of Sant Cubart, situat within our colledge kirk of Sant Geille within our said brugh, and for the common profeit of the neighboures thairof conteinand this effect :—

In the *first*, that na persounes presume them to be maisteris of the said Craft, to baik thair awin stuffe to sell without they be first prenteis, syne burges, and thairafter examynit be the maisteries of the said Craft, fundin able, and admitit thairto, and syne thairafter till pay thair dewties as uthir Craftis dois within this brugh ; and also that the said Kirkmaisteris and brether of the said Craft choise them ane sufficient chaplane at thair pleasure to make devyne service at thair said altar of Sant Cubart, upon ane competent pryce as they can agrie with the said chaplane, sicklike as uthir Craftis dois within the said brugh ; and that ilk brother of the said Craft furnish the said chaplane orderly as he sall happen to cum about to theme ; and quhen any persones of the said Craft happens to be chargit to forgather with the Kirkmaisters and principal maisters of the said craft to treit upon the common weill and profyte thairof, and absent thame but rationable cause, that persone to pay ane pund of wax to Sant Cubart's light at thair said altar ; and also quhatever he be maister of the said craft that beis apprehendit bakand falss and rotten stuff, or insufficient to sell again to our Soverane Lordis lieges, sall pay ane pund of wax to thair said altar the first tyme, and for the secund falt, two pund of wax, and gif he beis overtane in the third falt, he and his bread sall be brocht before the provest and baillies, and they to punish him thairfore as sall be thocht expedient with the advise of the Kirkmaister and worthiest of the said Craft as effeirs.

*Item.*—That quhatsumever persounes of the said Craft happens till disobey the Kirkmaister and the worthies uther persounes forgatherit with him of the said Craft for the honour and common weill thairof sall pay fourty shillings to Saint Geilles wark, and twa pund of wax to Saint Cubart's altar as said is.

*Item.*—That no maister of the said Craft sall take ony childer in service thairat ane or mae fra this tyme furth, but gif they be prentices and pay thair dewties as effeirs, and that na baxter take nor resset ane uther man's servand of the said Craft under the payne of fourtie shillings to Saint Geilles work, and twa pund of wax to Saint Cubart's licht, or else to be expellit frae the occupatioune thairof.

*Item.*—Anent the flour baiks and fadges that cumes fra landwart into this toune to sell (this afterwards explained), that they may be examit upone the guidnes of the stuffe and weicht for the toune weill sycklyke as thair stuffe is, sua that gif they be nocht fundin conformand in guidnes and weicht, with the avise of the officiaris and maisteris of the said Craft, that they be destroyit; and nocht to repair with sycklyke stuffe in tyme thairafter sen this caiss standis baith for the common weill and common profeit of our mylles, and also that they micht have facultie and priviledge yet as of before to make statuts and reules for the guyding of thair said Craft in honestie, and for the common weill of the said toune, accordand till equitie and reasoune.

With the quhilkis desyres we beand diligently avisit has consider it the samyn and fyndes them conformand to the honour and lovage of Gode and this guid toune and common profeit of our Souerane Lordis liegis repairand thairto; we ratiffie and confirme the samyn in all effect above written.

In witnessing of the quhilk thing to thir our present letteres we have gart append our common seal of cause of the said brugh at the samyn the twentie day of the moneth of March, the year of God ane thousand fyve hundreth and twenty and twa yearis.

A printed copy of the above seal of cause was granted to the Incorporation of Bakers in 1825. The original, therefore, must have been lost.

From the foregoing seal of cause it would appear that the Incorporation of Baxters is by far the oldest civic incorporation of Edinburgh. The document referred to states that it is a new charter of incorporation, the body having for some reason or other forfeited its previous one. That there was a previous charter is self-evident from the minutes of the Town Council, which, in so far as they have been preserved, are about a century older than the seal of cause which has been quoted. The writer will give a few examples of them. For instance, in 1443 (April 9), there is the following entry :—

It is statute and ordainit that na baxter baik na mayne breid to sell fra hine furthwart, saiffing allenarly at Whitsounday, Saint Geillis messe, Yule and Pasche ; and that the said breid sall nocht be sauld at nane of the said festivall tymes bot endurand aucht days, that is to say begynnand at the evin of ilk ane of the said feists and endurand quhil that day awcht dayes, and gif any mayne breid be sauld any uther tyme it sall be chete, and the said baxteris sall nocht bake the said mayne forotyn pase to be given to thame to the baillies.

Again on 13th September 1456, regarding the entrance of their members as burgesses or freemen, there is the following entry :—

The quhilk day it was grantet be the provest, baillies and counsale of the toun in favoures of the haill Craft of the Baxteris that thair sall na man of that Craft be maid burges or freman, without the avys and consent of the maist pairt of the worthiest of the craft, and that it sall be sene that he be worthie and sufficient to labour, and that he haif cunnying and power to labour, and that thai pay their dewteis to the altar lyk as the laif of the Craft dois.

On 10th November 1482 all Baxters within the burgh were forbidden to purchase flour, whether for baking of bread or to sell in small quantities, without paying to the "fermorar of thair common mylnis" the multures (multour thairof as efferis). It would appear that in those days the Bakers had the privilege of selling flour in small quantities to the poorer people; because the same Act of Council ordains that no merchant within the burgh take upon him to tap or sell any flour "in small bot in greit, under the pane of escheit of the samyn quhair evir it may be foundin or ourtane."

On the 10th of November 1492 the Baxters were ordained by the Town Council to pay multure on all imported flour, and they were forbidden to sell flour in large quantities—this privilege being reserved for the merchants. The regulation regarding the Baxters grinding corn at the town's mill seems to have been in existence before the date mentioned by Maitland. By an Act of Council on 28th July 1514, the Magistrates and Council re-enacted the rule which had previously obtained that during times of scarcity of water each neighbour thereof should have the facility and privilege of grinding four "laid of quheit" (wheat) and eight "laid to be broken in his roume as accordis," so that each neighbour one after the other should be served; and when any failed to take his turn it should be lawful to the next person to occupy the place for the time. Whoever should be found guilty of breaking this statute should be fined in the sum of twenty shillings, of which fifteen shillings should go to the "Kirk werk," and five shillings to "their awin altar." Alexander Gray, the "serchour," was to be recompensed for his labour, and had to collect the multure.

The minute of the Town Council to which Maitland refers re-enacts former rules in regard to the grinding at the mills, and specially forbids the Incorporation of Baxters grinding at any other mills except those of the city.

Down to the year 1518 the Incorporation of Baxters appear to have had a monopoly in the sale of bread to the inhabitants. The Lords of the Scottish Parliament, however, altered this state of matters, and permitted outsiders to bring in bread to be sold on the market days. This caused the Incorporation to apply to the Town Council for protection from the invaders, by asking that rules should be laid down for the strangers regarding the terms on which bread could be sold. The following minute, of date 15th October 1518, was passed by the Lord Provost, Magistrates, and Town Council in regard to this matter :—

It is statute and ordainit be the president, baillies, and counsale that foresamekill as it is statute be the lordis of Parliament that it sall be lesum (lawful) to strayngeris to cum with their breid to this burgh and sell the samyn on twa mercat dayes in the owlk, Wedinsday and Fryday, and becaus the saids strayngeris and vnfremen [nother] stentis waikis nor wairdis nor beris na vther portabill chairges within this burgh, that thairfore it is statute that iiijd. laif of quheitt breid sawld be the said vnfremen sall wey iiij vnces mair than the iiijd. laif baikin within this burgh, and that the samyn be of fyne stufe weeill baiken and dryet, and the gray breid vj vnces mair than the gray breid baiken within this burgh vnder the payne of escheitt of the breid.

The Magistrates and Town Council seem to have exercised strict surveillance over the Baxters' fraternity, as well as those who sold or bought meal. They, therefore, did not leave the matter to be adjudicated upon by the members of the Incorporation as was to be found in the case of the Hammermen. This will be evident from the following minute of the Council, of date 4th April 1503 :—

Thir ar the personis and regrattouris (retailers) vnder writtin of meill (meal) that ar convict be ane assys for the bying of the samyn in greit quantitie, mair than may sustene thair self to thair awin meit, and selling of the samyn to the puir folkis vpoun proffeit-wynning, causand greit darthe.

*Item.*—Thir ar the personis caik-baxteris regrattouris vnderwritten that ar convict be ane assys for the baikin of caikis, nocht kepand the pais vait and wount, that is to say, that the caikis for the penny sould wey vther half-tymes almekill as the penny quhit breid, viz., the quhit penny laif weyand xvj vnce, the vther to wey xxiij vnce, and swa les or mair pais [as] accordis; and attour the baillies ordanit and chargit gif thir personis aboue written will baik ony caikis in tyme to cum, or the laif that are convict, that thai obserue and keep the statutis maid thairvpon as accordis.

The Town Council also passed ordinances regarding the quality of the bread baked, as well as in regard to the weight and the price. One of these is to the following effect :—Ordains all masters of the Baxter Craft, and all Baxters within this burgh, to bake their bread "sufficientlie and weill dryit" under the pain of "tynsall of their freedome and escheiting of their breid that dois in the contrare, and to be merkit with thair irnis as abefoir vnder the said payne." Another is to this effect :—The Town Council finds and declares that, by the price of wheat as found at the last market day at 12s., that the Baxters bake commonly to our Sovereign Lord's lieges 12¼ ounces well baked bread and dried sufficient stuff for one penny; and that they furnish the town with 2d. bread and 1d. bread, and that they sell "nocht to the tovne vnder the payne of spaining fra the occupation yeir and day; and that thay cum to the clerkis buith and tak thair tikket heirvpon." There are also ordinances regarding "fages" of wheat bread and the "fowattis of Musselburgh," all which must be regulated by "the wecht of Leith." From time to time, according to the Town Council records, the civic body fixed the price at which bread was to be sold within the burgh.

The Baxters seem always to have had some fatality about them as to their history and their records; because the chief historical volumes of the Corporation have not now any existence. It is understood that these were destroyed some years ago by one of the chief officials of the Corporation, whose appreciation of the minute books seemed to rank them no higher than the value of waste paper. With that act of vandalism perished a good deal of matter that might have shed some light on the civic history of the period.

It ought to be stated, however, that the Incorporation of Baxters was at one time a very wealthy fraternity, that built and owned for many years several mills on the Water of Leith, viz., the West Mill, Mars Mill, the Greenland Mill, etc. There they ground their own grain, and that of other bakers of Edinburgh, who were not members of the Incorporation, and who carried on business in the town after the exclusive privileges of trade were abolished within the burgh.

G

These mills were eventually a great loss to the body. In fact, they absorbed nearly all the funds of the Incorporation other than the funds specially reserved for the widows. It is understood that not less a sum than £40,000 perished in this adventure. The great cause of the eventual failure of the Water of Leith mills was the creation of a milling industry in the town of Leith, when steam took the place of water power. The bakers in general ceased to purchase grain and send it to the mill for grinding. They found it was more profitable for them, and gave them less trouble, to purchase the flour ready made from the millers. A baker was thus enabled to start business, and work upon a smaller capital. To show how unprofitable the Water of Leith mills had become, it may be stated that during the last year of the Incorporation's proprietary interest in them, they were let to a Mr Allan without any rent, but on condition that he paid to the City of Edinburgh the feu-duty exigible for the ground.

The Incorporation, however, was more careful about the money set aside for their widows. This was strictly guarded by a special Act of Parliament passed in the year 1813. The fund is therefore dispensed in accordance with the provisions of this statute, and is now a valuable inheritance to those who possess the right under it.

There are on the average quarterly meetings of the body. Mr Alexander Ramage is the present Deacon, and he has recently been appointed Convener of the Trades. Mr Edward Sawers is Treasurer, and Mr R. B. Ranken, W.S., is Clerk of the Incorporation.

# THE INCORPORATION OF "FLESCHOURIS."

AT a very early period in the history of the Scottish burghs, a due surveillance seems to have been kept over the markets, and as to the sale and purchase of perishable food. Laws regarding these are fully set forth in the *Leges Burgorum*, *i.e.*, the Laws and Customs of the Four Burghs of Scotland—viz., Edinburgh, Roxburgh, Berwick, and Stirling. They are contained in the most ancient MS. now preserved (the Berne MS.) among the public records of Scotland in Her Majesty's General Register House in this city. These four burghs constituted a court of consultation, in which the Great Chamberlain of the Kingdom presided, and where he was assisted in the adjudication of disputes by commissioners from the four burghs referred to. Some of these laws in reference to the "fleschouris" are to the following effect :—

Clause 68 provided that whoever sells flesh shall sell "gude and halthsum flesh, sic as ky, oxen, and swyne," at the sight and consideration of the good men of the burgh (*proborum hominum villae*). It enacted also that the same should be exposed in their windows or in the open market, so that the goods might be common to all willing to buy. And if any foul beef or salmon was brought into the market, the "serjand" of the burgh was to seize the same, and "send it incontinent to the puire or leprose folk," or otherwise dispose of it as he thought fit, "without ony question, favour, or grace." If the seller had received any money for the same, he was compelled to pay it back to the purchaser "without difficulty or delay." In the event of his refusing to do so, he "sall be distrinzeit be ane unlaw."

The same clause also enjoins the Fleschouris to serve the burgesses in slaughter-time, from Martinmas to Yule. They were to serve them "in slaying, dichting, and ordouring of thair flesche to lay in thair lardner." During the time they were so occupied in serving the burgesses they were to "sit and eat with thame at thair awin buird, and thair servandis with thair servandis." The fee to be paid was as follows:—"For ilk kow and ox, ane half-penie; ane swyne, ane half-penie; and for fyve scheip, ane half-penie." There is also this general injunction—"Gif the Fleschouris grathis not the flesh weill, they sall restoir the damnage and skaith to the awineris thairof."

By clause 69 a prohibition was enacted against slaughtering beasts or selling flesh during the night, but only during "fair daylicht," under pain of unlaw.

By the statutes of the Gild, "apprysouris" were appointed to set a price upon flesh (stat. Gild 53), who were sworn to appraise the same faithfully, and in doing so to spare no person for "fee, favour, or dread."

Laws are also enacted regarding the purchase and sale of fish.

The "*Iter Camerarii*," which contains the Prohibitions of the Lord High Chamberlain, has (c. 8) the following "*Challenge of Fleschouris*":—

In the first, that they sell not the flesh conform to the price set thairupon be the honest men of the burgh.

*Item.*—That they sell the flesh befoir it be prysit, as thay pleise, or efter it is prysit they sell it dearer, and of ane greater price.

*Item.*—That thay buy and slayis beistis within time of nicht, aganis the law of the burgh.

*Item.*—That thay foirstall the burgh, buyand without, in ane town in the countrey.

*Item.*—That thay sell flesh without ane token or signe, or befoir the putting out of the samin.

*Item.*—That thay sell guid flesh to strangeris, and evil flesh to nichtbouris, or contrary wayis.

*Item.*—That thay conceale or denyis the price of flesh to thame that desiris to knaw the samin.

*Item.*—That thay sell flesh in secret, and not in thair buith ; or in thair buith, not havand thair window opin.

*Item.*—That thay mak lardner in griet, and sellis it out to tavernis in small, aganis the law of the burgh.

*Item.*—That thay deny to the apprysouris how thay buy thair beistis in the countrey, contrare thair aith, swa that thay may not be laucchfullie prysit.

*Item.*—That thay tak tar ledderis aff the hides, and thairafter affirmis the samin to be haill and not dismemberit.

*Item.*—That thay mix togidder auld flesh and new sayand all is of ane, or ony unhalthsum flesh.

*Item.*—That thay blaw the flesh and cause it seem fat and fair, throw the quhilk sindrie men takis seiknes, and utherwayis are beguylit.

*Item.*—That thay have not all mauer of flesh reddie to sell as effeiris for the tyme.

The first allusion to the duties of the Flesher Craft which appears in the minutes of the Town Council of Edinburgh—in so far as these records are extant—goes back to the year 1483, and, strange to say, it has reference to the selling of fish. It is as follows :—That " na fische be halden nor keipit into houssis, nor brokin into houssis, bot in the mercat vnder the pane of escheit, and vnlaw of vijs. *Item.*—That " na fische be halden ouer nycht and presentit the morne to the merket, vnguttit or clengit, vnder the said pane." One of the Bailies (weekly in turn, especially during the season of Lent), accompanied by one Coun-cillor and two sergeants, had to visit the market to see that the regulations were kept, and also to observe that the fleshers broke the fish honestly for the fee paid to them for so doing.

The remuneration paid to the flesher was as follows :—"*Item.*—Ilk fleshour sall haue to his fie for braiking of ilk killing, lyng, skait, jd. ; and for the turbet iiijd. ; and for pellock sald derrer nor xxti. schillingis xijd., and within xxs. vjd. ; and for ilk salmond ijd., and sicklike of all vther griet fische." It would thus seem that the salmon was in those early times accounted of very little repute. In the recently published Memoir of Sir George Burns, Bart. (the Patriarch of Wemyss Bay), it would appear that upwards of 300 years afterwards the salmon was still being regarded as a very common fish; because, in his "father's native town of Stirling, it was a customary stipulation by servants that they should not be fed on salmon more than twice in the week."

The duty of the flesher was simply to cut up the fish; he was not permitted in those days to sell or retail fish. The prohibition against his doing so is as follows:—" *Item.*—That na fleschour bye na fische to sell and regrait agane, bot to brek thame allanerlie for thair fie as said is, and handell thame honestlie."

A few years after the above ordinance of the Town Council, the Fleshours applied for a Charter of Incorporation. Their seal of cause is dated the "allewint" (11th) day of April 1490.

The circumstances under which it was granted are as follows:—On the foresaid day there compeared in the Chambers of the Tolbuith of Edinburgh, in the presence of the "richt nobill and worschipfullmen"— viz., Thomas Tod, Prouest for the time; George of Touris, James of Cubing, and Thomas of Yhare, Bailies; John Foular, dene of Gild; John of Teudy, thesaurer; and "the laiff of the counsall" of the town and burgh of Edinburgh; and presentit a supplication and bill of complaint—the following—viz., Richard Furde, "deykin" of the Fleschouris for the time, Robert Gray, Johnne Coky, John Malcolm, eldar, Riche Gray, Androw Tait, Patrick Andersoun, John Malcolm, younger, Adam Edgear, Androw Sillar, John of Fyfe, Johnne of Loche, John Towart, Robert Gilry, Dauid Johnstoun, Richard Phillop, Dauid Airth, Gilleis Ker, and others, the principal masters of the said Flesher-craft, desiring the said Provost, Bailies, and Council of the town, that having regard to the great trouble and vexation that the officers had experienced hitherto by the "evill reull, multitude of dyuerssis persouns vnhabill

contenit in the burgh [quha] sclander and blaspheme men of the toun
and the haill craft throw evill payment and vther wrangous iniuris and
deidis" used among the Craft, to the great hurt and prejudice of the
town and common profit of the same, that such things might be set
right and reformed by the Provost, Bailies, and Council of the town
with the advice of the deacon and principal masters of the Craft, by
passing such statutes and rules and ordinances as the said Craft thinks
expedient, with the advice of the said town. The which bill of
supplication and complaint having been openly read, heard, and seen by
the said Provost, Bailies, and Council, they therewith, in absence of the
Craftsmen, advised and considered the bill, and found it was profitable
and needful for the common profit—that amongst themselves for the
proper control of the Craft, that they should make certain statutes,
which the good town, with the deacon of the Craft and the masters of
the Craft should use, execute, and punish the trespassers as effeirs,
according to the laws of the burgh.

The said deacon and masters of the Craft then presented to the said
Provost, Bailies, and Council their desires, statutes, and rules, and
caused them to be read and considered in the Tolbuith, with the terms
of which said Provost, Bailies, and Council were advised. The tenour
of them is as follows :—

*Imprimis.*—We the deykin and principale maisteris of the Fleschouris Craft within
this burgh, thinkis it expedient for the comoun proffeit that all vnfreeman, laidies and
boyis, vsand our Craft be expellit thairfra bot gif he outhir will be ane vomannis prenteis
or ane feit man, gif he can work for certune yeiris, efter the tennour of the auld actis of
the toun maid of before, sua that na man handill menis sustentatiouns wther at his stok
or vtherwayis, but honestlie be the maister him selff, or his seruand, or prenteis allanarlie
as effeiris, and nane vthers vnder the pane of xl s., the tua pairt to be raisit be the
officeris of the toun to the Kirk werk, and the thrid pairt to be raisit be the deykin of
Craft to the reparation of thair awin altar vnforgevin ; and sicklyk all the vnlaws of
thair statutes vnderwritten beiris.

2. We think it expedient for the honour and honestie of freemen of this Craft, that ar of small substance, quhill God refresche them, that thairfor sic a burges bot na vther persoun marrow him with ane maister of substance, and lay his penny to his, and sua far as it will reik the pennyvorths to be bocht betwixt them, and they to dele thairvpon vyning and tynsell as effeiris, and sua far as ilk pairt reikis ; and gif this freemen gettis credence in the cuntrey of ony stufe, he to bring it to the guid toun and sell it oppinlie in the mercatt, the said fremen first fyndand souerty at the Craft sall nocht be blasphemit through his evill payment, nor yit the officeris of the toun to be wexit for administratioun of justice, vnder the pane xl s. for ane vnlaw to be disponit and raissit as first saidis be the officeris of the toun and the deykin of the Craft for the tyme.

3. We think it expedient that the deykin and best of the Craft daylie serche the Craft, gif ony of them owther byis slais or sellis ony infectit flesche or fishe with or keippis rottyn purit beistis, cassin or deid be the selff, or ony ither insufficient sustentatioun owther of fishe or flesche ; and quha that beis apprehendit theairwith to be depryvit of his fredome, the guids to be escheit to the seik folk in almous (alms) and he to be baneist the toun and Craft, by the officiars at thair discretioun for evir mair.

4. We think it expedient that na freman of this Craft dele nocht be pairties man with ane unfreman, becumis his guidis under cullour of his awin contrair his aith, under pane of depriuand of his freedome, and putting fra the Craft, and escheting of the stufe that he collouris.

5. That na flesche be brokin nor sauld in hiddillis nor in bak houssis, bot oppinlie in the hie mercatt, quhair it may be sene and sercheit be the deykin and the Craft, with ane officer of the toun, that the falt may be sene and pvneist and the guidis falteis to be escheit and delt ; and siclyk quhair ony nolt hydis or ony vther infectit flesche bene brokin to sell amangis guid stufe to the Kingis leidgeis, that stufe to be escheit, and the persoun pvneist at the discretioun of the Provest, Baillies, and Counsale, and be awyse of the deykin and the heidis men of the Craft.

6. We think it expedient that na man of Craft, candlemakers, nor vthers, in tyme to cum, but fremenis soneis of the Craft vse the Craft, and that can handill in himselff baith in slaing and breking as a Craftisman honestlie at his stok, and as he hes been leirnit and brocht vp thairwith vnder a maister, vnder the penalty of xl s. and escheitting of thair guidis as said is, and banysing of the Craft.

7. We think it expedient that na man of this Craft pas outwith the toun,

nor send their seruands to by ony stufe fishe or flesche, beif, mwttoun, veill, lameis, swyne, nor kiddis, frae Pashe to Mydsomerday, that all beistis may be in ply, vnder the pane of escheit; and gif a maister sendis his seruand to landwart to fesche ony beisties to sla at his maister has coft himselff, and nocht be his seruand vnder cwllour, he sall first certifie the deykin and vther maisteris of the Craft that thai guidis was coft be the maister his selff, and nocht be the seruand quhilk sall haiff authoritie nether to by nor sell.

8. That na maister ressaue ane vther manis seruand or prentois in seruise quhill the ishe of thair termes, and it be weryfeit (verified) to the deykin the tyme of his leive taking.

9. We think it expedient that ilk prenteis desire of the deykin and maister that lykis to vse the Craft that first thai desire and obtene the fredome of the toun, and gif he [be] fund abill to be ressauit to the Craft, and to pay his dewteis to the Craft and alter as efferis.

10. We think it expedient that the deykins serche all falis, and to pvnishe tua faltis, and the third falt to be pvneist be the toun with all rigour.

11. That na fleshe that hes [been] presentit [in] the mercatt tuyis and has tynt the sessoun be put to the mercatt agane vnder the pane of escheit; nor yit that ony of our Craft by ony fishe fra the vyffies (fishwives) nor regratours of the toun duelland in Leith.

12. That quhat persone of the Craft disobeyand the deykin in the vsing of his office foirsaid, that ane officer pas and pvneis his persoun as effeiris, and quha that beis obstinat to be put in ward quhill he amend the falt.

These statutes and supplication having been read, seen, and considered by the said Provost, Bailies, and Council, they found the same consistent with reason, and for the common good, as well as for the increase of " guid sheip, fish, and fleshe " in the town, as well as for good government of the burgh. They, therefore, ratified and approved of the same, " in sua far as in them was in all thingis, according to the common proffeit, and in sua far with the help of God will autoreis (authorise) the samyn." The Seal of Cause concludes with the following :—" Written vnder the Seill of Cause of the said burgh, in corroboratioun of the same, day year and place aboue written."

It would thus appear that the restriction previously placed upon the Fleshers not to sell fish, was removed by the terms of the charter granted to them by the Town Council. It is interesting to note, in connection with this privilege, that a union of flesher and fishmonger in trade is now very seldom seen. Each of these, however, is frequently found to combine with their own business that of poulterer. It is also worthy of comment that although the fish industry has always been a great institution in Scotland, it did not obtain in the city of Edinburgh, in the olden times, so prominent a place as to be among the incorporated trades of the burgh. This fact is all the more remarkable when brought into contrast with the London Guilds, where the Fishmongers' Company is one of the oldest and wealthiest institutions of the Metropolis.

The form of prayer made use of, in constituting a meeting of the Incorporation, was as follows :—" Almighty God,—Be Thou mercifully present with us who are here convened, and grant, we beseech Thee, that our meeting together may tend to Thy honour, and to the standing of this, our ancient, free and honest craft. Most Blessed God, we humbly pray that no persons here present may endeavour to promote their own private interest, to the prejudice of their brethren or liberty of this Craft; but as sworn brethren, conform to our oaths, may we all, in one voice, honestly and faithfully proceed in all doings as true members, united in one Craft, and in our Lord Jesus Christ, to Whom, with the Father and Holy Spirit, be ascribed eternal praise and glory—AMEN."

The following was the form of oath taken and subscribed by each freeman, on occasion of his admission to the Incorporation :—" Here I protest, before God and the Incorporation, that I shall be a faithful brother of the Incorporation; that I shall observe the haill acts thereof, made and to be made, and shall not discover or

divulge what is done in the convening-house or meetings of the Incorporation ; that I shall not colour unfreemen's goods under colour
of my own ; and shall obey the deacon and all his calls in relation
to the affairs of the trade ; and shall pay whatever shall be determined in case of my disobedience ; and shall not use any endeavour
to be free or exeemed from what shall be determined, otherways than
by application to the Incorporation ; and shall defend the officer of
the trade in the execution of his office ; and, finally, shall not do or
attempt anything hurtful to the interest of the Incorporation, under
the tinsel of my freedom. So help me God ! and by God himself."

It would appear from the Council Records that the sole right to
sell butcher meat in the market was strictly reserved to the Members
of the Incorporation. There is no information extant as to the cause
for any change, except what is recorded in the minutes of the Town
Council. From the terms of the minute, the statute seems to have
been passed on the 26th of October 1514, and the alteration took
place at the instance of the Incorporation itself. The terms of the
minute are :—

The quhilk day, in presens of the President (sic), Baillies and Counsall, comperit the kirk maister and the laiff of the maisters of the flescheoures fremen and
burgesses within this burgh, and thair of thair awin beneuolent will, at the avyse
of the said president, baillies and counsale, thai haif consentit and grantit that the
vnfremen flescheoures sell their stuffe of flesche, beif and mwttoun, and vthers
siclyk stufe, pertenand to thair facultie vpoun the Sonday and Mononday as commoun fie merkat day is to thame, and in lyk wy is all vtheris fie merkitt tymes
sic as proclaimit fairis, to haif na vse of selling of sic stufe flesche, nor siclyke bot
on the said merket dayes and vther privilegeit tymes, vnder the paynis contenit
in the facultie of the towne grantit to the maisters of the said Craft of before.

There seems from the records to have been no provision for a public
slaughter-house, unless the following entry bears upon the subject :—
" 10th November 1545.—The Fleschhous is set to Laurence Tailliefere

and John Levingtoun for the sowme of ten pundis ilk ane of thame dettour for vtheris." If this was in reality a public slaughter-house, under the authority of the municipal body, its arrangements did not appear to give satisfaction ; because on the 9th August 1524, the Town Council enacted an ordinance, along with the deacons of the various crafts, and apparently with the consent of the general public, whereby the Fleshers obtained the power to slaughter oxen and sheep on their own premises, and to pay maill for the same under certain conditions. The following contains the terms of the ordinance :—

> The quhilk day, the baillies counsale communitie and dekynnis of craftis discernis and ordanis, and als thinkis expedient for the common weill of this gude toun, and all our Sourane Lordis lieges reparand thairto, that all the fleschouris quhilk vsses the land mercat, fremen and vnfremen that duellis within this toun, haiff full free facultie and licens til slaa their stuf, nolt, and scheip, within thair awin houssis that thay pay maill for on Setterday and vther dayis neidfull, and to sell the samyn commonlie in the mercatt till all our Souerane Lordis lieges on the tua mercat dayis lymmyt thairto, viz., Sounday and Mononday allanerlie, without any stop or impediment to be maid to thame thairfore be the Fleschour Craft or vtheris in thair names in tymes to cum ; and ordanis that the Act maid to the said Craft of Fleschouris the ix. day of October the yeir of God jm. iiijc. xxxxxvj. yeris haue na strenth force nor effect in tyme to cum, because it wes vnderstandin that the samyn wes maid and is aganis the commounweill and proffit of this gude toun.

The Town Council of the day seems to have employed an officer to see that the behests of the Magistrates and Council were carried out in all respects. On the 13th August 1524, they ordained that "Jhonne Stevinsoun, fleschour," or the chieftain of the said Craft, should go with their officer, through all the houses of the unfreemen of the Flesher Craft and search them, and certify the authorities as to the same, so that justice should be administered to them ; and if any of the unfreemen "steikis thair durris wilfullie" so that no entry could be had, the officer had authority by force to obtain an entrance.

On the 10th of October 1551, the Town Council passed an ordinance that the fleshers should not sell tallow to strangers or inhabitants of other towns, but only to their neighbours and the candlemakers in the burgh, under the pain of escheat of their stuff, besides a payment of five pounds to the "commonwarkes" and banishment from the town.

From time to time other regulations were passed by the Magistrates and Town Council regarding the trade; but these have not as yet been printed in the volumes of the Burgh Records.

Fountainhall (1. p. 467) tells us that in 1540 "the Privy Council allowed the landward fleshers to bring in their meat to Edinburgh all the days of the week, and that the town appoint them slaughter-houses at the North Loch side; and discharges the town or the Edinburgh Fleshers to exact any imposition from them." He then adds :—"This, on the matter, dissolves the Fleshers of Edinburgh's seal of cause from being a deaconry or incorporation."

Whether the slaughter-houses at the North Loch side, above referred to, were the premises well known among the older citizens of the present day as "the shambles," at the foot of the Fleshmarket Close, until these were removed, from the fact of the site having been utilised for railway purposes by the Edinburgh and Glasgow (now merged in the North British) Railway Company, must remain a matter of doubt. The minute-books of the Incorporation of "Fleschouris" seem to have undergone the fate of many of the ancient records of our city. The following minute to some extent shows this :—"13th April 1773.—John Mellis, deacon, informed the Society that the last sederunt book, which contained the minutes of their proceedings from 12th September 1767, had been lost or mislaid in carrying from the convening-house to the clerk, and that every method had been taken to recover it, but without success; and, therefore, he promised that a minute-book should be made out by the clerk from the notes and materials in his hands from the date mentioned; and that the same when made out should be reported to and examined by the Society, and if found right, that the same should be approved of, and declared to be their sederunt book in time coming." This was agreed to, and the clerk was instructed "to frame the minutes from the period aforesaid as justly and exactly as could be done from the notes."

The new minute-book of 1773 contains the signatures of all the members of the Craft at the time, and brings down the history of the Incorporation to 14th December 1820. There is abundant evidence contained in this volume to show that "the shambles" were the undoubted property of the Incorporation of Fleshers. They were disposed of to the Edinburgh and Glasgow Railway Company in 1844.

Previous to 1850 the Civic Corporation seem to have had no proprietary interest in slaughter-houses. The slaughter-houses which then existed were mostly in the hands of private persons, and were scattered over the whole older parts of the city. Many of these old slaughter-houses were kept in a deplorably filthy condition.

The removal of "the shambles" subjected the chief fleshers in the town to great inconvenience as well as loss in the carrying on of their business. In 1849, a memorial, signed by a large number of these, was presented to the Town Council, requesting the Corporation to obtain Parliamentary powers for the erection of public slaughter-houses. A bill was accordingly prepared with this view. It was introduced during the session 1849-50, promoted by the Town Council, and supported by the leading fleshers in the city.

The Bill, which was opposed by the owners of private slaughter-houses, was passed by Parliament during July 1850, during the civic reign of the late Sir William Johnston. Proceedings were at once taken for establishing the new slaughter-houses on an area of ground of about 4¼ acres in extent, at Fountainbridge, and these were opened for business during May 1852, when the late Mr Duncan M'Laren was Lord Provost of the city.

By the terms of the Act already referred to, the property of the slaughter-houses is vested in the Lord Provost, Magistrates, and Town Council, who have the management of the undertaking. They frame rules and orders for the control and regulation of the slaughter-houses and those persons resorting thereto, subject, as in the case of the markets, to the approval of the Sheriff of Mid-Lothian.

The Fleshers are entitled, within a specified time, to petition the Sheriff with regard to the annual charges for management or the accuracy of the accounts, and as to the periodical fixing of the slaughter-houses dues. The decision of the Sheriff in all these points is final.

During 1889 the number of animals slaughtered was as follows :— Oxen, 40,638 ; swine, 6095 ; calves, 7400 ; sheep, 173,127 ; deer, 88— total, 227,348. The receipts for the same year were £4557, 4s. 6d., while the expenditure was £4413, 5s. 2d., showing thereby a surplus of £143, 19s. 4d. In the expenditure is included a sum of £1000 by way of annuity to the City of Edinburgh, in terms of sections 12 and 18 of the Act of 1850.

It is proper to state that the old Incorporation of " Fleschouris " suffered the fate of the other Incorporations when the privileges of these were removed by Parliament. Their affairs were practically wound up except for the annuities and other claims upon the body. The remanent members still have a yearly meeting to appoint a deacon and other office-bearers. The deacon has still a vote in the election of the Convener of Trades. Mr John Boyd Morham is at present the Deacon ;

Mr Alexander Henry Morham is the Treasurer; and Mr John Hastie, S.S.C. (of J. & A. Hastie), is the Clerk.

It is proper to note that for many generations all fleshers were prohibited from serving on juries. This prohibition was long since done away with by an Act of the Privy Council.

Although the functions of the Incorporation of Fleshers have long ceased, the Craft is not without its representative in the Master Butchers' Association, a very powerful company for the protection of the interests of the trade. The same remark applies also to the Fishmongers of the city.

# THE INCORPORATION OF MARY'S CHAPEL.

THE Incorporation of Mary's Chapel, which at first included only the Wrights and Masons, is at the present time the strongest, most important and most flourishing of all the civic organisations of former days. Its seal of cause dates back to the 15th October 1475. After that time the trade of the Coopers was added on 26th August 1489. These grants were ratified by Andrew Forman, Archbishop of St Andrews, on the 29th June 1517, and they were confirmed by a charter of King James V. on the 12th January 1527. By a grant from the Town Council of Edinburgh, of date 18th April 1633, several others Arts were added to the Incorporation. These additions were confirmed by a charter of King Charles I., on the 8th of August 1635; and by a Decree of the Court of Session, pronounced on the 5th day of March 1703, there were added to the Masons, the Arts of Bowyers, Glaziers, Plumbers, and Upholsterers—while to the Wrights there were united those of Painters, Slaters, and Sievewrights, together with that of Coopers already mentioned. In fact, the Incorporation of Mary's Chapel includes all those who take part in rearing or making beautiful an edifice. As the late Mr Dick, plumber, the poet laureate of the Incorporation used to sing in one of his original compositions, when referring to the body :—

What are the uses?
Building our houses.

I

The seal of cause originally granted to the Wrights and Masons by the Town Council of Edinburgh, in 1475, had reference not only to religious ordinances, but also to the customs to be observed by the Craft in regard to trade. In so far as religion was concerned, the following are the terms of the Charter:—

Till all and syndry quhom it efferis quhais knawledge thir present lettres sall cum.—The Prouest, Baillies, Counsall, Dene of Gild and Dekynnis of the hale craftismen within the burgh of Edinburgh, greting in the Sone of the glorious Virgine.

Wit ye ws in the honour worschipe and glore of Almychte God and of the glorious virgin Sanct Mary, and of our patrone Sanct Gele, and for the furthering helping eiking and suppleing of diuine seruice daily to be done at the Altar of Sanct Jhone the Evangelist, foundit in the College Kirk of Sanct Geile of Edinburgh, and for reparatioun beilding and polecy to be maid in honour of the said sanct of Sanct Jhone, and of the glorious sanct Sanct Jhone the Baptist, to have consentit and assignit, and be thir our present lettres consentis and assignis, to our lovit nychtbouris the hale Craftismen of the Masonis and of the Wrichtis within the said burgh, the Ile and Chapell of Sanct Jhone fra the ald hers of irne inwarts als frely as it is ouris, with all the fredomis proffitis and esementis thairto pertenand at we haf or may haf richt to, nocht doand nor committand ony preiudice or skaith to Sir John Scaithmure or his successouris in his first feftment or priuileges that he has broukit or joisit of befor. To be haldin and to be had the said Ile and Chapell of Sanct Jhone fra the irne hers inwart, with the pertinentis to the saidis Craftismen, the Masonis and Wrichtis of the said burgh, and to thair successouris for euir, with power to edify big reparell and put it ony pairt thairof to polesy or honour of the saidis sanctis outhir in werk or diuine seruice quhatsumeuir at the altar or vther weyes, nocht hurtand the auld feftment. And the saidis Craftismen to vse occupy and aduory the said Ile as thair avin proper ile, siclyk as vtheris Craftismen occupiis within the said College Kirk, nocht doand ony preiudice to our patronage or to the auld feftment or to the auld laus in the said Ile. And that the said craftismen sall adoury and haf the day of Sanct Jhone the Baptist and to thig to the licht of the said Altar as vtheris dois in the Kirk Yerlie. And this till all thame quhom it efferis we make it knawin be thir our present lettres. And in witnessing hereof our commoun sele of caus of the said burgh, togidder with the selis of Alexander Turing, David Quhytehed, Bartillo Carnis, balyeis for the tyme, and Alexander Richardson, sele dene of the gild, in token of gevin consent and assignatioun to the saidis Craftismen of the said Ile, be the handis of the dekin for them all, are to hungin at Edinburgh the xv. day of the moneth of October, the yeir of God j$^m$· four hundreth seviuty and five yeris.

The Seal of Cause, in so far as it was intended to regulate the affairs of the body, in matters of trade and otherwise, was to the following effect :—

Till all and syndry quhom it efferis quhais knawlege thir present lettres sall cum ;— The prowest baillies counsall and the dekynnis of the hale Craftismen of the burgh of Edinburgh gretin in God euirlestand, Wit your vniuersiteis that our comburgessis and nychtbouris all the Craftsmen of the Masonis and the Wrichtis within the said burgh quhilkis presentit to ws in jugement thair bill of supplicatioun desyring of as our licence consent and assent of certane statutis and reullis maid amangis tham self for the honour and worschip of Sanct Jhone in augmentatioun of devyne seruice, and richt sa for reuling, governyng of the saidis twa Craftis, and honour and worschipe of the towne, and for treuth and lawte of the saidis Craftis proffitable baith for the wirkaris and to all biggaris, the quhilk bill togidder with thair statutis and reullis befor ws red, and thair-with we beand well awysit, considerit and fand that thai war gud and loveable baith to God and man, and consonand to ressoun, and thairto we assentit and grantit tham thair desyris, togidder with the Ile of Sanct Jhone iu the college kirk of Sanct Gele to beild and put to polesy in honour of the said Sanct, and for the sufferage of devyne seruice, and thir ar the artikallis and statutis at we haf approvit, and for ws in sa far as we haf power.

In the first, it is thocht expedient that thair be chosin four personis of the best and worthiest of the twa Craftis, that is to say twa masonis and twa wrychtis, that sall be sworne, quhilkis sall serche and sa all wirkis at the Craftismen wirkis, and that it be leley and treulie done to all biggaris.

ITEM, gif ony man beis plentuous of ony wirk or of ony wirkman of the saidis Craftis thai to compleyne to the dekin and the four men or to ony twa of tham, and thai persouns sall caus the scaith and wrang to be amendit, and gif thai can nocht the prowest and baillies to gar if be amendid as efferis.

ITEM, gif ony persoun or persouns of the saidis Craftis cummis of newe after this act to the guid towne and schapis to wirk, or ta tak wirk apoun hand, he sall first cum to the said four men, and thai sall examyn him, gif he be sufficient or nocht and gif he beis admittit he sall lay downe to the reparatioun of the altar a merk.

ITEM, that na master nor persone of ony of the Craftis tak ony prentis for les termis than sevin yeirs, and ilk prentis to pay at his entre to the said altar half a merk, and gif ony prentis quhatsumeuir of the saidis Craftismen, or yit his feit man, pasis away or the ische of his termes but leif of his master, and quha that resauis the prentis or feit man, thai sall pay to the altar ane pund of walx the first falt, the secund falt twa pundis of walx, the third falt to be pvnist be the provest and baillies of the towne as efferis; and allswa quhen ony prentisses has completit his termis and is warne out, he sall be examinit be the four men gif he be sufficient or nocht to be a fallow of the Craft, and gif he be worthy to be a fallow he sall pay half a merk to the alter and brouke the priuilege of the Craft, and gif he be nocht sufficient he sall serf a master quhil he haf lirit to be worthy to be a master, and than to be maid freman and fallow.

ITEM, gif thar be ony of the Craft that disobeyis or makis discord amangis the Craftismen of ony of the Craftis, or that ony of them plenyeis apoun them sall be brocht befor the dekynnis and oucemen of the Craftis, and thai to gar amend it be trety amangis thamself, and gif thai can nocht be faltouris to be brocht and pvnist be the prowest and baillies of the towne for thair trespas as efferis. Alswa the saidis twa Craftismen sall caus and haue thair placis and rowmes in all generale processiouns lyk as thai haf in the toun of Bruges or siclyk gud townes, and gif ony of the Craftismen of outher of the Craftis decesis and has na guds sufficient to bring him furth honestly, the saidis Craftis sall vpoun thair costes and expensis bring him furth and gar bery him honestlie as thai aucht to do of det to thair brother of the Craft; and allswa it sall be lefull to the saidis twa Craftis and Craftismen of Wrichts and Masounis to haue power quhatsumeuir vtheris actis statutis or ordinancis that thai think mast convenient for the vtilitie and proffet of the gude towne and for tham to statut and ordane with awys of the hale Craftis and of our successouris, thai to be ratifiet and apprufit siclik as thir actis, and to be actit and transsumpt in the common buke of Edinburgh, hafand the samyn forme, force and effect as this present writ has.

The following is the deliverance of the Town Council:—"The quhilkis actis ordinance and devys shewin to ws and considerit, we appruf ratifyes and for us and our successouris confirmis and admittis, in so far as we haf power.

"In witnes of the quhilk thing to thir present lettres we haf to affixt our commoun sele of caus, togedder with the seles of the baillies of the said burgh for the tyme, in tykynyng of appreving of all the things aboue writtin, the xv. day of October the yeir of God jm. iiij° seventy and five yeirs."

The Seal of Cause granted to the Coopers, in August 1489, permitting them to become members of Mary's Incorporation, is in the following terms :—

Till all and syndry quhais knawledge thir present lettres sall cum, the provest, baillies, and counsall of the burgh of Edinburgh gretin in God euirlesting, wit ye that the day of the making of thir present lettres comperit befor ws sittand counsally gadderit and for jugement within the Tolbuith of the said burgh, in the inner chalmer of the samyn, thir persouns vnder written, Alexander Browne cowpar, Jhone Richart-soun, William Coupar, Jhone Jhonsoun, and Gilbert Turnour, masters of the Cowpar Craft within the said burgh, and thair presentit till ws thair supplicatioun and bill of complant makand mentioun that diverssis personis of the said Craft quilkis ar and has bene of lang tyme obstinat and inobedient in obseruying and keeping of gud reull ordinance and statutis maid and ordaint of befor and confirmit be our predecessorires to the maisteris of the wrichtcraft for the uphald of diuine seruice and augmentatioun thairof at Sanct Jhonis altar situat in our College Kirk of Sanct Gele, within the said burgh, and speciale in the withhalding and disobeying in the deliuering and paying of the oukly penny to God and to Sanct Jhone and to the reparatioun of the said altar, and als in the disobeysance in the payment making of thar prentis siluer at thair entre, quhilk is five shilling, to the reparatioun and polesy of the said alter, nor yit will nocht pay thair dewteis at the wpsetting of thar buthis siclyke as the masters of the wrychtis ar ordaint and statut to pay, considering the said Cowpar Craft is conformit to thairis and bunden with tham to fulfill the reulis and pay siclyke dewteis to the Sanct and altar as thai and thai lymmit togeddir, aud [adionit] to gadder and inbring the samyn dewteis and mak cowpt and rekynnyng thairof to thair dekyn and Kirk-maisters of the Wrichtis as efferis, and siclyke as is vsit amangis vther Craftis of the said burgh, and as anentis the outlandis folkis that the maisteris of the Cowpar Craft complanit vpoun lauborand and vsand thair Craft and practik thairof in this tovne, passand fra hous to hous mendand and spilland nychtbouris wirk and stuf, hafand nother stob nor stake within this touue, nor yit walkis nor wardis nor yit beris sic portable chargis with tham as extentis and vtheris quhen thai occur, nor yit beand sufficient in thair labour and werkmenschip, and thairthrow neuertheless hurtis and scaithis the saidis masteris in thair fredomes and priuileges contrar to all gud reull ordour and polecy within burgh, Quharupon the saidis masteris of the Cowpar Craft besocht ws of remeid for the honour and loving of God and Sanct Jhone, and the sustentatioun and wphalding of diuine seruice at his alter forsaid, patrone to the saidis Craftis.

The Town Council, having received the request of the Coopers, adopted the following resolution :—"The quhilk bill and supplicatioun beand red herd and vnderstandyn and diligentlie considerit by ws that thair petitioun was consonant to ressoun and to the lovage of God and thair patrone forsaid, and als consonand to the commoun proffet of the said burgh, we decret ordanis and deliueris concordant to thair resonable desyris and petitioun that all the poyntis and articlis contenit in the statutis of the Wrychtis confermit be the tovne be obseruit and kepit to the masteris of the Cowpar Craft, and be tham in all thingis accordant to thair Craft, and quha that disobeyis tham that ane officer pas with tham and tak a poynd of the disobeyar, and mak penny [payment] thairof to the awale and quantite of the dewteis awand to Sanct Jhone the altar and chaplane thairof for the tyme, siclyk as vse and wont has bene, and that the said officeris sall caus the masteris and ingadderaris of the said dewteis to be answerit and obeyit theirvntill, and thai to mak compt rekynning and payment to the dekin and Kirkmaster of the said altar, and that all the laif of the Wrichtis statutis forsaid be obseruit and kepit with tham and be tham according to thair faculte ; and anentis the outlandismen quhilkis prevenis tham in thair labouris and proffetis, that officeris pas with tham and forbid and put tham fra the occupatioun thairof in this towne, bot gif thai mak residence thairvntill, and be the masteris thairof, and to fulfill the statutis aboue expremit as efferis, so that the disobeyaris be pvnist be the officeris of the toune efter the tenour of the said wrichtis statutis maid of befor and confermit be our predecessouris.

In witness of the quhilk thing, we haue gart append our commoun sele of caus to thir present lettres of Edinburgh, the xxvj day of August the yeir of God jm. fourth hundreth aughty and nyne yeiris."

It was the duty of the Craftsmen in troublous times, on the requisition of the Magistrates and Town Council, to turn out, along with their servants or apprentices, in defence of their homes and hearths. The merchants also were enjoined to do the same, "weill prouidit in armour and wappinis, and ma gyf neid beis, induring in tyme foresaid." The minute of the 27th May 1558, ordains "the officiaris to pas and charge the dekynis of ilk Craft to consult and awys (advice) with the remanent of the fremen of his occupatioun to see quhat nomer of men thai may be furnising." The object of the call was to raise a local army of citizens, to assist the constituted authorities "for resistance of our ald inemies of Ingland, in cais thai persew this burgh." Every deacon was enjoined by himself to "gif in the nomer that thai may be in roll to the baillies and counsall vpoun Thurisday nixtocum, to the effect thai may knaw quhat the haill toun may do."

There was an ordinance passed by the Town Council on 30th May, that no one was to leave the City, if there should be invasion, but should take their share in defence, under penalty of having their goods "escheit, confiscat, disponit and deltt to the wyffis and bairnys of thame that sall happin to remane quhilkis beis hurt mutilat or slane in the defence of the toun." They were also to be "dischargit thair fredome, and banyst this toun for evir."

On the 10th June 1558 the Minute of Town Council is to the following effect :—"The saidis President, Baillies and Counsale ordanis Dauid Grahame, dekyn of the Masouns, of his awyn consent, to giff in the roll of the maisteris and habill men seruandis of the said Craft, on Wednisday nixtocum, vnder the pane of wardyn."

On the same day, there was a roll submitted of the Merchants and their Servants, numbering 736 capable men; and of the Crafts and their Servants there were reported 717. The Surgeons, the Fleshers, and the Members of Mary's Incorporation are not included. There is no further notice of this matter in the Minutes of the time.

Like most, if not all, the other Incorporations, the proceedings of each meeting were opened by the Deacon offering up the following Prayer, which has been attributed to the pen of John Knox:— "O! Lord,—We most humbly beseech Thee to be present with us in mercy, and to bless this our Meeting, and whole Exercise which we have on hand: O! Lord, enlighten our understandings, and direct our hearts and minds, so with Thy good Spirit, that no partial respect, either of feed or favour, may draw us out of the right way; but Grant, that we may so frame all our purposes, and conclusions, as they may tend to the Glory of Thy Name, and all the welfare of our Brethren,— Grant these things unto us, O Lord, and what else Thou seest necessary for us, and only for the sake of Thy Dear Son, Jesus Christ our alone Saviour and Mediator, to whom with Thee, O! Most Merciful Father, and the blessed Spirit of Grace, we render all praise, honour, and glory, for ever and ever—Amen."

The following contains the words of the Prayer to be said before dismissing the meetings of the Incorporation:—"O! Lord,—We most humbly acknowledge Thy goodness, in meeting with us together at this time, to confer upon a present condition of this world; O! Lord, make us also study Heaven and Heavenly mindedness, that so we may get our souls for a prey. And Lord, be with us, and accompany us the rest of this day, now and for ever more—Amen."

One great source of the success of the Incorporation has been the scrupulous care which has been exercised in regard to the management of its financial affairs, whereby its Widows' Fund has been carefully preserved and augmented. At the beginning of the present century, the Membership must have been very large. Contests frequently took place at election times, as to those who were to be nominated office-bearers. This led to the contending parties getting their personal friends and supporters to become Members of the Incorporation. The strongest example of this kind on the records is in relation to the election of 1809, at which time there were added, within little more than a month previous to the election, one hundred new Members, and a large addition to the Capital Stock. Since all special privilege was abolished, the Incorporation has been continued, like most of the others, only as a benefit society, the admission money being based on actuarial calculation. The numbers who now claim admission are becoming very few.

The laws of the "United Incorporation of Mary's Chapel," as it is now designated, have from time to time been changed, according to the circumstances of the times. The latest edition of these was published in 1885. It provides for a General Meeting of the body to be held annually, on the third Monday of October, for considering and passing the Annual Accounts, and for the election of Deacons, Treasurer and other office-bearers for the ensuing year. There are also four quarterly Meetings held during the year, at the terms of Martinmas, Candlemas, Whitsunday and Lammas. Extraordinary Meetings may be summoned for special business, on the order of the Deacons, or on a requisition addressed to them, or either of them, signed by five members and stating the purpose of the Meeting. There are two Deacons connected with the body. One of these represents the mason craft, and the other the wright craft. They regularly alternate in taking the chair—the Deacon of Masons taking the precedence. Nine members constitute a quorum; but, if unanimous, a smaller number may proceed to business. Both Deacons have a vote in the Convenery.

K

The old oath has been abolished for a very long time; but the Entrant must subscribe a declaration to the following effect:—"I declare and promise that I shall faithfully keep, observe and fulfil all acts, ordinances and statutes, made, or to be made, for the utility and welfare of the United Incorporation of Mary's Chapel, in all points, in so far as consistent with the laws of this realm."

The Incorporation is limited in the Investment of its Funds to the purchase of heritable property, superiorities and feu-duties, Government or public funds, bank or banking companies' stocks, or shares of the capital stocks of such joint-stock companies, or it may lend out its funds on heritable securities, or in debenture bonds of railways or other public companies, all as the members of the United Incorporation, at any of its General Meetings, shall consider to be eligible.

There are now only Representatives of the Mason and Wright fraternity, all the others having died. The Incorporation at present owns a Hall in Burnet's Close, High Street, which is denominated "St Mary's Chapel," but which is now let for religious worship. This is not the original Chapel. The original Chapel was in Niddry's Wynd, where for many generations the Members used to hold their meetings. This most interesting and beautiful Chapel, by its charter of foundation of 31st December 1504, which was confirmed by a charter of King James IV. on the 1st of January 1505, appears to have been founded by Elizabeth, Countess of Ross, and had its name from its having been dedicated by the pious Foundress in honour of the Virgin Mary. Some of the old furniture which used to garnish the original Hall was transferred to the Trades' Maiden Hospital, Rillbank, Meadows, for preservation at the time when the building was purchased by the City Improvement Trustees under the Act passed at the instance of the late Lord Provost Chambers. Among the rest will be found several chairs (arm, devotional, and ordinary), and an old oil painting representing Craftsmen of the Incorporation at work in front of Holyrood Palace. It is not known by whom this work of art was executed; but it is regarded as a creditable specimen of the period, and is decidedly quaint.

The present office-bearers are :—Deacon of the Masons, Mr George James Beattie ; Deacon of the Wrights, Mr William Field ; Treasurer, Mr Donald Walker Beattie ; Clerks, Messrs Macandrew & Blair, C.A.

WRIGHTS.     MASONS.

# THE INCORPORATION OF SKINNERS AND FURRIERS.

**T**HE Skinners (which included the crafts of the Furriers and the Glovers) would appear to have taken precedence of most, if not of all, of the other Trades Incorporations. The first record of their existence is to be found in a document written in mediæval Latin * of date the 12th January 1450, in which they request that certain statutes made by them for the maintenance of the Altar of Saint Christopher, founded in the Parish Church of St Giles of Edinburgh, according to the rule of the said Church, should be forthwith engrossed by the common clerk, notary, and scribe of the burgh, in the common book of the Gild of the said Burgh. It is recorded that the request was complied with, and it was ordained by the Provost Thomas of Cranstoun, and by the Baillies, John of Halkerstoun, Mathew of Chambers, and Richard of Farnley, Adam Cant, Dean of Guild, John Lamb, Treasurer, the Council and dusane

---

* Pro altari Sancti Cristoferi fundato in ecclesia parochiali Beati Egidii de Edinburgh juxta formam eiusdem ecclesie pro pellipariis artis subscriptis in instrumento sequenti dicti vero pelliparii condiderunt statuta ad sustentacionem dicti altaris vt patet per eiusmodi instrumentum quiquidem pelliparii requisiuerunt instanter communem clericum notarium et scribam burgi regestare et inscribere dictum instrumentum in libro communi gilde dicti burgi, et ita fieri decretum est per prepositum Thomam de Cranstoun, et balliuos Johannem de Halkerstoun, Matheum de Cammera, et Richardum de Farnele, Adam Cant decanum gilde, Johannem Lamb thesaurarium, concilium et duodenam dicti burgi, tenor vero instrumenti sequitur et est talis :—

In Dei nomine Amen. Per hoc presens publicum instrumentum cunctis pateat euidenter quod anno ab incarnacione domini millesimo quadringentesimo quinquagesimo, indictione decima quarta, die vero mensis Januarij duodecimo, pontificatus sanctissimi in Christo patris ac domini nostri domini Nicholaij diuina prouidentia pape quinti anno quarto in mei notarii publici et testium subscriptorum presentia personaliter constituti prouidi et honesti viri videlicet :—Willelmus Skynner, Gillcrist

of the said burgh.  The document, as translated into English by the
Editor of the Burgh Records, is as follows :—

In the name of God, Amen : Be it known clearly to all by this present public
instrument, that in the year from the incarnation of our Lord, one thousand four hundred
and fifty, in the fourteenth Indiction, in the twelfth day of the month of January, in
the fourth year of the pontificate of the most Holy Father in Christ, and our Lord the
Lord Nicholas the Fifth, by Divine Providence Pope, in presence of me notary public
and the witnesses subscribing personally appeared discreet and honest men,—videlicet:—
William Skynner, Gilcrist Turnebulle, Hugh Tod, Alan Skynner, William Staltt, James
Harlaw, David Littell, Thomas Yule, William of Cambusnethane, Edmund Skynner,
John Mathe, David Wilky, Thomas Salman, William Lachlane, John of Kympill,

---

Turnebule, Hugo Tod, Alanus Skynner, Willelmus Staltt, Jacobus Harlaw, Dauid Littill, Thomas
Yule, Willelmus de Camusnethane, Edmundus Skynner, Johannes Mathe, Dauid Wilky, Thomas
Salman, Willelmus Lachlane, Johannes de Kympill, Willelmus Ramsay et Andreas (*blank*), pelliparii
infra willam de Edinburgh, una cum consensu et assensu obligati sunt in forma que sequitur videlicet:—
Quod [ad] seruicium et sustentacionem vnius capellani ad celebrandum apud altare Sancti Cristoferi
nouiter fundatum per supradictos infra ecclesiam Beati Egidii de Edinburgh et ad reparacionem
ornamentorum dicti altaris quilibet dictorum pro toto tempore vite sue ac secundum facultatem
bonorum manus adiutrices apponet.  Item quilibet accipiens prenticium ad artem pelliparii soluet
ad reparacionem dicti altaris quinque solidos monete tunc currentis, ac etiam quod nullus prenticius
[per] quemcunque ipsorum accipietur ad dictam artem pelliparii nisi consimiliter obligatus fuit post
lapsum annorum sui prenticii ad libertatem vt supra manus suas adiutrices secundum facultatem
bonorum ad reparacionem dicti altaris vt supradictum est apponi.  Item quod quilibet prenticius
antequam ad artem pelliparii recipietur jurabit et obligabitur vt quam cito venerit ad libertatem sui
prenticii quod non recipiet quemcunque prenticium ad artem pelliparii nisi ad reparacionem dicti altaris
vt supradicimus soluat quinque solidos et sic de similibus imperpetuum.  Item ordinatum est quod
si contingat aliquam debatam discordiam aut controuersiam infra dictos pelliparios quoquomodo
imposterum [exoriri] ambe partes discordes determinacioni et ordinacioni artis sociorum eorundem et
decreto concilii et doudene burgi stabunt et subibunt sine quacunque contradictione aut demanda,
ac vt etiam supradicta appunctuamenta inviolabilia perpetuis temporibus obseruent quilibet dictorum
pellipariorum per se compari juramento obligatus est.  Super quibus omnibus et singulis petiit sibi
fieri dictus Willelmus Skynner nomine communi pellipariorum tunc presentium et nominatorum vnum
vel plura instrumentum seu instrumenta per me notarium publicum infrascriptum.  Acta fuerunt
infra ecclesiam Beate Marie de Campo hora tertia post meridiem anno die indictione mense et pontificatu quibus supra presentibus probis et discretis viris dominis Alexandro Hundby, Johanne Moffat,
Johanne Hendirsone, cappellanis, et Thoma Broun, mercatore, cum aliis testibus ad premissa vocatis
specialiter et rogatis.

William Ramsay, and Andrew (blank), skinners within the town of Edinburgh, with one consent and assent, are obliged in manner following, videlicet:—That for the service and support of a chaplain to celebrate at the Altar of Saint Christopher, lately founded by the above-written within the church of St Giles of Edinburgh, and for the repair of the ornaments of the said altar, each of the said persons for the whole period of his life, and according to his means, shall put to helping hands: ITEM, Every one receiving an apprentice to the Craft of Skinners shall pay to the repairs of the said Altar five shillings of the money then current, and also that no apprentice shall be received by any one of them to the said Craft of Skinners, unless he has been in like manner taken bound that, after the expiry of the years of his apprenticeship to freedom, he shall put to his helping hands, according to his ability, to the reparation of the said altar as aforesaid: ITEM, That every apprentice, before he shall be admitted to the Craft of Skinners, shall swear and become bound, so soon as he shall come to the freedom of his apprenticeship, not to receive any apprentice to the Craft of Skinners, unless he shall pay five shillings to the repair of the said altar as aforesaid, and so in like cases for ever: ITEM, It is ordained that if any debate, discord, or controversy among the said Skinners shall henceforth happen to arise in any manner of way, both the contending parties shall abide by and submit to the determination and judgment of said matters by the brethren of the Craft, and to the decree of the Council and dusane of the burgh without any contradiction or appeal; and, moreover, that they may observe the above-mentioned appointments inviolably, each of the said Skinners, for himself, has been bound by a like oath. Upon which, all and sundry, the said William Skynner, in the common name of the Skinners then present and named, asked one or more instruments to be made by the notary public subscribing. (And ane Johne Hogo preist in the dyosie of Glasquow is notar heirto.) These things were done within the church of Saint Mary in the Field, the third hour in the afternoon, of the year, day, indiction, month, and pontificate as above, in the presence of good and discreet men, Sir Alexander Hundby, John Moffat, John Hendirsone, chaplains, and Thomas Broun, merchant, with other witnesses specially called and required to the premises.

Connected with the above offer of the Skinners, to endow the altar of St Christopher, it may be interesting to note that during the same year, viz., 9th November 1451, King James II. granted a charter, under his great seal, for removing the customs on skins and salt. The substance of it is to the following effect:—For the singular favour he bore towards his beloved merchants, burgesses, and community of the city of Edinburgh, in respect of the manifold free services rendered by them to His Majesty, he granted and perpetually confirmed to the burgesses and community, and their heirs and successors, burgesses of the said burgh, that in all time thereafter, they should be free absolved and quit from all payment of the custom of salt, and of the skins underwritten, commonly called "schorlingis, skaldingis, futefellis, lentrinwere, lamb skynnis, tod skynnis, calf skynnis, cunning skynnis, otter skynnis, and fumart skynnis." He also granted to the said burgesses and community free power and faculty to sell, barter, or exchange, as well strangers and unfreemen, as to any other persons whatever, and as well within his kingdom as without, the foresaid wares of salt and skins, without any custom to be paid by the said strangers or others whatsoever, in all time coming, so that no custom should be paid by the strangers out of said salt and skins, bought and purchased from the burgesses foresaid, unless only the small custom due and in use to be paid by strangers and unfreemen to the said burgesses and community off the said salt and skins in former times. This concession was likely to have given a great impetus to the skinners' trade.

The Seal of Cause granted by the Town Council to the Skinners is of date 2d December 1474, and is in the following terms :—

Til all and sindry quhais knawlag thir present letteres sal cum The prouost bailyeis and consale of the burgh of Edinburgh greting in the Sone of the glorios Virgine : Sen it efferis to ws jugis be verteu of our office to declar schew and bere suthfast witnessing to the verite of the thingis led pronunsit determit and ordanit be ws or befor ws in jugement, sa that innocentis be nocht throu the hiding of verite hurt nor scaithit in our defaltis. Herefor it is that to your vniuersite we mak it knawin and declaris that the daye of the makin of thir presentis, in the chawmer of the Tolbuth of the said burgh comperit, befor ws we sittand in jugement the craftismen of the Skinnaris of the self burgh that is to saye John of Cranston dekin, Robert Haithwy, William Ramsaye,

Thomas Salmund, Thomas Grahame, Thomas Frew, Robert of Duscon, Alane Skinnar, John Mathe, James Tod, William Trumbule, Henry Haswele, James Greg, Robert Lauerok, John Scot, Thom of Harlawbankis, Robert Wilschot, Thomas Evinson, Alexander Red and William Craufurd for thaim and in the name of the hale Craf, present to ws thair bill of complaynt of certane thingis that was vsit amangis the craftismen, quharthrou the tone had a sclander and lak, the Craft sustenit gret scaith and hurt and the commounis dissauit, and als that diuine seruice and sufferage of Sant Cristoforis alter is mynist, and reparatioun of the said alter nocht beildit nor helpit efter the avis statutis and ordinance of the toue and of the said Craft vsit of befor; and als anentis the dissobeying of thair dekin in the cumming and gaddering befor hym and the Craft quhen thai ar warnit, for the comonning and avising for the gude of the hale Craft, and for stanching of deformaris and babillaries of the werk baith in kirkis and in tone and for the reformatioun to be had of thir thingis and diuers wtheris concerning and rying [referying] to the hale Craft. The quhilk bill beand in presens of ws and diuerse of the Craft red herd, and thair desire resonable considerit to the forti-feing and obseruing of the said desiris and statutis vnderwritten we have assentit: In the first, as tuiching the rasing of the Monondais penny of him or them at werkis thair awin laubor, it is statut and ordanit be the dekin and the laif of the Craft witht awis of ws that the said penny be rasit wolkly on the Monundaye outhir be the dekin or ony at beis ordanit to gidder it, of al personis lauborand thair awin werk and quha that dissobeyis the gadderar to pund hym thairfor quhil it be pait. Alswa that all personis of the Craft sal compere befor the dekin and the Craft quhen thai ar warnit for the gude of the sammin and quha that dissobeyis and absentis hym in the tym withoutin lief or a resonable assonye he sal paye to Sant Cristoforis alter half a pund of wax. And alswa quha that beis fundin or attayntit brekand schepe skinnis on the ryme sidis outher for poyntis or for gait leddir, or at sellis the samin poyntis for raphell outhir in priue or in a perth fenyeit and fals stuf the committer sal be brouch and the stuf at is fundn takin witht him befor the prouost bailyeis and consale of the tone, and thai sal witht avis and ordinance of the dekin and four or five of the worthiest and best of the Craft mak the said persone or personis to be pvnyst as efferis; and richt swa of the bauchlaris of the said laubour, outhir in the opin gate or in the kirk, quha at beis tayntit tane thairwitht on halidais or werkdais the dekin sal rais on him for the first falt half a pund of wax, the secund falt a pund of wax but fauour to the reparatioun of the said alter of Sanct Cristofor, and the thrid tym the dekin sal bring him and the werk before the consale of the tone, and thair the prouost bailyeis and consale sal pvnis it witht avis of the dekin and the best of the craft,

The following is the ratification of the said Charter by the Town Council :—" The quhilkis articls and desiris we appruff ratifeis and for ws and our successouris in sa fer as afferis ws or sa fer as we haf power confermys ; and this til all thame quham it efferis we mak knawin be thir oure presentis ; and for the mare witnessing hereof the common sele of cause of our said burgh is to hungin togidder witht the subscripcione manuale of oure common clerc William Farnely at Edinburgh the secund day of the moneth of December the yer of our lord athousand foure hundreth sevinty and four yere. FARNLY."

Another Seal of Cause was granted to the Incorporation of Skinners and Furriers on 22d August 1533. It was to the following effect :—

Till all and sindry quhais knauledge thir present letteres saltocum, the provest baillies and counsale of the Burgh of Edinburgh greting : Witt youre vniuersiteis that the day of the dait of thir present letteres comperit before ws sittand in iugement the kirkmaisteris and the laif of the maisteris and brether of the Skynnar craft and Furrour craft of the said burgh, and present till ws counsaly gaderit thair bill of supplicatioun of the qubilk the tenour followis :—My lordis provest baillies and worthy counsale of this guid toun, vnto your richt honorabill discretionis humlie menis and schewis the kirkmaisteris and the laif of the maisteris of the Skynnar Craft and Furrour Craft within this burgh viz., William Akinheid kirkmaister, Stevin Bell, Henry Cranstoun, Robert Huchesoun, Henry Lille, Johnne Gibsoun, William Loch, Thomas Bischop, Johnne Huchesoun, William Scott, Robert Haithwy, James Ramsay, Thomas Clerksoun, George Hammiltoun, Johnne Park, Andro Romannos, Johne Watsoun, William Coldane, William Watsoun, William Wallange, Adam Wricht, Thomas Quhite, James M'Lellane, Thomas Hervy, James Andersoun, Johnne Auld, Johne Fairlie, Thomas Wischart, James Forat, James Huchesoun, skynnaris ; the names of the furrouris Robert Bischop dekin, David Ferry, Johnne Craig, Archibald Loiche, Alexander Duncane, William Duncane, Adam Makcalyeane, Thomas Singiltoun, William Carnys, David Younger, Walter Somervell, Thomas Andersoun, Matho Cant, and Richart Henrisoun, that quhare, first, for the loving of Almichty God, the honour of the realme, the worschip and proffit of this gude toune and all oure Souerane Lordis lieges and vtheris reparand thairto, and in exempill of vtheris and for the augmentatioun of divyne seruice at the altare of Sanct Cristofer our patrone of the samyn altare situate within youre College Kirk of Sanct Geill of the said burgh, we desire that we micht haue thir statutis, articulis, and rewlis eftir following grantit and gevin till vs be youre autorite quhairthrow gude rewle and giding may be had amangis ws of the saidis craftis, baith maisteris and seruandis, and oure successouris thairof in all tymes tocum, becaus it is said be commoun autorite that multitude but rewlis makes confusioun, and for till eschew the vice thairof, and to be eschewit in tyme tocum, we desir thir rewlis eftir followand :

In the first, that sen all increment of vertew practikis and knaulege standis in gude begynning and foundment, and fra thinfurth to continew in vertew and perseuerance to finale end, that fra thynefurth na maner of personis of the saidis craftis of skynnaris and furroris be sufferit to set vp buth nor pull skynnis within this burgh without he be first freman and burges of the samyn, fundin sufficient and abill in werkmanschip and vthirwayis, and admittit thairto be the provest baillies and counsale and sworne maisteris of the craftis, and than for his vpsett to pay, gif he be ane skynneris son burges within this burgh ten schillingis, and gif he be ane vthir mannis son to pay for thair vpsett the sowme of fyve pundis vsuall money of Scotland, to the reparatioun and vphalding of divyne seruice at oure said altare ; and at na maner of maisteris of the saidis craftis tyest hous [or] herbery any vtheris maisteris prentice or servand ; and gif ony dois in the contrar he sall pay ane pund candill of walx, and thaireftir als oft as the falt happennis at the discretioun of the provest baillies and counsale the persoun falctand to be pvnist ; and at ilk maister haldin buth within this said burgh of the saidis craftis sall pay his oulklie penny to the reparatioun of the ornamentis of oure said altare and sustene the preistis meit thairof as it cumis about :

Item, that na fals stuff be sauld till our Souerane Lordis liegis vnder the pane of half ane pund candill of walx to oure said altare als oft as it beis ouretane ; and at the fals stuff be present to the provest baillies and counsale, and thai to remeid and reforme the samyn as thai sall think expedient for the tyme ; and gif ony personis of the saidis craftis intromettis or withhaldis the gudis of the said altare or craftis, and sustenis pley thairintill, he to pay and deliuer the samyn with the expensis of his proper gudis gif he be fundin in the falt ; and at the saidis kirkmaisteris and principall maisteris of the saidis craftis that sall happin to be for the tyme may haif full faculte leif and preuilege, with ane officar of the tovne to pas with thame for to poynd and distrenye gif neid be for the taking rasing and inbringing of thir dewiteis forsaid to the sustentatioun and vphalding of Goddis seruice as said is, but danger stop or impediment, and that all the maisteris of the saidis craftis that takkis ony persoun in prenteis with thame sall pay to the reparatioun of the said altare the sowme of twenty schillings :

Quharfore we humlie beseik youre lordschip and wisdomes, sen we ar twa craftis and vnite oure self in cherite togiddir to the vphalding of Goddis seruice and for the honour of this gude toune and proffit of all oure Souerane Lordis liegis, and sen thir oure sempill desiris and petitionis ar resonable and conforme to equite and are consonant to the gude reule honour and polecy according to the vsis and consuetudis of grete townis of honour of vthir realmes and provinces, that ye wald grant to vs thame ratifyit approvit and confermit be yow vnder youre commoun sele of caus, in perpetuall memoriall of gude reule to be had in tyme tocum, with youre ansuer heirapoun we humilie beseik.

The following is the Town Council's deliverance:—"The quhilk supplicatioun and desiris before expremit beand red in iugement, and we thairwith beand ripelie avisit, we thocht the samyn consonant to ressoun, and thairfore ratifyis approvis and confermes the samyn for ws and our successouris als long as thai salbe sene expedient speidfull and proffitabill for the commoun proffit to the provest baillies and counsale of this burgh that sall happin to be for the tyme ; and this till all and sundry quham it efferis we mak it knawn be thir oure letters. In witnes of the quhilk thing we have gart append to thir presentis our commoun seall of caus. At Edinburgh, the twenty-twa day of the moneth of August, the yeir of God ane thousand fyve hundreth threty and thre yeris."

Here follows attestation in Latin, as translated in the Burgh Records :—*

This is a true and undoubted copy of the principal letter of statutes

---

* Hec est vera et indubitata copia principalis litere, statutorum communitati Pellipariorum et Foderatorum burgi de Edinburgh per prepositum balliuos et communitatem eiusdem eiis concessis, et per eosdem roborate et confirmate sub eorum communi sigillo, fideliter copiate et collationate per me notarium publicum subscriptum nil addito vel remoto quod facti substanciam mutaret aut intellectum variaret, sub meis signo et subscriptione manualibus.

Ita est, Andreas Richartsoun notarius publicus manu propria premissa asseruit.

to the community of Skinners and Furriers of the burgh of Edinburgh, granted to them by the Provost, Bailies, and Community of the same, and by them ratified and confirmed under their common seal, faithfully copied and collated by me, notary-public subscribing, under my sign and subscription manual, nothing being added or taken away which could change the substance of the deed or vary its meaning. So it is. Andrew Richartsoun, notary public, certifies the premises with his own hands.

Nearly a century thereafter, viz., during the year 1630, the Incorporation of Skinners approached the Town Council for an amended charter, in which they desired to have certain regulations passed for the better government of the body. This is the only Charter quoted by Maitland, who had some difficulty in obtaining information as to the Incorporation. It is to the following effect :—

1. Forsamekill as certane Brether of the said Craft, nocht having Regaird of the Comoneweill, followand thair awin privat Lucre, hes ressavit ane Multitude of Prenteisis of ther awin Appetyt, quhilk they could nocht be abill to undertak be instructing of them in the said Craft, and susteinin of them as they aucht to do.

For Remeid therefor, to statute and ordane, that it sall nocht be lesum in Tyme cuming to any Brother of the said Craft, to ressave ane new Prenteiss, quhill the first zeir of the last Prenteis quhilk he ressavit immediatlie befoir, be compleitlie outrown, and that under the Payne of Fyve Pund to be payet to the Collectouris of the Townis Unlawis, in the name of the Towne, so often as they failze, the Buithe to be closet and steikit up, and nocht be sufficient to work quhill the sam be reformit.

2. That na Maister ressave in Service any Servand of the said Craft, that hes nocht bene ane Prenteis with ane frie Maister within this Burgh, except he first cum with the Deykin and quates Maister being for the Tyme, and caws him be buiket in the Townis Buikis, to be ane bound Servand for the space of thrie Zeirs, efter the quhilk thrie Zeirs outrown, the said Servand sall be frie to serve quhair he pleisis, with ony frie Maister within the Towne ; and this to eschew the Abuse that hes been throw the Multitude of Servandis daylie resorting and repairing within this Burgh, and lernin of the said Occupation ; and thereafter passing furthe therof, to remaine quhair they pleis

under the Pane of Fourtie Schillings to be payet to the said Maister, so oft as he failzeis, as said is.

3. That nane of the Maisters of the said Craft ressave in Service ony uther Maister's Prenteis, without the said Prenteis or Servand first have satisfiet the last Maister for his Service, and have obtenit his Discharge therupone, at the least, without he have ane sufficient Caws, knawin and tryet to leave his Maister foresaid, under the Pane foresaid.

4. That na Prenteis of the said Craft shall be ressavit or admittit to his Upset and Friedome, without he have servit for the Space of thrie Zeirs at the leist, efter the utrunning of his Prenteischip with sum frie Maister, that he may be the mair abill, and that he may serve oure Soverane Lordis Lieges.

5. That na Skinner Wark be sauld within this Burgh upon the Hie-streites or other publict Places outwith Buithis, except upone the *Monondayis* Market, upone Puine of Escheit of the same to the good Townis Use.

6. That nane be admittit nor ressavit Frieman of the said Craft, except first he give his Assey to the Deykin and Craft, and suche as they sall appoynt thereto; and that the samyn be fund sufficient be thame, utherwayis nocht to be maid Frieman.

7. That the Provest and Baillies, at the Desyre of the Deykins, or any Brother of the said Craft, sall put the said Articles to Executione, and reforme all uther Enormities of the said Craft, and gif Command to thair Officers to that Effect.

The following is the Town Council's deliverance upon the same :—"Quhilk Articles beand read and considerit, after lang Conference and Consultation had thereupone, and therwith beand ryplie advyset, the said Provest, Baillies, and Counsall, and Deykins of Craftis findes the same mest ressonabill, lawfull, and profitabill for the Honor, Weill, and Profit, and Pollicie of the said craft, and therefore rattifies and approvis the samyn haill Clausis and Circumstances thereof, be thir Presentis interponing their Authoritie thereto; and decerning thame to be observit and Keipet in all Tyme cuming, with a Command to the Officiars present and to cum, to the samyn, to dew Executione in all Poyntis agains the Contraveners and Brekkers therof, and to uplift the Paynes contenet therin, to be imployet in Maner above mentionat."

The above Charter was confirmed on the 26th November 1630, by the Town Council, subject however to the following restrictions:—

1. "That none of the Trade presume to brock Sheep-skins on the Rim or Flesh-side, either for Points or Gaitt-leather, or to sell the same for Raphall, under the Pain of Punishment, at the Discration of the Town's Council, by the Advice of the Deacon and Brethren of the Craft.

2. "That none presume to sell a bad commodity, under the Pain of an arbitrary Punishment as aforesaid.

3. "That no member of the Corporation presume to bachill any Wark in the Gaitt or in the Kirk, neither on Holy-days or Wark-days, on the Penalty aforesaid.

4. "That no Person hang up Bachall or Exampill of his Work to publick view within the Town, or hang out the Sign of the Glove before his Shop, unless he be a Freeman of the Company.

5. "That no Freeman of the Corporation shall take upon him to alum, grow, or lime Sheep, Kid, Lamb or Calve Skins, or peel the Wool from off the same for Sale; except such as belong to *Paul's Work*, and others who hereafter may be permitted by the Common Council.

6. "That no Unfreeman presume to wash, collour, Buttoun, or dress any Gloves, or work with Sheers, Needles, Grind-stones, or other Implement belonging to the Craft or Art of Skinners, except such as have bought Gloves by way of Merchandise, who may help or mend unmarketable Goods.

7. "That no Unfreeman sell any Sort of Gloves, within *Edinburgh*, but on the Market-days.

8. "And for the better avoiding Frauds in Skins, all Persons are strictly injoined to bring the Skins with the Carcasses to Market, to be openly sold, being first searched, under the Pain of Forfeiture; and

the said Skins to have the Wool on, under the Pain of Forty pennies for each Skin which is either pulled or cut. And to prevent all ingrossing and clandestine Bargains, all Persons that shall buy Skins out of the Market-place, shall be amersed in the sum of Ten Pounds *Scotish*, and the Seller in Five Pounds of the same Money.

9. "That no Unfreeman presume to make Gloves, exercise the Trade of a Glover, or hang out a Sign before or in his Shop, relating to the Craft, within *Edinburgh*."

Some difficulty afterwards arose among the members of the Incorporation, on account of many of the Skinners' workhouses having been transferred to the banks of the Water of Leith, lest they should lose their right of citizenship and the privileges flowing therefrom. The result of it was the granting of a Deed of Obligation on the part of the Members of the Craft, to the Town Council of Edinburgh, so as to avoid the necessity of raising an Action of Declarator in the Court of Session. This was done on the 22d June 1765.

The deed narrates that the business or craft consists of two branches:—the one of manufacturing various skins into leather or furs, and therefore named Skinners and Furriers ; and the other of manufacturing the leather or furs into gloves, breeches, muffs, and the like, and therefore named Glovers. The Glover Craft, with their families and servants, resided within the city's bounds, while the Skinners had to betake themselves to a running stream, and past the memory of man they had their workhouses at the Water of Leith. They alleged that the great improvements they were constantly making in their business necessitated close attention to their workhouses, and that for some years past they and their families and servants had dwelt near to their works, and had notwithstanding this enjoyed all the privileges of the Incorporation. But doubts having arisen as to the legality of their position, it was with a view of solving the difficulty that the Deed of Obligation was granted. The Deed bound all the parties to be subject to the jurisdiction and laws of the city of Edinburgh, and to all Acts and Regulations of the Magistrates and Town Council, and of the Guildry and Convenery, and of our own Corporation of Skinners and Furriers, and to be subject to all services, burdens, and taxations imposed by the Stentmasters, as if their actual residence were in the city. The Skinners' Hall, or the Weigh-house of Edinburgh, were to be held as the domiciles for all citation purposes, and that a schedule or copy of citations affixed on a conspicuous place on the inside of the wall of either of these buildings should be deemed good service, and as effectual as if it were delivered at one's dwelling-house.

One of the first statutes of the Town Council preserving the rights of the Skinners to sell their skins in the Market is as follows:— "15th May 1530. — The quhilk day, the Provest, Baillies, and Counsall statutis and ordanis and als commandis and chargis that na maner of brokharis nor forstallaris of woll, hydis nor skyn, man nor woman, be fund nor sene on the Merket day in the place quhar ony woll, hyd or skyn are to sell, nother spekand, standand, nor commondand with the sellaris tharof in na tyme to cum, vnder the pain of," etc.

Another statute, of date January 24, 1532, prohibits a flesher from buying skins for sale. It is to the following effect :—" The quhilk day, in presens of the Provest, Baillies and Counsall, Jhonne Lawsoun, fleshour, comperit and granttit that he sauld and delieurit to Alexander Mauchane the xj scheip skynnis, and oblist him to warrand the said Alexander thairof at all handis, as accordis vpoun the law, and als the said Jhonne oblissis him of his awiu consent neuir till by onye skinnis till sall agane to ony merchand, vther nor his awin slauchter, vnder the pane [of] banissing the toun."

The ancient Market for the sale of Hides and Skins was at the Tolbooth, but on the 11th February 1558, it was shifted. The Town Council's order was that it should be "sett and haldin beneth the Salt Trone, betuix Walter Scottis Close and Nudries Wynd on bayth sidis, induring the townis will allanerlie, and that for guid caussis, considerationis and motives moving thaim thairto, at this instant tyme, and that officeris put this present act to execution with all diligens." There is a further Act of Council to the following effect:— "4th Sept. 1559.—The Baillies and Counsall foirsaid ratefeis and apprevis the Act made of befoir for doun taking of the skyn merkatt fra the place quhair the samyn wes vsit to be had to the Freir Wynd heid, and fra thyne furthe to the Nether Bow, and ordanis the samyn to indure efter the tenour of the said act, and the samyn to be putt to executioun in all poyntis, and all persons havand skynnis to sell to keip mercatt in the place foirsaid, vnder the pane of escheitting of the samin."

The Furriers seem never to have been erected into an Incorporation, although there are most unmistakable proof of their having at an early period exercised considerable sway among the various arts. They were not without cause of complaint; and they sought redress at the hands of the Town Council of the period. For example, on the 7th of September 1593, they state that "it is not unknown to them (the Council) that they are an ancient Free Craft, with as old liberties and privileges as any other occupation within Edinburgh, paying Scot and bearing Lot with the rest of the inhabitants; but of late are greatly decreased both in the number of their members and the profits of their trade, chiefly occasioned by the Skinners and Tailors practising divers branches of their business;" which being taken into consideration by the said Town Council, they hereby strictly enjoined all persons, not being freemen of the Furrier Craft, that they do "not fur cloaks or

M

gowns, nor dress Lamb-skins or Schorlings, under the Penalty of Forty Shillings Scotish Money for each offence."

This order of the Corporation was not found to answer the desired end; because on the 5th of April 1665, another Representation came before the Lord Provost, Magistrates and Town Council, to the effect "That there are sundrie Persones within this Burgh, Cannogait, Town of Leith, Barronies of Portsburgh and Broghtoun, who take upon them the Exercise of the Furriers' Trade within the said boundis, being Unfreemen in calling, as making of Muffs, furring of Coats and Caps, and working of furred skins, and hanging out of the saymn in open view for selling thairof." The Narrative goes on to say that such conduct causes His Majesty's lieges to be abused; the Craft injured by being disenabled and frustrated from receiving those benefits which should belong to them; that it is contrary to all equity and reason, and to the liberty of Free Burghs, and their "awin auld Richts and Privileges who have been a Calling of ane very antient Standing within Burgh."

The Representation further proceeded to desire that the Town Council would prohibit and discharge any person or persons whomsoever to use or exercise the said Art of Furrier Craft, as making of Muffs, furring of Coats or Caps, working of furred Skins, and hanging out in open view for sale, or using any other point of the said Calling within this burgh and liberties thereof, in all time coming, under the penalty of Twenty Pounds, *toties quoties;* the one half to be paid to the Magistrates and the other half to the use of the Craft,—besides imprisoning their persons at the discretion of the Magistrates. It then desired a general concurrence, that the Deacon and his successors should "searche, seik, take, and apprehend all such Persones and their Warke within the said Boundis, who sall be found Transgressors; and the Baillies to punishe the Transgressors according to their Fault, as the said Supplicatioun in itself at mair Lenth beires."

The Lord Provost, Magistrates and Town Council, taking into consideration the fact that the supplication and desire of the Furriers was reasonable, passed the following resolution :—"They doe heirby prohibite and discharge all Unfriemen, or any uther Persone whatsomever, to use and exerce the said Furrior Craft, as making Muffs, furring of Coatts or Caps, working of furred Skinns, or hinging out of the samen in open view for selling, or useing any uther Poynt of the Calling within this Burgh or Liberties thereof in na Tym comeing under the Pain of Twentie Pund, *toties quoties*; the ane Halfe to be payit to the Magistratts and the uther Halfe to the Calling, besyde the Imprisonment of their Persones at the Discratioune of the Magistratts. And siklyk, gives generall Concurrance to the present Deakon and his Successors, Deakens of the said Calling, to imploy Officars to searche, seik, take and apprehend all such Persones and thair wark within the said Boundis, who sall be found Transgressors ; and the Baillies of the Boundis to punish the Transgressors according to their Fault, as said is ; whereanent thir Presents sall be their warrand."

It will be observed that the first notice of the Furriers being included in the Incorporation of the Skinners is in the Seal of Cause granted to that body by the Town Council on 22d August 1533, which bears to be "Seal of Cause to the Skinners and Furriers." Again in the Deed of Obligation already referred to as having been granted on the 22d June 1765, the tenor is as follows :—"The business or Craft consists of two branches :—the one of manufacturing various skins into leather or furs, and thereby named Skinners and Furriers," etc. It would appear, therefore, that down to this date there was no separate Incorporation of the Furriers. They seemed to have gone straight to the Town Council with their complaints. Another case of this kind occurs on 5th April 1665. This complaint has not been published by the Burgh Records Society. It is probable that it was like the one of

1593 : because the Deed of Obligation of 1765, being one hundred years afterwards, states specifically that the Skinners and Furriers were Members of the same Incorporation.

The following is the Prayer which is regularly read before beginning the business of any meeting :—"O Almighty God! Who of Thy tender love towards mankind, hath graciously promised to hear the prayers and petitions of those that ask in Thy Son's name, we humbly beseech Thy blessing upon this our meeting for the preservation of brotherly love and concord amongst us. And grant, O Lord! that no malice, resentment, or selfish views may bias the wills or influence the resolutions of any here present; but that Thy Good Spirit may direct, sanctify, and govern all our actions and resolutions, to do always what is good in Thy sight, for Thy glory and for the good and welfare of this society. And this we beg, O Lord! in the name of our Advocate and Mediator, Jesus Christ, Amen." This form of prayer has been made use of since the year 1749.

The Incorporation had originally a Hall and other property situate in Skinners' Close, High Street. But these were disposed of in 1832.

Mr Robert Legget is the present Deacon of the Skinners, and Mr Andrew M'Cullagh, the Deacon of the Furriers, is Treasurer and Clerk. Both Deacons enjoy the privilege of voting at the election of the Convener.

SKINNERS.

FURRIERS.

## THE INCORPORATION OF CORDWAINERS (CORDINERS).

THE word Cordwainer (or Cordiner, as it was eventually called) was derived from the word *Cordovan*, a kind of leather made of goats' skins in the city of *Cordova*, in Spain. The Cordiners were, according to Maitland, at first erected into a fraternity or Incorporation, by a Charter from the Town Council of Edinburgh, on the 28th July 1449. That Charter had no reference to trade purposes. It is not to be found in the City Archives, and consequently does not appear in the Burgh Records which have been recently printed by the Scottish Burgh Records Society. Like the first Charter of the Skinners' Incorporation, which is of date the 12th January 1450, it had reference exclusively to religious purposes. Each master of the trade who kept a booth or shop within the town was enjoined to pay weekly one penny Scots, and the several servants of the Craft one halfpenny towards the support of their altar of *St Crispin* and *Crispiani*, within the Collegiate Church of St Giles in Edinburgh, and the maintenance of the Priest who officiated thereat.

Maitland again states that by a second Seal of Cause, dated the 26th November 1479, power was granted to certain masters and chief men of the trade to search and inspect the various kinds of work brought to the market by the Shoemakers, to prevent the people being imposed upon by having bad work or inferior leather supplied to them. This Seal of Cause, likewise, is not to be found among the existing muniments of the city. Neither of these Charters are produced by Maitland.

There is, however, a reference to the latter Seal of Cause in an Act of Council, dated 6th December 1513, a note of which, to the following effect, is to be found in one of the volumes of the Burgh Records Society. It refers to the same Charter, and is in the following terms :—

They limitt and ordanet certane persouns, maisteris and oversmen of the said Craft, sworne in thair presence, quha suld every market-day diligentlie serche, visie and sie all maid wark and barked ledder cummand and presentit in the market, and if that they find sufficient till mark it; and quhair they find fals feyngyeit wark or barket ledder, the sercheris till bring it to the provest and baillies for the tyme, and at the will of thame to escheit the stufe faltive, and the persouns to pvneis as effeiris, sua that the King's lieges be nocht dissavit, and that na sic stufe be sauld on the market-day quhill the sercheris have visit the samyn. Nor yit that nane be stoikkin up to sell quhill seven houris at somer and nine houris in wynter before none, vnder the payne of escheit and pvnesing the persouns as said is. And that no outlands folk dwelland without this burgh, nor unfreemen by any rwch hydes nor barkit ledder, within this toun, bot on the market-day allenarlie, vnder the payne above written. And attour, for certane reasonabill causis moving thair predecessours, bayth for honestie of the said burgh, and profit of the said stufe, maid wark and others perteinin to the said Craft, they locat, limitt, and ordanet the market place for selling of thair wark and vther stufe foresaid in the market-day in the Kowgaitt, fra the new well to the Grayfreris allenarly, as at length is containet in the said letter, or seal of cause.

The oldest Seal of Cause that appears on the records of the Burgh is of date 4th February 1509. It is in the following terms :—

Tyll all and sundry quhais knawlege thir present lettres sal cum, the provest baillies and counsaill of Edinburgh greting in God euirlesting. Wit your vniuersities that the day and the dait of the making of thir present lettres comperit before ws counsally gatherit—John Dauidsoun, Kirkmaister, Thomas Quhitehill, Nicholl Bynnyn, Andro Quhite, Alexander Willesoun, Peter of Murray, Williame Hamyltoun, Richert Nicholsoun, and the laif of the maisteris of the Cordinar craft, within this burgh, and presentit to ws thair supplicatioun contenand certane Statutis Articulis and Reulis diuisit be thame and affermit be ws for the loving of God Almychty, the honour of the realme, the wirschip and proffet of this guid toun, and the proffet of all our Souerane Lordis Lieges and vtheris reparand thairto; of the quhilk supplicatioun the tenour folowis :—My Lordis Provest Baillies and worthi Counsaill of this guid toun, vnto your honorabill discretionis richt humlie menis and schewis the Kirkmaister and the laif of the maisteris of the Cordinar Craft within this burgh, that quhair first for the loving of God Almychty, the honour of the realme, the wirschip and proffet of this guid tovne, and the proffett of all our Souerane Lordis Liegis and vtheris reparand thairto, and in exampill of vtheris, and for augmentatioun of divine seruice at the altar of Crispine and Crispyiniane situat within the College Kirk of Sanct Geill of the said burgh, we desire that we micht haif thir Statutis artikillis and reulis folowing grantit and gevin to ws be your autorite, quhair throu guid reull and gyding may be had amang ws of the said Craft, baith maisteris and seruandis, and our successouris thairof, in tyme to cum ; considering it is said be commoun autorite that multitude but reull makis confusioun, and for to eschew the vice thairof, and to be eschew it if in tymis to cum thir folowand ar our resonabill desiris : In the first senc that all incresment of vertew practik and knawlege standis in guid begynnyng and fundament and frathinfurth to continew in vse and perseuris to finale end, that frathinfurth all maner of prentissis to be tane at the said Craft sall stand in prentischip for the space of seven yeris and nales, without the dispensatioun of the principale maisteris of the said craft, and specialie in fauouris of the sonis of the said Craft; and ilk prentis to pay at his entre to the reparatioun and vphalding of divine seruice at our said Altar sex schillingis aucht pennis ; and that nouthir thir prentissis nor nane vthir persoun of the said Craft be sufferit to sett up buith within this said burgh without he be fundin sufficient habill and worthi thairto in practik and vther wayis, and admittit thairto first be the sworne maisteris of the said craft, and maid freman and burges of the said burgh, and than for his vpsett to pay four merkis, except burges sonis of this tovne to pay twa merkis to the reparatioun and vpholding of divine seruice at our said Altar; and that ilk seriand sall pay his vlkly halfpenny to vpholding of divine seruis as said is; and gif ony man of the said craft cummis nocht to the quarter comptis four tymis in the yeir als aft as thai be, thai bein lauchfully warnit be thair seriand thairto, thai sall pay twa pundis of walx vnforgevin, without thai haif ane lauchfull impediment, and the saidis twa pundis walx to be delieurit to our said altar within twa dayis efter the falt be notourly knawin before the said sworne maisteris of the said Craft; and that na maner of maister of the said Craft lift hous herbery nor ressaue ony vther maisteris prentice or seruand, vnder the pane of paying of twa pund of walx to our said Altar vnfoirgeven; and that ilk maister haldand buith within this burgh of the said Craft sall pay his vlkly penny to the reparatioun of the ornamentis of our said Altar, and sustene the Priestis meit thairof as it cummis about; and that the said Kirkmaister and ane certane of the principalis maisteris of the said Craft that sall happin for the tyme sall haif full faculte leif and priuilege with ane officiar of the toune to pass with thame, poynd distrenye gif neid be for the takin rasin and inbringing of thir dewiteis forsadis to the sustentatioun and vpholding of God's seruice as said is but danger stop or impediment: and gif thair be ony fre maister of the said Craft that makis impediment in the paying of his said dewiteis, quhair throw ane officiar of this guid toune may be haldin to poynd him, he sall pay the officiaris feo for his laubouris als weill as the principale dewiteis that he is owin to the said Altar; and gif ony Maister of the said Craft disobeys the Kirkmaister that sall be for the tyme to pay twa pundis of walx for ik tyme he disobeyis vnforgevin to our said Altar: Quairfor my Lordis sen thir our resonabill and simpill desiris and resonis conformis to equite, and are consonant to honour and policy accordinge to the vse and consuetudes of greit tounis of honour in vther realmis and provincis, that ye wald grant to us thame and ratifeit and apprevit and confermit be you vnder your seill of caus, in perpetuall memoriall of guid reull to be had in tyme to cum, with your answeir heirupoun we humbilie beseik.

The following is the deliverance of the Town Council on the same:—" The quhilkis Artikillis, Statutis and Reulis being red (sic) hard and vnderstand and diligentlie considerit be ws that thai ar first for the loving of Almychty God, and sustentatioun of Divine Seruice, and for gud Reulis to be had in tyme to cum amangis thame of the said Craft, in augmentatioun and supple of the commoun proffitt, for to eschew misgidit wayis that has beyn vsit in tymes bygane, we haif ratifeit apprevit and confermit, and be thair presentis for us and our successouris ratifeis apprevis an confermis the samyn in all poyntis and artikillis to the saidis maisteris and thair successouris of the said Craft, in perpetuale memoriall in tyme to cum foreuirmair, and this to all quhame it effeiris we mak it knawin, be the tenour of thir our lettres. In witnes of the quhilk thing to thir our present letteres, our commoun seill of caus of our said burgh we haif gart append at Edinburgh, the ferd day of Februar, the yeir of God ane thousand five hundreth and nine yeris."

In so far as these Seals of Cause referred to religious matters, it is right to state that all these ordinances and obligations were abolished at the time of the Reformation, and the following Constitution, which is now regarded as the chief Charter of the Incorporation, was granted by the Town Council of Edinburgh, on the 1st day of February 1586. Strange to say, although it appears in Maitland, it finds no place in the Burgh Records Society's Volumes, and it may therefore be assumed that it is not to be found in the City Archives. The terms of the Charter are as follows :—

1. Forsamekill as the Predicessoures of the Provest, Baillies, Counsall and Deykins of guid Memorie, diligentlie considering and understanding upoun the Supplicatioun gevin in to thume be the Masters and Heidismen of the said Craft for the Tyme, thair Nichtbouris and Burgesses, that oure Soverane Lord's Lieges ar greitumelie skaithet and defrawdet be insufficient Wark of ignorant Persouns, Lawbourira, bayth in black Wark and barket Ledder, be thame daylie boucht and sauld within this Burgh, alsweill be Friemen als Unfriemen and Owtlandsmen on the Wolk dayes, alsweill as on the Market-dayes, the Friedome and Privileges of Burgesses destroyet thairthrow, contrare to the Commonweill. For Reformatioun thairof, be thir Lettres patent, under thair Seill of Caus, limit and ordanet certane Persouns, Maisters and Oversmen of the said Craft, sworne in thair Presence, quha suld every Market-day diligentlie serche, visie and sie all maid Wark and barket Ledder, cummand presentit in the Market, and that thay find sufficient Persouns to mark it ; and quhair they find fals feyngzeit Wark, or barket Ledder, the Sercheris till bring it to the Provest and Baillies for the Tyme, and at the Will of thame to escheit the Stufe faltie, and the Persouns to puneis as effeiris, swa that the King's Lieges be nocht dissavit : And that na sic Stufe be sauld on the Market-day quhill the Sercheris have visit the samyn. Nor zit, that nane be strikkin up to sell quhill seven houres in Somer, and nyne houres in Wynter before None, under the

N

Payne of Escheit, and punesin the Persouns as said is.   And that na Outlandsfolk, dwelland without this Burgh, nor Unfriemen, by any rowch Hydes or barket Ledders within this Toun bot on the Market-day allanerlie, under the Payne above writtin.   And attour thay, for certane resonabill Causis moving thair Predecessours, bayth for Honestie of the said Burgh, and Profit of the said Stufe, maid Wark and uthers perteining to the said Craft : They locat, limit, and ordanet the Market-place for selling of thair Wark, and uther stufe foresaid on the Market-day in the *Kowgaitt*, fra the new Well ta the *Grayfrieris* allanerlie, as at length is contaiuet in the said Lettre of the Dait, the sext day of December, 1513 Zeires.

The quhilks being of sic Antiquitie, and for ane Comounweill, the said Deykin and Breter desyre thair Lordschips to ratifie, approve, authoreis, and allow in all Poynts, and ordane the samyn to be observit, keipit, and obeyit in all Tyme cuming ; and to mak, creat, and constitute the Deykin, and sex Quarter-maisteris of the said Craft, and thair Successouris zeirlie, to be generall Searchers for paiting the samyn to execution be the Assistance of thair Officeris, except and heirin the place of Market of barket Ledder, to be in the nyther Kirk-zaird, quhair the samyn is presentlie plaicit, induring the Townis Will allanerlie ; and that it sall be lesum to the Burgesses of this Burgh and Friemen to sell thair barket Ledder, at all Tymes, the samyn beand guid and sufficient Stufe.

2. For putting Remeid to the present Derth, and eschewing the lyke in Tyme cuming, that all Forestallers, Regraiteris, and Cowperis of barket Ledder be discharget ; and do statute and ordane, that na Maner of Persouns present any barket Ledder to the Market, bot sic as buyes the samyn rowch, and barkis the samyn be thameselffis or thair Servands ; and that nane of the said Ledder be huirdet or keipet in Housses, but be brocht altogidder to the Market, at the Houres before mentioned, that the samyn may be tryet be the Serchers to be sufficient Stufe to serve the King's Lieges, under the Payne of escheiting of the said Ledder ; and that the Friemen of the said Craft be nocht sufferit to sell insufficient Stufe mair than the Outlandsmen.   Thairfore, that they lykewayes that bark any Ledder within this Burgh, present thair barket Ledder or ane resonabill Pairt thairof to the Common Market appoyntit ; to the effect that the samyn may be serchit and markett as the Outlandsmens Ledder is, under the Payne foresaid.

3. That na Unfrieman cum to the Market to by any Ledder before elevin Houres be past, to the effect that Friemen may be first stockit that beirs portabill Chairges, under the Payne of wairding of the said Unfrieman, and paying of an unlaw of Twintie Schillingis.

4. That all maid Stufe be presentit to the Market, and be sauld to the Lawboreris thairof, or thair Servands, that the samyn may be tryet, gif it be sufficient or nocht for serving the King's Lieges, be the serchers foresaid, and the insufficient Wark escheitt. And that all Wark unsauld be removit at twelf Houres every *Mononday*, conforme to the auld Ordour, under the Payne of Fourtie Schillings.

5. That na Unfrieman bring any Buits or Schone, or uther maid Wark to sell within the Friedom of this Burgh, bot on the *Monondayes*, and present the samyn to the Market in Tyme and Place appoyntit, under the Pain of Escheitt thairof.

6. That all Buithes within this Burgh be serchit owlklie, or swa oft as neid is, be the said Serchers, and the insufficient Wark escheitt.

7. That on the *Sondayes* na Buithes be oppin after nyne Houres in the morning; and that na Wark be wrocht at any Tyme the said day, under the pain of Twentie Schillings.

8. That na habill young Men be sufferit to keip ane Cobleris Buith, bot onlie the samyn to be permittit to thame that ar past threttie zeir awld, that the Friemen may have their Servands to serve thame; and that the said Cobleris sell their auld Wark in the *Kowgaitt* on the *Monondayes*, and nocht at the Croce, nor on the Hie Streitt, in Dishonour of the guid Toun, under Payne of escheitt of thair Stufe.

9. That na Frieman of the said Craft, being Burgess, pack nor piell, nor be Partiner with Unfriemen, nor mak Conventioun with thame, under the Payne of Ten Pund and Tynsell. And that na Frieman and Burgess of the said Craft, owt with the Friedome of this Burgh, nor wirk his Wark owt with the Friedome, under the Payne foresaid.

10. That na Maister resett ane uther's Prenteis or Servand without leif, or ane resonabill caus first schawin and tryet, under the Payne of Twentie Schillings.

11. At the taking of any Prenteis, that Tryall may be tane, gif the Resaver be worthie to tak ane Prenteis, and to instruct him and giff him Meitt and Drink sufficientlie; to statute that all Indentouris be subscryvit be the Deykin or his Clerk, utherwayes the Prenteis nocht to be buiket in the Toun's Prenteis-buik. And that na Maister of the said Craft tak any uther Prenteis, quill thair be thrie Zeires owtrun of his former Prenteis, to the effect that the awld Prenteis may be habill to teache the Servand for eschewing of unsufficient Warking, under Payne of Fyve Punds.

12. That nane be maid Maister of the said Craft, except he haif bene ane Prenteis

for fyve Zeir, and servit ane Frieman for Meitt and Fie thrie Zeires thairafter, or ellis marie ane Burgess Dochtor, under the Payne of Ten Pund to be payit be the Deykin and Craft-maister that admits him maister; and alsmekill be thame that procures the same.

13. To ordane ane of thair Lordschips' Officers to put the Premisses to Execution, be passing with the Serchers, and ane of the Tounis Collectors of the Unlawes, and wairding or poynding for the Unlawes, and intromitting with the Escheitt Guids, to be delyverit be him to the said Collectors, to be imployit be thair Lord-schips, and according to the Decreit arbitrall, and the saids Collectors to gif zeirly Compt thairof.

The Minute of the Town Council, approving of the above terms, is to the following effect : — The foresaid Laws and Articles having been duly considered, the Provost, Bailies, Council and Deacons of the Craftsmen, having given commission to certain merchants and crafts-men, to "intreat, considder and resoun upoun" the said articles, and the said persons having met together, and reasoned and consulted thereupon, and made emendations on certain points and clauses thereof, —They made this day their report of the same to the said Provost, Bailies, Council and Deacons of Crafts who caused the Articles to be read in open Council : And they been advised regarding them after mature deliberation, found them to be "guid, honest, and profitabill" for the said Craft, and all our Sovereign Lord's lieges. They, there-fore, ratified and approved of the same, interponing their authority thereto. They likewise decerned them to be observed and retained as perpetual Laws in all time coming, under the penalties contained therein, with "reddy executioun to follow thairupon." And having granted to the said deacons and brethren and their successors this Act and Ordinance, they ordained that their seal of cause should be appended. Provision was made, however, that if any question should arise upon the Articles, or any of the points or clauses, the interpreta-tion, execution, and mitigation of the same should be at the discretion of the Provost, Bailies and Council for the time, "according to the qualities and circumstances of the Persounes, Tyme, Maner and Places."

This Seal of Cause granted by the Town Council was afterwards confirmed by James VI., on the 6th day of March 1598, in consideration of "the Goodwill and thankful service done to us by our Servitor, *Alexander Crawfurd*, present Deacon of the said Cordiners and his Brethren."

The Cordiners obtained another Seal of Cause from the Town Council on 17th September 1533, which does not appear in Maitland, and refers to a desire to raise more money for upholding the altar of St Crispine and Crispiani, whereof the tenor follows :—

Till all and sindry quhais knaulege thir present literis sall tocum, the prouest ballies counsale communite and dekynnis of Craftis of the burgh of Edinburgh greting in God euirlesting, Wit youre vniuersiteis that the .day of the date of thir present lettres comperit before ws sittand in jugement the dekyn kirk maisteris and brether of the Craft of Cordinaris within the said burgh, videlicet, Thomas Mureleyis dekin, James Litiliohnne, Richart Nicholson, Robert Borg, and the remanent of the haill brether of the said Craft, and presentit before ws thare bill and supplicatioun in maner and forme as efter followis, that is to say ; To yow my lordis prouest bailies and worthy counsale of this gude town, humlie menis and schawis your dailie seruitouris the dekyn kyrkmaisteris and brether of the Cordinaris within this burgh, that quhair it is weill kend to all your wisdomis how for the lowing of God and vphalding of dewyne seruece we mak grete reparatioun and expens at oure altare of Sanctis Crispine and Crispiani situat within your College Kirk of Sanct Geill, and has na lowing to vphald the samyn and daly chaplane thairat bot oore ouklie penny gaderyt amangis the brether of the said craft, quhilkis ar bot a few nommer, to the regarde of vther greit craftis within this burgh, quhilk has grantit to thame ouklie one the merket day ane penny of all stuf belanging thare craftis brocht fra landwart Canongait or vther placis to be sauld within this burgh, for sersing of the gudnes and fynes tharof, sua that oure Souerane Lord and his lieges be nocht begylit tharewith anent the vnsufficientnes of the samyn, and to that effect oure said Souerane Lord of his speciall grace has direct his writingis to yow praying yow effectuislye and als chargeing that ye grant and geve syklike priuelege and fredome to the dekyn and maisteris of oure said Craft of Cordinaris within this burgh that we may ouklie on the merket day haue and tak aue penny to the reparatioun of our said altare and vphalding of dewyne seruice tharat of all barkit leddir and maid stuf belanging oure craft that beis brocht fra landwart, Cauongait, or vther partis, to be sauld within this said burgh, for sersing of the gudnes, fynes, and warkmanschip of the samyn, sua that oure Souerane Lord and his liegis be nocht begylit tharwyth as saidis; Beseking heirfor youre lord-schippis and wisdomes that ye wald grant ws be your autorite till haue and tak ouklie on the merket day ane penny of ilk dakyr of barkit leddir, and of ilk stand of maid stuf belanging till oure said Craft, that beis brocht fra landwart, Cannongait, or vther pairtis, to be sauld within this burgh to the reparatioun of oure said altar, siklyke as vther Craftis within this burgh has, sen it is for the commoun weill and with the grace of God we sall do sua for the honoure of God and vphalding of devyne seruice at oure said Altare and for the vniuersale weill of oure Souerane Lordis liegis, that youre lordschippis salbe contentit tharof, with your deliuerance heirintill humlie we beseik; and als the saidis dekin and maisteris producit oure Souerane Lordis lettres vndir his signet and subscriptioun manuall of the date at Striuelyng (Stirling) the secund day of Merche, and of his rigne the tuenty yeir desyrand and chargeand ws till consent to the samyn.

The following are the terms of the Minute of Council in reference thereto :—The foresaid Supplication and Bill having been openly read before us sitting in judgment, and we having been ripely advised regarding all points and articles contained in them; find the same consistent with reason, and for the common good of our Sovereign Lord's lieges of this Burgh and those repairing thereto : Therefore we consent, give, and grant, for us and our successors, to the said Deacon, Kirkmaster, and brethren of the said Craft of Cordiners now present, and their successors in all time coming, full faculty and freedom, that weekly on the Market Day, they have and take One Penny to the repair of their said altar of Saint Crispin and Crispiniani, and to the upholding of Divine Service at said altar, off "ilk dakyr of barkyt leddir and siklyk of ilk stand of maid stuf belangand thare Craft that beis brocht fra landwart, Cannongait," or any other parts to be sold within this said Burgh : for searching as to the goodness, fineness, and workmanship of the said stuff, so that our Sovereign Lord's lieges may

not be imposed upon through the insufficiency of the same, conform to
the command and desire of our Sovereign Lord's letters and writings
directed to us on this subject, and this in the same way as each other
Craft does within this Burgh : Discharging them and their successors
from taking such pennies from any person residing in the Burgh : And
this to all and sundry whom it may concern, be it known by these
presents.—" In witnes of the quhilk thing we haue to thir present lettres
hungin oure commoun scill of caus, at Edinburgh the xvij day of the
moneth of September, the yeir of God ane thousand fif hundreth thretty
and thre yeris."

Three years thereafter, the Town Council seem to have again
granted them another Charter, viz., on 22d September 1536. This
also is not to be found in Maitland. The terms are as follow :—

Till all and sindry quhais knawlege thir present letteres salcum, Robert Lord
Maxwell, ane of the regentis of this realme the tyme of oure Souerane Lord the Kingis
absence, and provest of the burgh of Edinburgh for the tyme, George Henrisoun,
William Adamsoun, Johnne Carkettill, and William [Littil] baillies of the said burgh
for the tyme, counsale and communite of the samyn, greting in God euirlesting. Wit ye
ws, at the instance and requeist of Thomas Mureleyis dekin for the tyme of the Cor-
dinare Craft of the said burgh, Richart Nycholsoun, Robert Borg, Johne Wilsoun,
Johnne Freland, Johnne Prestoun, and Robert Dikesoun, maisteris of the said Craft,
and vthers thair brethir and maisteris of the Cordinaris of this toun, and for increment
of the commoun weill of this burgh, policy of the same and agmentatioun of devyne
seruice, to haue gevin and grantit to thame and thair successouris Cordinaris within this
toun thir priuilegis under writtin :—that is to say, all maner of prentesis to be tane to
the said Craft sall stand in prentischip for the space of sevin yeris and nay les, without
dispensatioune of the principall maisteris of the said Craft, and speciallie in fauoris of
the sonis of the said Craft, and ilk prenteis to pay at his entre to the reparatioun and
vphalding of devyne seruice at thair said altar tuenty schillingis vsuall money of this
realme; and that nodir thir prentesis nor nane wthir persoune of the said Craft be
sufferit to set wp buith within this said burgh without he be funding sufficient, habill
and wourthy in practik and wthir ways, and admittit thareto be the kirk-maister and

sex maisteris of the Craft, and maid burges and freman of the said burgh, and bring his tiket thairupone, and than for his wpset to pay fyve pundis, except burges sonis of this toune to pay fyfty schillingis, to the reparatioun and wphalding of devyne seruice at thare said Altar; and that ilk seruand sall pay his wkly halfpenny to the wphalding of devyne seruice as said is, and gif ony maister of the said Craft cumis nocht to the quartar comptis four tymes in the yere als oft as thai be, thai being lauchfullie warnit be thare seriand thareto, thay sall pay twa pundis of wax, unforgevin, without thai haue ane lauchfull impediment, and the saidis twa pundis walx to be deliuerit to thare said Altar within twa dayis efter the falt be notourly knawin befoir the said maisteris of the foirsaid Craft; and that na maner of maister of the said Craft tyst hous herbery resaue nor gif him laubouris to ony wther maisteris prenteis nor seruand, wnder the pane of paying of twa pundis of wax to thare said Altar, wnforgevin; and that ilk maister haldand buith within this burgh of the said Craft sall pay his wkly penny to the reparatioun of the ornamentis of thare said Altar, and sustene the preistis meit thareof as it cumis about; and that the said kirkmaister and ane certane of the principale maisteris of the said Craft that sall happin to be for the tyme, sall haue full faculte leif and priuilege with ane officiar of the toun to pas with thame, poynd, distreynye gif neid beis, for the taking raysing and inbringing of thir deviteis foirsaidis to the sustentatioun and wphalding of Goddis seruice as said is, but danger stop or impediment; and als that the dekyn sall haue power to poynd for the preistis meit, that is to say aucht penneis on the day, gif neid beis, and gif thair be ony fre maister of the said Craft that makis impediment in the paying of his said dewiteis, quhairthrow ane officiar of this toun may be haldin to poynd him, he sall pay the officiaris fee for his laubouris alsweill the principale dewiteis that he is awand to the said Altar; and gif ony maister of the said Craft disobeis the kirkmaistare that salbe for the tyme, to pay twa pundis of wax for ilk tyme he disobeis, wnforgevin, to thare said altare.

The following is the deliverance of the Town Council thereon :—
" The quhilkis articulis statutis and rewlis we haue ratifiet apprevit and cornfermit, and be thir presentis for ws and oure successouris ratifies and apprevis and als confermis the samyn, in all punctis and articulis, to the saidis maisteris and thare successouris of the said Craft in perpetuall memoriall in tyme to cum for evirmair; and this to all quhome it efferis we mak it knawin be the tenoure of thir oure letteres.   In witness of

the quhilk thing, to thir oure present letteres oure commoun seill of caus of oure said burgh we haue gart append, at Edinburgh the twenty-twa day of September the yere of God ane thousand five hundreth thretty and sex yeris."

The Members of the Incorporation of Cordiners used to assemble in a handsome Hall of their own, situated at the south-west corner of the *Horse Wynd.* The Essay which each Member had, and still has to perform, is to make a pair of boots or shoes to the satisfaction of two Essaymen, one of whom is chosen by the Incorporation, and the other by the applicant. On admission he has to make the following declaration :—

I do solemnly and sincerely declare and promise that I shall defend the true Religion and Protestant form of Worship presently professed and practised within this Realm : that I shall obey the Deacon and Office-bearers of this Incorporation for the time being, and shall scot, lot, watch and ward and bear all manner of Burghal customs and charges with my brethren according to my ability, and that I shall keep all the general Statutes and Ordinances made or to be made for the welfare of the Craft, and shall not colour nor fortify any unfreemen : And I make this solemn Declaration conscientiously and honestly, intending to observe and fulfil the same in all points.

The Incorporation meets at least four times a year. Its business consists of the management of the Funds, and the election of Office-Bearers. It is represented in the Convenery by the Deacon. Mr Walter Park, 14 College Street, is the present Deacon ; and Mr John Whitehead, S.S.C., is the Clerk.

o

# THE INCORPORATION OF TALZOURIS.

HE charter of the Incorporation of Talzouris or Taylors (now Tailors), dates so far back as the 26th day of August 1500. Nevertheless, there is abundant evidence to prove that its existence as a Society was antecedent to that date. For a long time prior to their application for a Seal of Cause from the Town Council, the body supported an Altar dedicated to St Anne. Before the Reformation in Scotland, the revenues of the Craft were freely devoted to the salary of their Chaplain in St Giles, and the upkeep and repair of the Altar. When Altar worship was, however, abolished at the change of religious views which took place at the time, the revenues of the Talzour Incorporation, like those of the other Crafts, were judiciously employed in providing a fund for the Widows and Orphans of the various members of their respective Incorporations.

Desirous, however, of having certain articles passed for the better Government of the fraternity, they approached the Town Council with the view of obtaining from them a Seal of Cause, as several of the other Incorporations had already done. In this they were successful. The following are the terms of the charter referred to, which will be found chiefly to relate to the maintenance of divine service :—

Till all and sindry to quhais knawlege thir present Letters sall cum. The Provost, Baillies and Counsall of Edinburgh, gretings in God evirlesting.

With zour Universities, that the Day and Dait of the making of thir present Lettres, comperit before us in Counsall gatherit, John Steill, Kirkmaster (Deacon), George Bell, William Hockburne, Johne Quhyte, Robert Richartsoun, Johne of

Lauder, William Lamb, Thomas Foulare, William Dick, Morice Slenny and the Laife of the Maisters of the Talzour Craft, within this Burgh, and put till us thare supplicatioun contenand certane Statutis and Rewles devisit be thame, to be affirmit be us, for the loving of God Almichty, the Honour of the Realme, the Worschip and Profit of this gude Toune, and the Profit of all other soverane Lordis, Lieges, and utheris reparand thareto; of the quhilk supplicatioun, the Tenore followis.

"My Lordis Provest, Baillies, and Worthie Counsale of this nobill Toune, unto zoure honorable discrationis, richt humily menis and schawis the Kirkmastir, and the Laife of the Maisteris of the Talzouris Craft, within this Burgh, that first for the loving (Praise) of Almichty God, the Honore of the Realme, the Worschip and Proffit of this gude Toune, and the Profitt of our Soverane Lordis, Leigis, and utheris reparand thareto, and in Exempill of utheris, and for the Augmentatioun of Divine Service at the Altar of Sanct An, our Matrone of the samen, situate within the College Kirke of Sanct Geils of the said Burgh. We desyre that we micht have thir Statutis, Articulis, and Rewlis followand, grantit and gevin till us be zour Autoritie, quarethrow gude Rewle and gyding, may be had amangis us of the said Craft, baith Masteris and Servandis, and oure successoris; considering it is saide be comone Auctorite, that Multitude but Reull maks confusion, and to eschew the vice thereof, and be estimit in tyme to cum, thir followand ar our rationable desyris.

"In the First, That for the several Encrements of Vertue, Practick and Knawlege standis in gude Begyning and Foundment, and fra think furth to continew in Vertue, and persevere to final End. That fra thinc furth all Manir of Prentice to be tane at the said Craft, sall stand in Prenteischip for the space and termes of sevin Zeirs, and na less, without Dispensatioun of the principall Master of the said Craft, and Specialie Favour of the Sonnys of the said Craft, and ilk Prentice to pay at his Entrie, to the Reparatioun and Uphalding of Divine Service at oure said Altar, Ten Schillings, and that nouther thir Prenticis, nor nane othyr Persoun of the said Craft, be sufferit to set up Buth within this said Burgh, without he be fundin sufficient habill and worthy thairto, in Practick and utherwayis, and admitted thairto, first be the sworne Masters of the Craft, and maid Freman and Burgess of the said Burgh; and for his Upsett to pay Forty Schillings to the Reparatioun and Uphalding of Divine Service at oure said Altar.

"And that na Maner of Master of said Craft, to hous, harber, or resett any uther Master's Prentice or Servand; and gif he dow, he sall pay ane Contribution and Taxt to oure said Altare, at the Discratioun of oure said sworn Masteris principall, of the saids Craft, and the Cause thereof to be reformit be thame: And that ilk Master haldan Buth, within this said Burgh, of the said Craft, sall pay his wolkly Penny to the Reparatioun of the Adhornementis of oure saids Altare, and to sustene the Preistis Mete thereof, as it cummys about; and that the said Kirkmaster and certane of the principall Masteris of the said Craft, that sall happin to be for the Tyme, may have full Facultie, Leife, and Privilege, with ane Officare of the Toune to pass with thame for to poind and distrenzie, gif Neid be, for the taking, raising, and inbringing of their Dewities foresaid, to the Sustentatioun and Upholding of Goddis Service, as said is, but Danger, Stop, or Impediment.

"Quharfore, as this our rationable and simpil Desyris and Petition is conform to Equitie, and ar consonant to Honore and Pollecey, according to the Usis and Consuetudis of great Antiquitie in uther Realmys and Provincis; that ze wald grant till us thame ratifyit, approvit, and confirmit be zou, under zour Sele of Cause, in perpetual Memorial of gude Rewle to be had in Tyme to cum, with zour Answere hereupon we humily beseik."

The Town Council's deliverance thereupon is to the following effect:—The aforesaid Articles, Statutes, and Rules having been heard, read, and diligently considered by us; and seeing that they are for the love of Almighty God and the Sustentation of Divine Service, as well as for good Rules being observed in time to come among the Members of the Craft, in augmentation and supply of the common profit, and for the purpose of "eschewing misgydit wayis that has bene usit if time begane": Therefore we have ratified, approved, and confirmed the same, in all points and articles, to the said Masters and their successors of the said Craft, in perpetual memorial in time to come for evermore. And this to whom it concerns we make known by these our letters.— "In Witness of the quhilk Thing, to thir oure present Lettres, oure comone Sele of Causs of oure said Burgh, we have gart append: At Edinburgh, the 26th day of the moneth of *August*, in the Zere Ane thousand and five·hundreth Zeres."

The Town Council about thirty years afterwards granted the

Incorporation another Charter, viz. :—on the 20th of October 1531, of which the tenor follows :—

"Tyll all and syndry, quhais knawlege thir present letters sal cum, the provest, ballies, and counsall of Edinburgh, greting in God euerlesting : Wyt your vniuersite, that the day and the dait of the making of thir present letters, comperit befor ws counsally gaderyt, Thomas Stanhous, kyrk-maister, Thomas Arthour, Andro Edgar, William Pacok, Alexander Frostar, Andro Persoun, Alexander Robesoun, Robert Spittal, Johne Cowpar, Johne Kraik, Johne Bayne, and Thomas Thomesoun, and the laif of the maisterys of the tailyeor craft within this Burgh, and present till ws thair supplicatioun, contenand certane statutis, articulis and reulis, dyuysyt be tham to be affirmyt be ws, for the loving of God Almyghty, the honour of the realme, the worshype and proffyt of thys gud tovne, and the proffyt of all oure soverane lordys liegis, and vtheris reperant thairto, and in exampell of vtheris, and for the agmentatioun of dyuyne seruice at the alter of Sanct An, situat within our College Kyrk of Santt Gele of the said Burgh, and thairfor desyryt that thai mycht haue thir statutis articulis and reulis followand grantyt and gevyn to the saidis brether and thair successouris be ws and our authorite, quhairthrow gud reule and gyding may be had amangis thame of the said craft, bayth maisterys and seruandys, and thair successouris thairof in tyme to cum, considering it is said be commonis authorite, that multitud but reule makys confusioun and for till eschew the vice thairof, and to be eschewyt in tyme to cum, the quhilk desyr we thocht consonant to resoun, and thairfor has grantyt and gevyn to the saidys brethir, and thair successouris, thir statutis, articulis and reulis followand :—

"Item, in the first, that sen all entresment of verteu, practik and knawlege, standys in gud begynyng and fundiment, and fra thynfurth to continew in vse and perseuire till fynale end, that fra thyn furtht all maner of prentis [that] sall be tayne at the said craft sall stand in pryntischype for the space of sevyn yeris, and na less, without dis- pensatioun of the principall maisterys of the said craft, and specialye in fauours of the sonys of the said craft, and ilk prentis till pay at his entry to the reparationis and wphald of dyuyne seruice at thair said altar, or ony prentis be sett upoun the tailyeor burd, ten shillingis.

"Item, that na maister resaif ane seruand that hes nocht bene prentis within this Burgh with ane free maister of the said craft, without he pay ten shillingis to the said altar, and that he [be] bund prentis to the maister that resaiffis hym for ane certane of yeris, as the sayd maister and he can aggre.

"Item, that nane of thir saidys prentissis be ressauit, without the dekyn, the four kyrk maisterys and the chaplane that says prayers, till be for the tyme, be present for till put the saidys prentissis in thair prentis buk, and mak the indenturis of thair conditiouns amangys thame, under the payne of twenty schillingys, till be payt till Sanct Gelys werk, and twenty to the reparatioun of the said altar of Sanct An vnforgevyn als oft as thai brek ony punct of the said act.

"Item, that nowthir thir prentisis, nor nane vther persoun of the said craft, be sufferyt till sett wp buyth within this said Burgh, nor wyrk of the said craft, bot with ane fre maister of the samyne, without he be sworn maister, and fund sufficient, habyll and worthy thairto in practik and vtherywayis, and admyttyt thairto first be the sworn maisterys of the said craft principall, and maid fre man and burgess of the said Burgh, and than for his wpset till pay fyf pundys to the reparatiouns and wphald of dyuyne seruice at thair said altar with an honest dennar to the sworne maisterys thairof.

"Item, that na fre maister of the said tailyeor craft fie ane vther craftis man of ane vther craft to wyrk in his buyth, under pain of ten schillingys till be payit to Santt Gelys werk, and ten schillingys to Santt Annys altar, als oft as ony maister wses the samyne.

"Item, that na vnfreman of the said craft cum within the fredome of this towne that has ane buyth without the fredome of the samyne, till tak ony werk or stuff furth of the samyne till wyrk it, owder schappin or wnschappin, it sall be lesum till the dekyn and maisterys of the said craft for the tyme till tak the samyne werk fra thame, and gyf it be made werk, the price thairof till cum to the reparatioun of thair said altar of Sanct An, and gyf it be not maid, na fre maister of the said craft till mak the samyne to the persouns that the said stuf pertenys to, and take his price thairof, because the saidis vnfremen nowthir scottis, lottis, walkis nor wardis within our said fredome.

"Item, that na burgess, na fre man within this burgh, lord na lard, ressaif ane vnfreman of the said craft in thair houses nor lugenys till wyrk quyetly or oppynly, in defraude of the said craft, without the pricys thairof be payit to the said dekyn and maisterys, to the reparatiouns of thair said altar, and quhay doys in the contrar, that officiaris of this gud tovne pas with the saidis dekyn and maisterys, and mak thame oppyne durris, and deliver the stuf that they fynd wrocht and vnwrought, being in the saidis vnfremens handys for the tyme, to the saidis dekyn and maisterys, and till remayne with thame quhill the pricys thairof be payit to the reparatioun of thair said altar, and gyf ony burgesses, lordis, lardis, or vther fremen, induellers, or vnfremen within this burgh, uses the resett of sic vnfremen of the said craft in tyme cummyn, thai sall pay vnforgevyn twenty schillingys to Santt Gelys Werk, for ilk tyme thai be fund in thair forsaidys houses and lugenys, fra the first charge be gevyn be aue offycyar of this gud tovne, and to pay the officiaris for thair lawbouris, and ten schillingys to the said altar, for the costys and skayth it sustenys thairupon.

Item, that [na] maister of the tailyeour craft ressaif nor resset ane vther maisterys servand nor prentis of the said craft within this burgh, without he haue maid compt and raknyn with the maister he cumys fra, and that he be contentyt thairof, vnder the payne of ten schillingys to be payit to the said altar quha dois the contrar vnforgevyn.

Item, gyf ony fremaister of the said craft within this burgh brekis ony manys stuf vnordourly, or womanis, and spillis the samyne in his defalt of werkmanshype, the persoun that aw it sall cum to the dekyn and maisterys of the said craft for the tyme, and plenye thairupon, it beand seyn be ane certane of the said sworne maisterys, that the werkmen thairof has falyeit in ony punct, the said dekyn and maisterys sall cause the said man till recompens the complenyear thairof, of the skayth he has sustenyt thairthrow, and that thair be certane maisterys of the said craft be sworn apon all sic caissis, or thai decerne in the samyne, that thai sall lelely and treuly, without feid, fawour, or prejudice of party, depone and deliuer in the samyne, and cause the complenyear till be payit of his skayth.

Item, that na maister sall haue forman in his buyth till wyrk, bot ane allanerly within this fredome.

Item, that na maister sall dissobey the dekyn and maisterys for the tyme, in the gatheryn in of the dewteis to thair said altar, vnder the payne of twa punddis of walx till be payt to the said altar als oft as thai dissobey vnforgevyn.

Item, gyf thair be ony fremaister of the said craft that bydis away fra the quarter comptis, thai being lawfully warnyt be the seruand of the said craft, he sall pay ane pund of walx vnforgevyn, without he haue ane releuand excusatione, and that it be oppynly knawn.

Item, gyf ony maister of the said craft dissobeys the dekyn and the maisterys in ony thing that is for the commone weill of the samyne, quhairthrow they will not obey, without an officiar of this gud tovne be brocht to thame till pund for the samyne, thai sall pay twa schillingys to the officiar for his feys, ane pund of walx with the dewteis that are awyn.

Item, that ilk maister haldand butht within this burgh of the said craft, sall pay his wkly penny to the reparationis of the enhornamentys of the said altar, and susteyne the prestis meit thairof, as is cummys about, and that the said kyrk-maister, and ane certane of the principall maisterys of the said craft that sall happyn till be for the tyme, sall haue fulfeture, leif and preuilige, with ane officiar of the tovne till pas with tham for till pund and distrenye, gyf neid be, for the takyn, raising, and inbringyn of the forsaids dewteis to the sustentatione and uphald of Godis seruice, as said is, but danger, stop, or impedyment.

And attour, gyf it sall happyn ony maister or freman of the said craft, efter that he be maid maister to the saymne, abstrak him and disuse his said craft, and thairefter returne agane to the occupying of the saymn craft, that he sall pay all maner of dewteis bypast, sa he be thollyt till wyrk at the said craft, or ellis till pay his new upsett agane.

The terms of this Charter contain very ample privileges and immunities. The Minute of Town Council sanctioning the same is to the following effect :—The Articles and Rules, with the privileges above written, we, the said Provest, Bailies, and Council, for us and our successors, Grant to the said Deacon and Masters, and we affirm, ratify, approve, and confirm the same, in all points and respects to the said Deacon and Masters, "to be brukyt and josyt be thame and thair successors of the said craft, in perpetuall memoriall in tyme cummyn for euer mayr." And this to all whom it may concern, we make known by the purport of these our letters.—"In witnessing of the quhilk thing to thir our present letteris, oure commone seill of cause of our said burgh we haue gert append, at Edinburgh, the twenty day of the moneth of October the year of God ane thousand fyve hundreth and thretty ane zeris."

The terms of this Charter were afterwards confirmed by Kings James V. and VI. Indeed, the Incorporation of Talzouris had the honour to receive a Letter from James VI. The following is a copy of the said letter in which his Majesty requests that his own private Tailor, whom he kept exclusively for making and working the "Abulzements" of his own person, should be admitted gratis to the liberty and freedom of the "Talzouris" Incorporation :—

*" Dekin and remanent Maisters and Brether of the Tailzour Craft within oure Burgh of Edinburgh, we gret zou weill."*

" Forasmeikle as respecting the gude service of *Alexander Millar·* in making and working the Abulzements of oure awin Person, minding to continew him in that oure Service as ane maist fit and meit Persone. We laitlie recommendit him unto zow be oure Letter of Requeist, desiring zow to ressave and admit him *gratis* to the Libertie and Fredom of the said Craft, as a thing maist requisite for him, having the cair of oure awin wark, notwithstanding that he wes not Prenteis amangis zow, according to your ancient Liberties and Privileges had ·in the contrair. Willing zow at this oure Requeist to dispense with him thereanent.

" Quhilk lettre being presentit and red before zou, we have hard by gude Report of zour gude-will and mynd utterit to the fulfilling and obedience tharof ; sa the·same indurit not a Preparative, and was not ane Miens to ony uther Unfreman to sue and obteine the lyke Benefite, to the hinder of zowr privileges heirefter ; quhilk we esteeme maist ressonable for eschewing of confusioun and disorder ; always sen the said *Alexander* is burdenit with the chairge of our awin proper service and man only gif Attendance tharupon as he sall be commandit.

" It is oure Will, and we affecturuslie requeist zow zit as of befoir, that at this oure ernist requeist, ze will ressave and admit him to be ane Brother of said Craft amangis zow *gratis ;* seing it is maist convenient that he being oure awin Servand have that Privilege and Benefite ; assuring zow upon oure Promeis, that for evading of Preparatives and Prejudice of zowr Privileges, we sall not burden zow with the lyke for heirefter ; not doubting, bot upoun this conditioun, ze will agre to this

P

oure ressonable Desire, as ze will do us maist thankfull and acceptable plesur, we comit zow to God. Subscrivit with oure Hand at    the day of      1584.              JAMES R."

Of course Millar—who seems to have been the Scottish "Poole" of that period—required to be made first burgess and freeman, and this privilege could be conferred on him only by the Town Council. Although there is no mention of his name in the Burgh Records which have been published, there is sufficient evidence of occasional commands on the part of the King to give free admission to the Burgess Roll. For example, during the previous year, there is the following Minute of the Corporation :—" 14th June 1583.—At the request of the Kingis Maiestie, grantes and admittis Phinlaw Tailyeour, lacquay to his Maiestie, burges of this burgh *gratis*, and ordanis his name to be insert in the lokkit buik and his aith of burgess to be resauet."

The last Statute of the Town Council regarding the Body is of a somewhat lengthy description, and is dated 11th November 1584. It complains of the great number of unfreemen practising the craft, and asks a remedy. It is as follows :—

In presens of ane nobill and mychtie lord, James erle of Arrane lord Avon and Hammiltoun, chancellare of this realme, provest of the said burgh, and of the bailyeis, dene of gild, thesaurer, counsell and deykins, being convenit to consult vpoun the commoun effairis of the said burgh, comperit Alexander Owsteane, deykin of the tailyeouris of the samyn, and the said George Smyth, James Nicolsoun, Patrik Sandelands, Jhonn Murdow, Jhonn Young, Androw Cairnie, Nicoll Rynd, eldare, tailyeours, friemen of the said craft and burgessis of the said burgh, quha for thame selffis and in name and behalff of thair remanent brether, burgessis and friemen, exhibit and produceit dyuers heids and articles concerning thair said craft, desyring the said bailyeis, counsall and deykins, to interpone thair decreitt and authoritie thairinto. Quhilk heids and articles beand red and considerit, and the said bailyeis and counsall after lang and sufficient resoning being thairwith rypelie avyset, all in ane voice admittet, retefeit, and apprevit the heids and articles vnderwritten, as tending to the weill of the said brether and all our Souerane Lords lieges and agreand to all guid lawes, ordour and policie; and thairfore hes interponet, and be thir presents interponis thair authorite thairto; decerning and ordaning the samyn to be inuiolablie obeyet, kepet, and obseruet as perpetuall lawis in all tymes cuming amangs the present brether of the said craft and thair successoures and vtheris, burgessis, fremen, indwelleris of the said burgh, and all vtheris repayring and remaning within the samyn, vnder the paynis contenit thairinto. Followis the saidis heids and articles :—

In the first. Forswamekill as it is complenit be the said deykin and brether that thai ar heavelie hurt and damnefeit be ane greit number of vnfremen dwelland within this burgh, als weill mareit as vnmareit, quha ar nawayes under subiection of ony maisteris nor yitt subiect to ony stenting, watcheing, wairding, or vther portabill chairges with the friemen of the said craft, bot levis licentiouslie and workis all maner of wark that thai may purches in priuie howssis, lofts and chalmeris, and takkis pay- ment thairfore as thai wer admittet to thair friedome, and thairby hinders and preiuges the frie brether of the said craft quha ar subiect to all portabill chairges of thair commoditie and proffeitt; for remeid thairfore that gife onie sic vnfrie persouns of the said craft quha makis daylie residence within the toun beis apprehendit within this burgh, ather vpoun the Hie gaitt, priuie howssis, loftis, chalmeris or vther strettis in tyme cuming, nocht subiect to ane frie maister aither for meitt, fie, or owlklie waige, and his conditioun of seruice maid before the deykin and foure maisteris, that thai sall be tayne and put in waird quhaireuir they may be apprehendit, and gif thai be ony sic houssis that officeris of this burgh mak oppin durris quhill thai be apprehendit and mak payment of the sowm of fourtie schillings als oft as thai be apprehendit furth of the seruice of ane frie maister, viz., the twa pairt of the said sowm to the vse of the hospitall and the third pairt to the apprehendaris at the distributioun of the said deykin and maisteris being for the tyme.

*Item*, Becaus the said deikin and brethir complenit that thai ar havelie hurt and damnefeit be sindrie persouns of the said craft nocht beand friemen of this burgh duelland in the Cannogait, Potterraw, and West Port, and vther suburbs of the said burgh, quha daylie cumis within the fredome of the samyn and takis furth wark, schaipin and vnschaipin, pertening to the burgessis and friemen of this burgh, and wirkis the samyn in thair awin friedomis, and thairafter inbringis the said wark agane to this burgh to the awner thairof and takis thair pryce thairfore, and thairby also grittumlie hurtis the said deykin and brether of thair commoditie and proffeitt quhilk thai wald obtene of the said wark gif thai wer stoppet to vsurp thair fredome and libertie; for remeid thairof, the said provest, bailyeis, counsall and deykins, hes statute and ordanit that gif ony sic vnfrie persouns dwelland outwith the said fredome, nocht beand burgessis and friemen of the samyn burgh, beis apprehendit with ony sic wark in tyme cuming, ather schaipin or vnschaipin, in the owttaking or inbringing within this burgh, that it sall be lesum to the said deykin and maisteris, or ony of thame, with the concurrance of ane officer, to tak and intromett with the said wark fra the haver thairof quhaireuir the sam may be apprehendit within the fredome of this burgh, and to keip and retene the samyn quhill payment be maid of the soum of fourtie schillings be the warkmen that wirkis sic wark, and as thai be fund and apprehendit committing the said falt, the twa pairt of the said sowmes to the vse of the hospitalitie and the thrid pairt to the apprehendaris at the distributioun of the said deykin and maisteris being for the tyme.

*Item*, Becaus the said deykin and brether havelie complenis that thai ar grittumlie hurt of thair commoditie and proffeit be sindrie of thair awin brethrein, burgessis and friemen of this burgh, quha vnder cullour and pretence of ane seruand takis, resavis and resettis, within thair buithis, vnfriemen, uather being thair seruands nor prenteissis, and sufferris and permittis thame to wirk and inbring within thair buithis to thair awin behuiff and profeitt all maner of wark that thai may purches and obtene and to tak pryce thairfore and to dispone thairvpoun at their plesure and to vse all vther liberteis of the said craft as the said frie maister micht do himsellf, for granting of the quhilk pretendit libertie the said vnfrie personis ar bund and oblist for payment to the maisteris of craft that resettis and resauis thame of ane certane sowm of money, to the greitt abuse of the said craft and preiudice of the liberteis of the samyn ; for remeid quhairof the said provest, bailyeis, counsall, and deykins of craftis, hes statute and ordanit that na frie maister of the said craft sall be sufferit to hald, resett, nor resaue ony sic vnfrie persouns to wirk within thair buithis in tyme cuming, nor yett to hald nor resaue any seruand of the said craft in thair seruice without he be bund for certane yeiris to remayne in his said maisteris seruice for meitt and fie as his maister and he can agrie, and the condition of seruice to be maid before the said deykin and foure sworne fey maisters being for the tyme ; and gif it be fund verefeit and provin that ony frie maister of the said craft sall happin to do in the contrare, or that the said maister and seruand sall happin to mak any collusioun betuix thame to the hurt of the said craft, vtherwayis nor beis in thair appoyntment to be maid before the said deykin and brether, the said maister and seruand sall pay euerie ane of thame swa oft as thai failyie heirin the sowm of fourtie schillings money, the twa pairt to the hospitalite and the thrid thairof to the apprehendaris at the sicht and distributioun of the said deykin and brether.

t
`,
i-
ve
to

To the Incorporation of Talzouris, there belonged in ancient times the superiority and direction of all the tailors within the suburbs of Edinburgh and the Town of Leith. Latterly their jurisdiction was confined to Portsburgh, Potterrow, south side of the Canongate betwixt St John's Cross and St Mary's Wynd, and the ancient and extended Royalty of the City. They received fees from apprentices who were indentured in these districts. They also had the privilege of exacting certain fees from all *Mantua-makers*, for liberty to make up women's apparel within the city. The abolition of all special privileges has, however, put an end to this state of matters.

The Incorporation of Tailors is still in existence, for the purpose of paying annuities to those entitled to the same, and for electing a Deacon to represent the body in the Convenery. Mr R. G. Muir has recently been elected Deacon. Mr James Dundas Grant is the Treasurer, and Mr Alexander Wardrop (of Messrs Banks & Wardrop, S.S.C.) is the Clerk.

# THE INCORPORATION OF WOBSTARIS.

HE Websters, or Weavers, of the City of Edinburgh, having, in the year 1475, petitioned the Magistrates and Town Council to erect them into an Incorporation, their request was at once granted.

The following are the terms of the same :—Till all and sundrie quham it effeirs, quhais knawlege this present Letteris sall cum ; the Provest, Baillies, and Counsale of the Burgh of *Edinburgh*, greeting in God everlasting. To your Universitie we mak it knawin, that there comperit before us in our Tolbuith, we sittand in Jugement, the best and worthiest Personis of the haill Craft of Wobstaris within the said Burgh, quhilkis presentit to us thair Bill of Supplicatioun, in the quhilkis was contenit certane Statutis and Articles maide and avisit with thame, for the Honour and loving of God Almightie, and of his Modir, the Virgin *Marie*, and of *Saint Soverane;* and for the suppleing and uphalding of divyne Service, and appareling of thare Altar of *Saint Soverane,* foundit and uphaldin be thame in *St Giles'* Kirk ; and for the Governance of thare Warks and Laboure and gude Reule baithe for the Worship of the Realme, commone Profite, Laute of the Craftismen, and for other diverse and mony Causes of gude Motive, the quhilkis Bill we have sene, hearde, and gart be rede ; and tharewith beande riplie avisit considerande thare Desyres of us tharein, to have our Benevolence, Assistance, and Leif thareof, and to have our Affirmatioun and Ratificatioun thareupon, so far as in us is, or may be. We tharefore have considerit the said Desyris and Statutis, and find thame consonant to

Reason, Honour, and Worship to God and Hale Kirk, profitable to the Realme and Craft.

The following are their Desires and Statutes :—

(1.) In the first, that the haill Craftismen may zeirlie chese them a Deykin, like as uther Craftismen dois, quhilks sall reule and govern the Craft in all gude Reulis as effeirs; to the quhilk Deykin all the Leif of the Craft sall obey in all leifull and honest Thingis concerning the Craft; and this Deykin to be chosen with Freemen of the Craft that are Burgesses, and nane uther to have Voyce tharin.

(2.) That na Man occupy the Craft as Foremaster quhill he be made Burgess and Freeman, and to be examinate be the Deykin and Maisteris of the Craft, gif that he be worthie; and that he sall have gude and sufficient Graith and Warkloumis to be seene and considerit be four Men of the Craft; this brande, he sall pay Twa Marks and Twa Pund of Wax to the said Altare, and Upholde thereof; and gif he be a Burgess' Son, he sall pay half a Mark to the Altare foresaid.

(3.) Na Maisteris sall tak ane Prenteis for less Terms then five Zeirs, and sall pay at his Entrie to the said Altare, Five Shillings, or less, as can be tretit with the Craftismen gif he be nocht of Power, and the Mynisar of thir five Zeires sall pay Twentie Shillings quhen it is tayntit upon ony Maister.

(4.) Thare sall na Maister tak ane uther Maisteris Prenteis in Service, nor ane uther feid Servand quhilk be feid, or els have Leif of this Maister that aws him, under the Payne of Ten Shillings and a Pund of Wax, and restore the Prenteis and Servand again.

(5.) That na Man tak on Hand to resave nor wark ane uther Mannis warpit Zarne, nor Wark but Leif, but he sall pay ane Pund of Wax, or the Price thereof.

(6.) Ilk Man or Woman that occupies the Craft, sall gif the Priest his Mete, and ilk Owlk gif to the Altar a Pennie; and this to be gaderit be the Deykin; and ilk feit Servande sall gif in the Zeire Foure Pennies. And also, that the Personis that disobeys the Dekin, and will nocht underlie the Ordinance of the Craftis Statute for the Gude thareof; alse oft as he disobeys, he sall pay ane Pund of Wax, or the Price thareof, and to be tane but Favour.

(7.) That na Woman sall occupie the Craft as a Master to hold Warkhouss, but gif she be a Frieman's Wyfe.

(8.) That na Man sall tak ony Loumis to hyre for dout of spilling of them; but gif it be a Frieman, and qua that dois, sall pay a Pund of Wax ay quhen he can be tantit tharwith.

These desires, statutes, and articles, with all the various points contained in them, having been laid before the Provost, Magistrates and Town Council, and they having found these "lovable to God, and holy Kirk, honourable for all the Realme, and profitable for the Worship of the Craftismen,"—did admit the same: And for them and their successors in office, the Provost, Bailies, and Town Council did approve and ratify the above-written articles in all points, in so far as they had any power. And to make them more effectual, the following Minute was added:— "To all and sundrie quham it effeirs, we mak it knawin be thir oure Letteris; and for the maire witnyssing to the samyn we have to hungin oure commoune Seill of Cause. At Edinburgh, the last day of *Januare* the Zeire of our Lord 1475 Zeires."

This Charter was confirmed by the Town Council on the 27th day of February 1520, with an additional Right of receiving from every Country Weaver that wrought for the Edinburghers One Penny Weekly, towards the support of their Altar aforesaid. Both of these grants were during the same year confirmed by John, Archbishop of St Andrews, as they were subsequently done by the *Scotish* Parliament.

About the beginning of the sixteenth century, certain disputes having taken place between the Incorporation and the Waulkers in point of precedence, they both made an application to the Town Council to get the same adjusted. The Civic body, in order to avert all contests of a like kind in future, was pleased to make Regulations on the 15th day of May 1509, of which the following is a copy:—

15 May 1509.—The quhilk day the Provest, Baillies, Counsale, and Kirkmaisteris hes consentit and ordanit that in tyme to cum, baith the craftis, Webstaris, Wakeris and Scheraris, in all tymes of processioun quhair euir thair bannaris beis borne, that thai pas togedder and be incorporat vnder ane baner in als formis as thai pleis; and to be maid in this wys, that thair baneris of baith the saidis Craftis be paynitt with the imagis figuris and armis of the Webstaris, and principalie becaus thai ar found the

Q

elder Craft, and first placit; and with the ymagis figuris and armys of the said
Scheraris and Wakaris quarterrie rynnand togedder; and the armes of the Webstaris,
viz. thair signe of the spule to be vnmaist in ilk baner; and ilk ane of thair craftis to
haue thair bymarkis on thair awin bannaris that thai mak principale cost vpoun for the
keiping of the saymn; and the said Scheraries and Wakeris to pas vnder the bannar
of the Wobstaris quhill thai may gudlie furnis thair awin, and the armys of the said
Scheraries and Wakeris to be now put in the Webstaris bannaris gif thai may be gudlie
formit and gottin thairvntill.

Maitland states that this settlement of the question in dispute put
an end to all differences between the two bodies. In this respect, the
historian is wrong. Twenty years thereafter, viz., 21st June 1530,
there is a Decreet-Arbitral with much the same object in view between
the Websters, Waulkers and Shearers; as well as along with the
Bonnetmakers to have it determined to which of the Corporations there
should be an annexation. The Minute, like all formal documents of
the day, is written in mediæval Latin.* The translation of the Editor
of the Burgh Records is as follows :—

In the name of God, Amen. By this present public instrument let it appear
evidently to all, that in the year of the incarnation of our Lord one thousand five
hundred and thirty, on the twenty-first day of the month of June, in the third
indiction, and in the seventh year of the pontificate of the most holy father in
Christ and our lord the lord Clement the Seventh, by divine providence, Pope: In

---

* In Dei nomine, amen. Per hoc presens publicum instrumentum cunctis pateat euidenter quod anno
incarnationis Dominice millesimo quingentesimo tricesimo mensis vero Junii die vicesimo primo, indictione tertia, pontificatus sanctissimi in Christo patris et domini nostri domini Clementis diuina
prouidentia Pape septimi anno septimo: In mei notarii publici et testium subscriptorum presentia
personaliter constituti honorabiles et circumspecti viri Willelmus Raa, Andreas Edgar, Stephanus Bell,
Edwardus Thomsone, Johannes Arras, Jacobus Litiljohnne, Adamus Baxtar, Edwardus Hendirsone
et Thomas Andersone, burgenses burgi de Edinburgh, tanquam judices arbitratores et amicabiles com-
possitores de vniuersa secta et caterua artificum per subscriptas partes de consensu honorabilis et egregii
viri magistri Adame Otterburne prepositi de Edinburgh acetiam de consensu balliuorum et dominorum
consilii dicti burgi specialiter electi et jurati inter Alexandrum Michel decanum Textorum prefati
burgi et ceteros artifices et magistros eiusdem artificii ab vna, et Johannem Gray decanum Fullonum et
ceteros artifices et magistros eiusdem artis dicti burgi partibus ab altera, penes discrimina singula

presence of me, notary-public, and the witnesses underwritten, personally compeared, honourable and discreet men, William Raa, Andrew Edgar, Stephen Bell, Edward Thomsone, John Arras, James Litlejohnne, Adam Baxtar, Edward Hendirsone, and Thomas Andersone, burgesses of the burgh of Edinburgh, as judges, arbitrators, and amicable compositors of the entire set and company of craftsmen, specially chosen and sworn by the underwritten parties, with the consent of the honourable and worthy man, Master Adam Otterburne, provost of Edinburgh, and also with consent of the bailies and deacons of the council of the said burgh, between Alexander Michel, deacon of the Websters of the said burgh, and the rest of the craftsmen and masters of the same craft, on the one part, and John Gray, deacon of the Walkers, and the rest of the craftsmen and masters of the same craft of the said burgh, on the other part, anent sundry contentions and debates concerning these parties respectively, and chiefly anent the craftsmen of Bonnetmakers, as to which of the foresaid craftsmen they ought to be incorporated, annexed, and adjoined with, and in regard to the place and position of the same in general processions whatsoever, the men above-written, judges, arbitrators, and amicable compositors, not led by force or fear, but long reasoning and mature deliberation being previously had at divers times to the effect above-written, and being convened together, with unanimous consent and assent, without any disagreement or change whatever, with consent also of the aforesaid parties there present, who having touched the holy evangelists of God, they swore for themselves and their successors, henceforth to observe the decree of the said judges, and not to contravene the same in any way in time coming ; as in the said decree-arbitral made thereupon, in the common tongue, is more fully contained. The tenor of the decree-arbitral, of which mention is above made, follows word for word, and is thus :—

At Edinburgh, the xxi day of Junij the yeir of God j<sup>m</sup> v<sup>o</sup> and thretty yeiris, we Williame Raa for the brethir of the Smythis, Andro Edgar for the Tailyeouris, Stevin

---

et debatabilia ipsas partes respectiue concernentia et precipue penes discrimen artificum burrutorum vtri predictorum virorum artificum incorporari annexari et adungi deberent, et penes locum et locationem eorumdem in processionibus generalibus; quiquidem suprascripti viri judices arbitratores et amicabiles compositores, non vi aut metu ducti, sed longo temporis tractu et matura deliberatione prehabita diuersis vicibus ad effectum suprascriptum insimul congregati vnanimo eo consensu et assensu sine discrimine aut variatione quibuscunque, de consensu etiam partium predictorum ibidem presentium, tactis sacrosanctis Dei euangeliis, jurauerunt decretum dictorum judicum pro se et suis successoribus in futurum obseruare nec eidem aliquatenus contrauenire temporibus futuris imperpetuum, prout in suo decreto arbitrali in vulgari desuper lato sequenti, latius continetur : cuiusquidem decreti arbitralis de quo supra fit mentio tenor sequitur de verbo in verbum et est talia,

Bell for the Skynnaris, Edward Thomsone for the Baxtaris, Johnne Arras for the
Barbouris, James Litiljohnne for the Cordinaris, Adame Baxtar for the Wrichtis
and Masonis, Edward Hendirsone for the Flescheouris, and Thomas Andersone for
the Furrouris, as jugis arbitratouris and amicable compositouris coniunctlie chosin
sworne and admittit be avise and consent of the provest baillies counsall and the
haill communite of the craftismen of the said burgh betuix Alexander Michel dekin
of the Wobstaris and the laif of the masteris and brethir of the said Craft one
that ane part, and Johanne Gray dekin of the Walkaris and Scheraris and the laif
of the hedisman and masteris of the said Craft one that vther part, anent the con-
tentioun and debait betuix the saidis brethir and communite of the Wobstaris Walkaris
and Scheraris, and specialie anent the brethir of the Bonetmakaris to quhome thai
suld be incorporat vnit and annexit, to be vnderneth ane ouerman or dekin equalie
to be chosin yeirlie amangis thame, to proceid gang pay and fulfil thair dewiteis
with thame in reparatioun of ane altare, processionis and vthers conuentionis neidfull,
and to haue thair place in the samyn, conforme to all vthers craftis and sectais
within the said burgh, the quhilkis partiis beand oblist and suorne to stand abid
and fulfil oure decreit deliuerance and finale sentence anent the mater foirsaid ;
and we the saidis jugis takand the said mater in and vpone ws, and inlikuis oblist
and sworne to deliuir thairintill eftir oure vndirstanding and knawlege, all in ane
voce, the richtis resonis and allegationis of baith the saidis partiis be ws sene
vnderstand considerit and riply auisit and matur deliberatioun had thairupone, for
stanching of pley vnite concord and tranquilite to be amangis thame and thair
successouris in all tyme tocum, decretis deliueris ordanis and for finale sentence
arbitrale gevis that the Scheraris Walkaris and Bonetmakaris sall pas all togedder
vnder ane hedisman dekin or oureman equalie chosin amangis thame as said
is in all processionis generale and all vtheris conuentionis and counsallis neidfull amangis thame to be ouresene considerit and visiit and to obey to him as
thair oureman siclik as vtheris craftisman obeyis to thair dekin or oureman in
reparatioun of ane altare and sustentatioun of ane chaplane to the samyn, and in
all vtheris thingis vsit and wount in tymis bigane amangis thame, and to haue
thair place in all generalle processionis and conventionis with thair banneris and
serimontis betuix the Flescheouris and the Barbouris, becaus the saidis Scheraris
Walkaris and Bonetmakaris war incorporat vnit and annext all togiddir vnder ane
oureman of befor of thair avin desiring and consent with the auis of the provest
baillies and communite of the said burgh, as ane obligatioun and contract of thair
annexatioun vndir the common seill of the said burgh maid and gevin to thame

thairupone mair fullelie proportis; and that inlikuis the saidis Wobstaris pas all
togiddir vnder ane dekin with thair banneris and vtheris derayis in processionis
and generale conuentionis in thair auld place vsit and wount to thame of langtyme
bigane passit memore of man, that is to say betuix the Baxtaris and the Tailyeouris,
and that ilkane of the foirsaidis partiis stand afald lele and true in freyndlie luf
and kyndnes till vtheris in tyme tocum, and quhilk of the saidis partiis that makis
any incontentatioun troubill or impediment in the mater foirsaid and kepis nocht
this our decreit arbitrale and sentence in all thingis aboue expremit, the party
contendand or failyeand ony maner of way to be banist the toun or to be punist
at the discretioun of the provest baillies and counsaill of the said burgh for the
tyme as thai think cause, with assistance of the haill craftismen nixt eftir the
failye be notourlie knawin to the saidis provest baillies and counsaill of the said
burgh; and gif thair be ony terme doutsum or obscur in the premissis the inter-
pretatioun and declaratioun thairof to be referrit to the jugis arbitratouris forsaidis.
And for the obseruying fulfilling of this our foirsaid decreit arbitrale and deliuerance
aboue written and euery poynt thairof, baith the saidis partiis ilkane till vtheris
ar bund oblist and sworne inuiolably to obserue the samyn for thame and thair
successouris be the vphalding of thair richt handis, the haily Euangelis tuichit,
and neur tocum in the contrar vnder the panis aboue expremit, and of provit
infirmite and inabilite in presens of ane notar and ws jugis arbitratouris in ratificatioun and approbatioun of thair first aith maid to ws of befor thairupon. And
this our decreit arbitrale and final sentence to all and sindry quhome it efferis
we mak it knawn. In witnes of the quhilk we the saidis jugis arbitratouris hes
subscriuit this our decreit arbitrale with oure handis at the pen, day yeir and
place forsaidis, befor thir witness Andro Michel, Johne Bane, Archibald Mowbray,
Schir James Huntar, Schir Johne Hendersone, and Sir Williame Thomsone, chap-
lanis, with vtheris diuers. Sequuntur subscriptiones judicum arbitratorum super-
scriptorum de quibus supra fit mentio [Follow the subscriptions of the judges
arbitrators above written, of whom mention is made above] Androu Edgar, Edward
Thomsone, James Litiljohne, Edward Hendersone, John Arras, William Raa, and
Stevin Bell, with owr handis at the pen, and Thomas Andersone with my hand.

Upon * which, in all and sundry, the said parties for their own part, and each of

---

* Super quibus omnibus et singulis dicte partes hinc inde a me notario publico subscripto sibi fieri
petierunt et quilibet earum pro se petiit vnum seu plura publicum seu publica instrumentum siue instrumenta. Acta erant hec infra insula beati Johannis euangeliste infra ecclesiam collegiatam de Edinburgh

them for himself, asked from me, notary-public, a public instrument or instruments, one or more, to be made. These things were done in the aisle of St John the Evangelist, situated within the collegiate church of Edinburgh, at the twelfth hour before noon, in the aforesaid year, month, day, indiction and pontificate; being present discreet men, Sir James Moffet, John Hendersone, and William Thomson, chaplains, with divers other witnesses specially called and required to the premises.

On the 19th May 1531, there was presented before the Town Council of the city sitting in judgment, another Decree Arbitral between the parties. It had reference to the sums which the Incorporations should respectively pay to Saint Mark's altar, and the order in which they should pass in procession on "Corpus Christi day and the octaius tharof," and all other general processions and gatherings. The unanimous resolution of the Council was that the Deacons and Brethren of the Websters should receive and suffer those of the Waulkers, Shearers, and Bonnetmakers to "resort and pas with thame all togidder," in one place without any hindrance, and that they should display their respective banners; and that the place and room should be called the "Wobstaris place and rovm for euir." Further, that the Waulkers, Shearers, and Bonnetmakers and their successors should pay to the Websters the sum of thirteen shillings and fourpence yearly, aye and until they pay the sum of Ten Pounds "vsuall money haill and togidder, on ane day." This order and rule was to remain binding upon them to prevent variance and discord in time to come. The award was signed by Jo. FOULAR, notary public, clerk of the said burgh, on the above date.

On the 29th May 1532, the various parties again appeared before the Magistrates and Town Council, when they received the following discharge :—

---

situatam, hora duodecima ante merediem sub anno mense die indictione et pontificatu quibussupra; presentibus ibidem discretis viris dominis Jacobo Moffet, Johanne Hendersone, et Willelmo Thomsone capellanis, cum diuersis aliis testibus ad premissa vocatis specialiter atque rogatis.

The twentynyne day of the moneth of Maij the yeir of God ane thousand five
hundreth thretty and twa yeris, the quhilk day, in presens of the provest baillies and
counsall sittand in jugement comperit the dekin kirkmasteris and brethir of the craft
of Wobstaris on that ane pairt, the dekin heidisman and brethir of the Walkaris
Scheraris and Bonetmakaris on that vther pairt, and thare in presens forsaid the saidis
dekin heidisman and brethir of the saidis Walkaris Scheraris and Bonetmakaris contentit and paiit to the saidis dekin and brethir of the Wobstaris the sovme of ten pundis
vsuall money of Scotland for the annuell of xiij s. iiij d. quhilk thai war decernit to pay
yeirlie to the saidis Wobstaris, efter the forme of the decreit and act of the tovne maid
thairupon of the dait the nyneteyne day of Maij the yeir of God j<sup>m</sup> v<sup>c</sup> and xxxj yeris,
quhilk ten pundis the saidis dekin and brethir of Wobstaris grantit thame till haif
ressauit fra the saidis Walkaris Scheraris and Bonetmakaris for the said annuell of
xiij s. iiij d. yeirlie eftir the forme of the said act, and grantis the said merk of annuell
lauchfully redemyt fra thame, and tharfor for thame and thare successouris renuncis all
richt and titill of richt that euir thai had to the said xiij s. iiij d. yeirlie, and quytclamis
and dischargis the saidis Walkaris Scheraris and Bonetmakaris and thare successouris
thairof now and for euir, promittand neuir till clame nor thar successouris tharfor in
jugement nor vtouth jugement in na tymes tocum; and the saidis pairtiis craftismen
oblissis thame ilkane till vtheris that nane of thame sall perturb nor iniure ane another
nouthir in word nor deid in preue nor in pert in tyme tocum vndir the payne of that
persone that dois in the coutrair to be ryalii pvnist be the avise and sicht of the provest
baillies and counsall of this tovne to the rigour but fauouris.

The Weaving business, in former times, was extensively carried on
within the City and suburbs of Edinburgh, chiefly by Quakers—members of the Society of Friends. The far-famed Paisley Shawls, for which
that town eventually obtained notoriety, were originally contrived and
manufactured in the district of Sciennes, and were first named "the
Edinburgh Shawls," and were well-known all over the world. Potterrow, Brown Street, the Banks of the Water of Leith, the district where
Picardy Place now stands, and the West Port contained each of them
not a few manufactories. In fact, in the last-mentioned district, there
was a motto carved out on the front of one of the Factories; the
building has now been removed; but the stone containing the motto is

still in existence, having been appropriated for the purpose of embellishing a recently erected edifice in the district. It contains the words, "My life is as a Weaver's Shuttle." The names of Deacon Brown, whose manufactory was in the Water of Leith district, of the Wighams, of the Howisons, whose working-house was in a lane off Brown Street, the Hewats, the Scotts, the Simes, the Grays, and other noted weavers of their day, are still in the recollection of many Edinburgh people.

Regarding all these worthy citizens, it is now only too true that the place that once knew them knows them no more for ever; although we have still among us one of our most respected Lady Citizens, noted for her benevolence and her many good offices,—viz., Miss Eliza Wigham. The click of the looms which was wont to fall upon the ear of the passer-by, indicating industry, prosperity, and plenty, is now for ever silent. The factories are utilised for other purposes. Bailie Nicol Jarvie's trade has deserted our City. The financial affairs of the old Incorporation of Wobstaris were wound up under the direction of the Court of Session about fifteen years ago. The body is, however, still represented in the Convenery through its Deacon, who is a citizen of Glasgow,—viz., Mr Robert Brown, 17 Hope Street.

# THE INCORPORATION OF WAEKARIS.

THE Members of the Craft of Waekeris, or Waulkers, as they are now called, on the 20th day of August 1500, obtained a Seal of Cause from the Provost, Magistrates, and Town Council of the period. In the Petition which they presented to the Corporation, they alleged that their Craft had previously been incorporated, and they relegated their existence to a very remote period, viz. :—"very soon after the foundation of the city." This, however, would seem to be an entire mistake on the part of the Petitioners. The very terms of their request were not in accordance with their suggestion or rather allegation; because in their Petition, they ask the Town Council to grant them the liberty to meet for the purpose of managing and controlling the affairs of their own Craft. The business of the Waulkers might be said to consist chiefly in the dressing of cloths, the working-in of wool, or of fur, to make felt, etc. Hence the Craft of Sheermen (Scissorsmen) was engrafted upon it. And on the 13th September 1672, the fraternity of Hatters became incorporated with the Waulkers. In the Council Register of the City, there is a Seal of Cause to the Hatters on 18th February 1473. This by many is supposed to be a mistake, and should be read "Bonnet-makers," as Hats were not in use in Scotland until about the middle of the Sixteenth century, or about seventy years thereafter.

The Regulations laid down by the Provost, Magistrates, and Town Council in 1500 for the government of the Waulker fraternity, as well as for God's service at their Altar of Saints Mark, Philip, and Jacob in St Giles' Church, are as follows :—

1. In the first, that we may haue faculte and powere yeirlie to cheis our Kirkmaister of the said altar as vthir Craftis dois.

2. And at euery freman of our saidis Craftis pay for the vpsett of his buthe five croonis vsuall mony of Scotland, and or he sett wp buthe that he be examit be foure maisteris of the said Craft quhether he be abill and worthy thairto or nocht to serue the nichtbouris of the toone and vtheris reparand thairto, and gif he be fundin abill to sett vp buthe that he be worth of his awin substance thre pair of scheris and of powere to pay ane steik of hewit claith, awa that gif ony falt standis in him he to satefy the pairty sustenand the scaith.

3. And at euery master of our saidis Craftis that takis ane prenteis to pay at his entre ten schillingis to the sustentatioun of Godis seruice to be done at the said alter ; and gif it sall happin ony maister of the saidis Craftis to take or ressave ane vther masteris prenteis, seruand or wagit man, he sall pay tuenty schillingis Scottis mony to the said alter ; and gif ony personis of the saidis Craftis beis ouertane wyrkand with cardis notit or previt apone him he sall pay for ilk tyme he beis ouertane or tayntit thairwith fivetene schillingis Scottis mony, to be distribuit in this wys, five schillingis to Sanct Gelis werk, five schillingis to our said alter, and five schillingis to the findar quhat euir he be.

4. And at the kirkmaister for the tyme and ane honest man of the saidis Craftis with him may pas to the nichbouris tharof in sobir wys for the ingathering of thir dewiteis and sowmes aboue expremit to the vphald of Godis seruice at our said alter and the ornamentis of the samyn, buke, challice, vestimentis and siklike neidfull thingis, and gif neid beis tharfor till poynd and distrenye with ane officiar of the tovne as efferis.

5. And now becaus the communite of our Craft Walkaris and Scheraris within this tovne walkis wardis extentis and beris all vthir commoun chargis within this tovne, and the outland walkaris and scheraris duelland vtouth the fredome of this burgh takkis the werk of the nichtbouris and wynnyn tharof and beris na portable chargis within this tovne, that thairfor ilk out walkar or scherar of claith to landward cumand within this tovne and takand the stuf thairof till wyrk sall pay ilk oulk ane penny, quhilk is bot small valour, till vphald the devyne seruice at the said altar of Sanct Mark, Philip, and Jacob, to be ingatherit be the dekin and kirkmasteris of the saidis Craftis for the tyme.

Maitland adds another clause, but this does not appear on the records. It may, however have been in the original document in the hands of the Incorporation and seen by the Historian. It is, therefore, proper, because of its importance, that it should be quoted, viz., "That the Masters and Godsmen of the Craft may assemble and determine all Controversies that may arise among the Members of the Corporation."

The decision of the Town Council was to the following effect:— Having considered the before mentioned desires, Statutes, and Rules and these being deemed expedient and convenient for the "lovage of God, honour and policy for the said Kirk and this Burgh," and for the common profit for the same and of all our Sovereign Lord's lieges, we ratify and approve of the same, by these our present letters, so long as it shall be thought proper by us and our successors, Provost, Bailies, and Council of this Burgh: And we confirm them for the common weal and profit. We interpone our authority for their being kept and observed in so far as we have power, according to the desires of the said craftsmen. And this to all and sundry to whom it effeirs, we make it known by these our present letters, written under our Common Seal of Cause of the said Burgh, at Edinburgh, " the tuenty day of the moneth of August, the yeir of God ane thousand five hundreth."

To promote the trade and interest of the Hat-makers in Edin-burgh, the *Scotish* Parliament in the years 1641 and 1661, empowered them to choose an Overseer or Quarter-master to be elected yearly from amongst themselves by the Town Council; and the fraternity having petitioned the Corporation for this purpose, it was thought more expedient, and for the advantage of the said Craft, that they should be united to one of the fourteen Incorporations of the city. Having obtained the consent of the Waulkers to be conjoined with them, both Crafts made application to the Town Council for this purpose. This having been agreed to, as the only means to promote successfully their mutual interests, the civic Corporation granted them a charter wherein are contained the following Rules and Regulations :—

1. That the said Trade, Airt, and Handicraft, of making Hats within this Burgh, shall be united and incorporate with the said Calling and Trade of Waekers in Tyme comeing.  Lykeas the Council by thir Presents, unitts, annexes, and incorporates the Freemen of the said Incorporation of the Waekers and the present Hat-makers of this Burgh, viz. :—the said James Broun, first effectual Mover of the said Designe, George Andersone, etc., and their Successors respectively in the said Airts, into one Bodie and Incorporation, to meitt, sitt, and vote, and conclude in the Election of their Deacons and Officers of the said Calling of Waekers, and in all other Things relating to the Good of the said incorporated Calling.

2. Maks, constitutes and creates the foresaid Persones, present Hat-makers, and their Successors, in all Tyme comeing, Judges in the Tryell and Qualifications of the intrant Hat-makers conforme to the provisions undertaken.

3. In respect that the saids Trades of Waekers and Hat-makers are unite into one Bodie ; therefore the Council declairs that the Members, Freemen of the saids Callings, shall indifferently be capable of being lited Deacons and other Officers of the saids Callings, consisting of Waekers and Hat-makers.

4. That in respect all Tyme comeing, the Hat-makers of this Burgh are to be under the Rule and Government of one Deacon and Incorporation ; and that everie ane shall not have Libertie as formerly at his own Hand, without previous Tryall of his Qualification to exerce the said Trade of making Hats within this Burgh and Liberties thereof ; wherefore the Council, by thir Presents, in all Tyme comeing, prohibits and discharges all and whatsomevir Persones, except the Persones whose names are particularlie before exprest, to exerce and profess the said Airt and Trade of making Hatts within this Burgh and Liberties thereof, without they be lawfullie admitted and received Freemen of the said Incorporation, be the saids Persones, present Hat-makers, and their Successors in their Trade, conforme to the following Provisions, excepting alwayes such Persones, Hat-makers, who by Vertue of the Act of Parliament in favour of Manufactures, wes sett up before the Date of thir Presents, and actually

exerces the said Trade of makeing Hats, as Master of the said Calling, within any of the Liberties of the good Toun.

5. The Magistrates of this Burgh, present and to come, are to give concurrance to the present Deacon and his Successors, for apprehending all Unfreemen of the said Calling, and the Half of the Penalties and Fynes that they happen to exact from the Members of the said Calling is to be applied to Pious Uses, at the Discration of the Magistratts, and the other equall to belong to the Poore of the Calling.

6. That no Freeman of the said Trade of Hat-makers shall make insufficient Hatts, under the Paine of Escheit.

7. That the Tyme that a Prenteis shall serve to any Freeman of the said Trade of making Hatts, shall not exceed sevin Zeires.

8. That no Freeman of the said Calling shall take ane Apprentice but once in three Zeires, except they be Burgess Sones, and that they shall be booked in the Dean of Gild's Books, conforme to the Custome of Prentieces of other Crafts within this Burgh.

9. That none of the said Freemen of the said Trade shall take ane other man's Servand, without ane reasonable Caus.

10. That no Freeman of the said Calling of Hat-makers cullor any other Unfreeman to work in the said Trade.

11. That no Freeman of the said Calling dwell, or worke without the Toun of Edinburgh, in no Tyme comeing, except they be licensed by the Deacon and the Incorporation. And to the Effect, the granting of the foresaids Privileges in favour of the Hat-makers may not prejudge any just Interesses within this Burgh; therefore the Council ordaines the following Provisions to be insert therein, and to be holden as a Pairt thereof in all Tymes comeing, which the foresaids Hat-makers, for themselfs and their Successors, by their Acceptation of thir Presents consents hereto :—

(1.) That the importing of forraigne Hatts shall be free to all Burgesses, whether Merchands or Tradesmen; and to sell the samen in Chopes and Housses as thay think fitt.

(2.) That the retailing of Hatts made within this City, or any Pairt of this Kingdom, shall be free to all Merchands and Tradesmen that are only Burgesses.

(3.) That the retailing of imported Hatts shall be free to all Merchands and Tradesman that are Gild-brether.

(4.) That all Merchants and Tradesmen, and their children who shall happen to mary their Daughters and their Prentieses; and generallie all Persones that shall happen to be Burgesses, any maner of Way, and who shall be found, after Tryall, qualified to make Hatts, wherein they have learned the said Airt, whether within this Kingdom, or in forraigne Nations, and are desirous to be Members of the said Incorporation of Hat-makers; the said Incorporation is hereby obliged to admit and receive them Freemen of the said Trade, and that upon payment, viz.:—The Sones of Burgesses and Gild-brether that hes learned the said Trade abroad, the Soume of Twentie Marks for the Upsetts, and all other Expenses. And all others promiscuoualie to pay for the Upsetts, as the Waekers' Prentieses are in use to pay.

(5.) That no Persone be admitted Freeman of the said Trade of Hat-makers, without they be first actuallie entered Burgesses.

(6.) That albeit by the said Union and Incorporation of Hat-makers and Waekers into one Bodie, as to Government and Policie, and having one Deacon and other Officer in common; yet the said Waekers by themselfs, shall only admit and examine Freemen and receave Prentieses, and meddell with the Servands of their said Calling of Waekers, and cognosce upon what relates to their Trade of Waekers. And sicklye the saids Hat-makers shall only by themselfis examine and recave Freemen, and their Prentieses, and meddell with the Servands of their said Calling of Hat-makers, and cognosce upon what shall relate to their said Trade of Hat-making. And that the said Waekers and Hat-makers shall enjoy the Privileges and Liberties of their respective Trades, without incroaching or invading upon one ane others Liberties. And hereby it is not only expresslie declaired and provyded, that the Waekers' former Rights and Seall of Caus shall not in the least be waikned, infringed, or impaired by any thing contained in thir Presents. Bot also the Council grants full Power and Warrand to the said Hat-makers and Waekers, to make such Acts and Ordurs amongst themselfs, whereby cleare Limits, Bounds, and Marches may be made betwixt the saids respective Trades.

(7.) It is declaired, that notwithstanding the said Incorporation consists now of both Waekers and Hat-makers yet, that in all Tyme comeing the said Incorporation shall be called, termed, and denominated *The Incorporation of the Waekers;* and the Deacon of the said Incorporation to be called allanerlie, *The Deacon of the Waekers.*

(8.) It is alwayes expresslie provyded and declaired by thir Presents, that in all emergent and occasional Debates that shall happen to aryse betwixt the said incorporated Callings, or betwixt the Members thereof, or concerning the receaving of intrant Hat-makers, that the Council of this Burgh shall be competent judges thereto.

(9.) And, in respect the Council of this Burgh has been most full and free in granting the foresaids Privileges in favour of the Incorporation of the Hat-makers; therefore it is heirby declaired, that in Case at any Tyme hereſter, the said Incorporation shall happen to obtain from the Council of this Burgh, any furder Priviledges which may any Wayes be destructive to the foresaids Provisions: Then and in that Case, the haill foresaids Liberties, Immunities, and Priviledges granted to them shall, *ipso facto*, become voyd and null.

The Town Council, on the above conditions being fulfilled, considered that the Rules and Articles submitted by the Craft were just, lawful, and for the common good of the Burgh. They therefore ratified the same, and interponed their authority that they should be observed in future. They likewise took power to punish any offenders or breakers of these Laws. They further consented that the Deacon and Brethren of the Incorporation of Waekers, consisting of Waekers and Hat-makers, should endeavour to get a ratification of the same by the *Scotish* Parliament. In the meantime the Town Council ordered the Deed to be subscribed by their clerk, who was further enjoined to attach thereto the Seal of the Burgh.

It will be evident from a perusal of the above that the Town Council of the time entertained more liberal opinions, in the way of free trade, in so far as Hat-making or selling was concerned, than were held by many of their predecessors or successors in office.

Apart from the reference made to Decreets-Arbitral between the Websters, the Waulkers and the Bonnet-makers, in the notice already made regarding the former, the two latter Crafts frequently contended against each other, particularly in reference to the collecting of dues for the upkeep of the Altar. The matter was brought before the Town Council, who, on the 23d of November 1453, ordained that there should be "bot ane commoun box betwixt baith the saidis Craftis," and that there should be four keys, two of which should be put into the hands of the most honest and principal brethren of both Crafts respectively; also that the box should be kept by one member of one of the Crafts for one year, and pass on to a member of the other Craft during the following year; and if any of them refused to do so, the defaulting Craft should pay a fine of Ten Pounds to the reparation of the Altar beside their weekly contributions. They also ordained that one of the Waulkers and one of the Bonnet-makers should use all diligence in the collecting of the sums due, and that there should be a weekly or quarterly account kept.

The Incorporation of Waulkers (including the Hatters) is still represented in the Convenery. The present Deacon is Mr William Bell Mack, 2 Hunter Square.

# THE INCORPORATION OF BONNET-MAKERS.

THE Bonnet-makers, whose Craft was originally included in the fraternity of the Waulkers, on the 31st of March 1530, petitioned the Town Council of Edinburgh to give them a separate Charter of Incorporation. This the Civic Corporation readily consented to do; and in the Seal of Cause which they granted to them the following privileges were enumerated, viz. :—

1. That the Company yearly chuse, with the Approbation of the Town Council, an Oversman or Master to inspect the Work made by the several Members of the Trade, to prevent their imposing a bad Commodity on the People.

2. That persons shall not presume to work as Bonnet-makers unless they have served their apprenticeship to a Member of the Corporation; and that neither Master nor Mistress of the Craft shall employ the apprentice of another, without consent of his Master, on the penalty of Twenty shillings *Scotish* money.

3. That no Member of the Company make any use of unwarrantable stuff, under the Pain of Forfeiture, to be disposed of by the Town Council.

4. For the purpose of more effectually preventing any Frauds in the Manufacture of Bonnets, the Oversman or Master is to make a Search weekly throughout the Trade, and inspect their work.

5. That every Member of the Company, working either for himself or herself, shall pay at their admission, a Freeman or Freewoman, the Sum of Thirty shillings *Scotish* money, to be employed in the Support of the Altar of *St. Mark;* and for each Apprentice they take, the sum of Six shillings towards the same object. And so often as the Chaplaincy of the said Altar shall become vacant, the Bonnet-makers shall have their right equal with the Waulkers and Sheermen, in chusing a Chaplain for the same.

6. The said Craft shall have two Market-days weekly, viz., Monday and Wednesday, whereon to sell their Bonnets; and for the better carrying on of their Business with success, each person was bound to put his or her Mark on the goods which they severally made.

8

7. And that this Craft or Trade shall have a Key to the Common Box or Chest, wherein the Cash was deposited, as was also given to the Fraternity of Waulkers or Sheermen.

By the introduction of Hats, and their almost general use, the Bonnet-makers' Incorporation were reduced to very great straits. They were not able either to support their families or the expenses of their Company, without the assistance of some other of the Crafts. This would almost indicate that a Minute of the Town Council of 1473, which refers to the Hatters, should properly have been to the Bonnet-makers, seeing that the use of Hats had not been introduced at that period. By mutual consent, and that also of the Town Council, the Fraternity of Litsters or Dyers agreed to become conjoined with the Bonnet-makers.

The Litsters or Dyers had previously existed as a separate craft. But the Litsters, in conjunction with the Weavers and Waulkers, having committed great frauds in their respective occupations, to the great hurt and annoyance, and almost total ruin of the Woollen Manufactures of the City, the Town Council of Edinburgh, for the purpose of redressing these most pernicious practices, by virtue of an Act of Parliament made certain regulations to restrain the nefarious actions of the said Crafts within the bounds of their jurisdiction. The Litsters of the City, for the purpose of regaining their character, voluntarily appeared before the Town Council; and, with the view of effectually putting the said Regulations into execution, they, with one accord, bound and obliged themselves, in all time coming, to observe the following statutes of the Town Council :—

1. That thay nor nane of thame, in ony Tyme cuming, sall lit ony maner of Cullor of *Muster de Villois*, *French Gray*, or Russatis, with Brissell or Ursell, nor lit ony Blakis, with Cupprus, Gallis, Aller-barkis, or sicklike fals Cullors, bot the samyn to be littet with Mader, Alme, Glew, and sic trew Cullors as hes bene, and is usit amongis Men of

Honestie, Experience, and gude Conscience of the said Craft, under the Pane of Five Pund for the first Falt, Ten Pund the next Falt, to be disponit to the common Workis; and the third and last Falt, to be baneist the Toun and Fredome thairof for ever. And sa oft as sall happin ony of the saidis Littisteris or utheris of that Occupatioun, or taking that craft upoun thame, to spill, in thar Defalt, the Claith or Woole gavin to thame to lit, to pay to the Awiner the uttermaist Availl and Pryce that the samyn wald gif, in cace it wer perfitelie, compleitlie and sufficientlie wrocht and littit, provyding the spilt Claith and Wolle be gevin to the Littisteris Spillaris thairof, the uttermaist Availl, as said is, beand payit. And in cace they be nocht abill, the Availl, as said is, to be spanit from the Occupatioun, and baneist the Fredome of this Burgh, quhill the Partie damp-naget be satisfeit in Maner above written, and Cautioun found under Pains, at the Will of the Jugeis, for trew Labouris and trew Cullors in all Tyme cuming.

2. For the mare sure Tryall of the Honestie, Lawtie and sure Wark of the said Occupatioun that thair be made ane Stamp, and the Tounis Arms thairupon, quhilks sal be gevin in keiping to ane honest, trew sworne Nichtboure of Experience in making and colouring of Claith, quha sall be Oversear of all Claith littit and made within this Burgh, and sall stamp in Leid and utherwayis, quha sall have for his Labouris everie Pece of Claith stampit be him, as said is, Twa Pennies allanerlie; and that na Littister deliver furth of their House, ony Claith littit be thame, bot markit with thair awin Mark, under the Pane of acht shillings, to be distributit in Maner above written, sa oft as he faillies, bot Favour; and that the Keiper of the said Stamp be in Redynes at all Tymes for stamping of Claith, quhen he sall be requiret; and gif Neid be, then he sall seirche and seik the samyn to be stampit: and gif it happyns the said Stamp-Keiper to stamp ony Maner of Claith, not sufficiently coulrit, to pay Five Pund for every Falt, to be applyit, as said is, and to be puneist in his Bodie at the Will and Plesoure of the Provest, Baillies and Counsale for the Tyme.

And farder, That na Maner of Man nor Woman within this Burgh take upoun thame the Occupatioun of Litting, bot sic as be Burgesses and Fremen, and before their Admissioun, that thay mak thair Assay of Colouris, and deliver the samyn to the Provest, Baillies and Counsale of this Burgh, and they to call in before them the honest Nichtbouris, with the said Oversear, and tak thair Judgement of the Wordyness of the said Assay-gevar, and of the Justnes of the Coloure, under the Pane of baneishing of the Toun; and thir Ordinances to be observit in all Tymes cumming, togidder with the uther Statutis and Ordinances in the Actis made the Twentie-second Day of *Marche* last tuitching the making and liting of Wooll and Claith in all sorts, as said is.

At the time when the Litsters became incorporated with the Bonnet-makers, viz., in 1684, it was requisite that new Rules and Regulations should be passed by the Town Council for the proper government of the United Body. The following contain the Basis of Union and the various Clauses and Statutes relating to the same :—

1. The Counsell by thir Presents unites, annexes and incorporates the Freemen of the Incorporation of the Bonnet-makers and the Litsters, Burgesses of this City, viz., John Robertsone, etc., and their respective Successors in the said Arts into one Body and Incorporation perpetually in all Tyme comeing, with Power to them as one Body and Incorporation, to meitt, sitt and vote, and conclude in the Election of their Deacones and Officers of the said Calling; siclyke, and als freily in all Respects as any other Freemen of the Incorporation of any other Craft are in Use to do.

2. The Counsell makes, constitutes and erects the foresaid Persones, present Litsters and their Successors in all Tyme comeing, Judges of the Tryall and Qualificatioun of the intrant Litsters, conforme to the foresaid Act of Parliament, and the Agreement past between the said Bonnet-makers and them.

3. In respect to the saids Trades of Bonnet-makers and Litsters are unite in one Body; the Counsell heirby declaires, that for the first two years after the Tyme of the Electione of the Deacones of Crafts this nixt enshewing year, the Deacon of the said incorporate Callings, is to be elected out of the Bonnet-makers, in regard by the Sett; the Litsters now incorporate must be two years Masters of the Calling, before they be in a Capacity to be in the Leit to be Deacone; and efter the said two years is expyred, the said two incorporate Airts are to choyse sax Litsters for the List, which they are to present to the Counsell, out of which they are to have thrie for a Leit; out of which Leit, ther Deacone called *The Deacon of the Bonnet-makers* is to be elected, conforme to the said Agreement.

4. Conforme to the said Agreement, for the first two Years, that the Deacon must be a Bonnet-maker, the Boxmaster to the said two Airts now incorporate, is to be a Freeman Litster; and so furth two Years *per vices*. The List that is to be given in to the Counsell, in order to the Electione of the Lists of ther Deacones, the same sall consist of sex Bonnet-makers on two years, and sex Litsters on two years; and when the Deacone is a Bonnet-maker, the Boxmaster shall be a Litster; and when the Deacone is a Litster, the Boxmaster shall be a Bonnet-maker.

5. The Counsell, be thir Presents, in all Tyme comeing, prohibits and discharges all

Litsters whatsomever, except the Persones above-named, who are Freemen Litsters of this Cittie to exerce and profess the said Trade and Airt of litting and dyeing within this Cittie, unless they be admitted Freemen of the said Incorporation, be the foresaid Persones, present Litsters, and ther Successours that shall be lawfullie admitted Freemen of the said Incorporation, with Advice and Consent of the saids Bonnet-makers, to take Tryall of the Sufficiencie of the Work and Cullour dyed and litted by any of the intrant Freemen of the said Incorporation of the Litsters that shall heirafter be admitted, and to make Acts and Statuts amongst themselves for improveing of the said Airt, conforme to the foresaid Act of Parliament in favour of the said Litsters.

6. It is statut and ordained, conforme to the foresaid Agreement, that the Bonnet-makers and ther Successors, shall in no Wayes incroach upon the Airt of litting of Clothes and Stuffs, which is only proper to be dyed, litted, and drest by the Litsters; and that non of the said Freemen·Litsters, nor thir Successors in ther Airt shall medle with, nor incroach upon the making and dyeing of Bonnets, Night-caps, or any other Things that they bein in use to work and dye, or to have Liberty to doe, be Vertew of ther Seal of Cause.

7. The Counsell statuts and ordains, that in no Tyme comeing, any Litster shall have Liberty to exerce the Airt of Litting and Dyeing within this Cittie, or Priviledges therof, but such as are actuall Dyers and Litsters, Burgess of Edinburgh at present, or have been alreadie bound Prentices, and are booked in the Dean of Gild's Books as Litsters; and those shall be obliged, before they can exerce ther Art, to byde Tryall as to ther Qualificatiouns, before they be actually admitted to the Exercise of the said Airt, conforme to the Clauses mentioned in the said Act of Parliament; and after Tryall, before they exerce, unless they be of the Number of the Persons above-named, they are to be lawfully admitted Freemen of the said Incorporation, before they can exerce the said Art.

8. That no other Persones in any Tyme comeing are to be admitted Freemen of the said Incorporation as Litsters, wer they never so weill qualified, unless they serve a Freeman Litster of the said Incorporation, five years at leist, and be booked in the Dean of Gild's Books, and in the said Incorporation ther Books as Prentice, unless he be a Freeman's Son, or marie a Freeman's Daughter of the said Incorporation of the Litsters. And it is heirby speciallie provydit and declaired, that this present Grant, establishing and uniting the foresaids two Airts in one Corporatioun, shall be but Prejudice to the Merchants, Burgesses and Gild-brethir of this Cittie, to import any Cloaths, Stuffs, Stockings, or any other Wair in use to be dyed (which are not prohibited by Law) from

any forraigne Cuntrie, of whatsomever Dye or Cullour to this Cittie, or to the Burgesses of this Cittie, to import any Cloaths, Stuffs, or what els is in Use, to be dyed or litted within this Kingdom, or to any Place within the samyn, and to vend the same, sicklyke, and als freily in all Respects, as they have bein in use to do in any Tyme bygone, or may doe in any Tyme comeing, as Merchants, Burgesses, and Gild brethir of this Cittie.

9. It is declared, That all these that are actually exercing the Airt of Litting and Dyeing, shall have Liberty to come in, and be incorporate with the said Bonnet-makers and Litsters, provyding they be Burgess, and qualified in their Airt, albeit they be not of the Number of the Persons above-named; provyding they come in within the Space of three Moneths after the Dait of thir Presents; and sicklyke, that all that have bein bound Prentices before the Dait heirof to Freemen Litsters, Burgers of Edinburgh, shall be admitted Freemen of the said Incorporation, they being found qualified, and payin ther ordinary Upsetts as Prentices.

10. It is declared, That no Persone whatsomever have Liberty to sett up a Lit-house in any of the Suburbs of the Good Town, or within any other Pairt of the Priviledges of the same, or exerce the said Airt of Litting or Dyeing within the said Bounds, unles they have Liberty swa to do from the Incorporation.

11. It is heirby provydit and declaired, That when any of the Inhabitants of this Cittie shall take Occasione to export any Cloaths, Stuffs, or any Thing else, to be litted outwith the Priviledges of the Good Town, that they shall have free Liberty, without any Maner of Interruptione, to export the same, and import the samyn litted, as they have been of use to do, in any Tyme comeing.

The Town Council hereby interpones their authority for the above Articles, and decerns that they be inviolably observed in all time coming: That the Magistrates of this Burgh, present and future, give their concurrence to the officers of the City, to see them put into execution in all points, as against Contraveners and Breakers of the same: They consent that the Deacon and Brethren of the Incorporation of Bonnet-makers and Listers should obtain the ratification of these presents by Parliament: And they ordain an extract hereof to be given to them for that purpose, under the subscription of the Town Clerk, and the common Seal of the Burgh apponded thereto.

On the 23rd of June 1558, at a Meeting of Town Council held on that day, the Bonnet-makers lodged a complaint that the "out-landismen of Sanct Jonistoun and vthers vnfremen," were in the habit every day of passing through the town and openly exposing their bonnets for sale, to the great hurt of the members of the Incorporation and in violation of the law, considering the sums paid for watching and warding by the freemen. The Town Council issued a Statute wherein such sales were proclaimed illegal except on Market-days.

A complaint of a different kind fell to be disposed of by the Civic Corporation on 30th June 1563. It was against the Bonnet-makers on this occasion. They had been in the habit of working in the open street, causing the passers-by to be "fylit with the calk dust and flokis of the saids coittis and bonettis" which scandalised the "hale nobelitie and strangearis." The Council ordered them to desist and cease from this within sight of the High Street, and to carry on their work in their houses and workshops as formerly, under a penalty of Forty shillings.

Like some of the other Incorporations, the Bonnet-makers elected Honorary Members. For example :—

5 March 1746.—(Present—Deacon James Watson and ten other members). The Corporation being met and constituted, Considering that it will highly tend to the honour of this City that His Royal Highness William, Duke of Cumberland, be admitted and presented with the freedom of the several Incorporations of this City; yrfore the Corporation did and hereby do unanimously admit and present the said William, Duke of Cumberland, with the freedom of yr craft, and authorise and empower James Watson, present Deacon, jointly with the other Deacons of the several Incorporations of Edinburgh, to admit and present him with the freedom of the said Incorporations in the most ample form, and that the ticket be " wrote on velum," and delivered to him in a " Gold box."

The old form of Prayer made use of, as recorded in the Minute-Book of date 1637, is as follows :—

*The prayer usuallie said at ye meetings of ye saids deacones m*.*
*(maisters) and Brethraine of Crafts.*

O most gratious God and heavenlie father, who of thyne infinite goodness has ordained thir meetingis for the preservatioun of love, concord, and humane society :

Grant, O Lord, that nae particularitie nor partialitie over-reull the heartis of anny heir present, but that there may be the only object weill and prosperitie of everie brother wished and craved. And to that effect rectify our wills, memories and understandings to thy heavenly will, and be thou with us through thy comfortable presentis for Jesus Christ sake. To whom with thee and thy holie spirit be all prais, honour and glorie. So be it.

The Minute-Book is a fine folio in good preservation, bound in wood covered with calf, and surrounded by two iron bands, each with a separate lock. There is a mark impressed on the one side "For the Waikkers," and on the other, "For the Bannet-Makkers."

*The Oath taken on admission to the Incorporation was as follows:—*

I protest heir before God, that I am ane true professor of ye true religione pñtlie preachit in Scotland, as also I sall be leill and trew to our Soverane Lord, ye Kingis matie, and his hieness successors; to the Provvist and Baillies of yis burgh; to ye deacones and mⁿ. of ye Waikeris and Bannet-makers, and shall not hyde (?) nor conceill yare skaith in anny way, be night nor be day, but shall stope ye samen to ye uttermost of my power, and shall fortify and meantyne yame in all yair godlie affairs in whatsomever they shall happen to decerne or adjudge me to doe. I shall never come in the contrair before whatsomever Judge or Judges, and sall not take my bretherins house over yair heads, nor shall not fie nor seduce yair servantis by yair knowledge under the paine of perjurie and defamatioun for ever, and yis I promoise to keep in all poyntis. Sua help me God and be God himself.

The Bonnet-makers' Incorporation exists now only for benevolent purposes, and for appointing a Deacon who has a vote in the Convenery. Bailie Macdonald is the present Deacon, and Mr James Bruce (of Messrs Bruce & Kerr, W.S.) is the Clerk.

# LIST OF ALL THE DEACON-CONVENERS,

*From the First Institution of that Office in 1578, to the present day.*

Year.
1578. Robert Abercromby—Hammermen.
1579. Robert Henderson—Surgeons.
1580. Alexander Oustone—Tailors.
1581. Gilbert Primrose—Surgeons.
1582. Gilbert Primrose—Surgeons.
1583. John Watt—Hammermen.
1584.
*1585.
1586. William Hutchison—Cordiners.
1587. Patrick Sandilands—Tailors.
1588. Patrick Sandilands—Tailors.
1589. John Watt—Hammermen.
1590. George Heriot—Goldsmiths.
1591. John Bannatyne—Surgeons.
1592. Alexander Oustone—Tailors.
1593. George Heriot—Goldsmiths.
1594. George Heriot—Goldsmiths.
1595. Alexander Oustone—Tailors.
1596. John Watt—Hammermen.
1597. Alexander Millar—Tailors.
1598. William Symmington—Hammermen.
1599. Patrick Sandilands—Tailors.
1600. Patrick Sandilands—Tailors.
1601. William Wallands—Hammermen.

Year.
1602. James Wilson—Tailors.
1603. James Wilson—Tailors.
1604. Alexander Bunte—Hammermen.
1605. George Foulis—Goldsmiths.
1606. George Heriot—Goldsmiths.
1607. George Heriot—Goldsmiths.
1608. Edward Kerr—Tailors.
1609. John Inglis—Skinners.
1610. George Foulis—Goldsmiths.
1611. John Somerville—Skinners.
1612. Edward Kerr—Tailors.
1613. Edward Kerr—Tailors.
1614. Thomas Weir—Hammermen.
1615. James Henryson—Surgeons.
1616. Andrew Scott—Surgeons.
1617. Andrew Scott—Surgeons.
1618. Thomas Weir—Hammermen.
1619. John Inglis—Skinners.
1620. William Nemo—Tailors.
1621. William Carnegie—Skinners.
1622. George Crawford—Goldsmiths.
1623. Gilbert Kirkland—Goldsmiths.
1624. Gilbert Kirkland—Goldsmiths.
1625. Henry Aikman—Surgeons.

---

* There is no entry made in the Convenery-Book, from March 1584 to April 1586 ; no reason being subsequently assigned for this hiatus, it cannot now be ascertained whether or not there was any election in 1584 and 1585.

T

| Year | | Year | |
|---|---|---|---|
| 1626. | Thomas White—Hammermen. | 1662. | William Burnet—Surgeons. |
| 1627. | James Leslie—Tailors. | 1663. | John Milne—Masons. |
| 1628. | Andrew Scott—Surgeons. | 1664. | John Milne—Masons. |
| 1629. | John Hunter—Tailors. | 1665. | Arthur Temple—Surgeons. |
| 1630. | William Carnegie—Skinners. | 1666. | Arthur Temple—Surgeons. |
| 1631. | William Carnegie—Skinners. | 1667. | John Somerville—Skinners. |
| 1632. | Thomas White—Hammermen. | 1668. | John Somerville—Skinners. |
| 1633. | George Crawford—Goldsmiths. | 1669. | Arthur Temple—Surgeons. |
| 1634. | William Carnegie—Skinners. | 1670. | Arthur Temple—Surgeons. |
| 1635. | William Carnegie—Skinners. | 1671. | Edward Cleghorn—Goldsmiths. |
| 1636 | Thomas Weir—Hammermen. | 1672. | Samuel Chiefly—Surgeons. |
| 1637. | Thomas White—Hammermen. | 1673. | John Cunningham—Tailors. |
| 1638. | Richard Maxwell—Hammermen. | 1674. | John Cunningham—Tailors. |
| 1639. | Richard Maxwell—Hammermen. | 1675. | William Hamilton—Tailors. |
| 1640. | Thomas Paterson—Tailors. | 1676. | William Hamilton—Tailors. |
| 1641. | Thomas Paterson—Tailors. | 1677. | Alexander Reed—Goldsmiths. |
| 1642. | Robert Meiklejohn—Skinners. | 1678. | Alexander Reed—Goldsmiths. |
| 1643. | Robert Meiklejohn—Skinners. | 1679. | Edward Cleghorn—Goldsmiths |
| 1644. | Robert M'Kean—Skinners. | 1680. | Edward Cleghorn—Goldsmiths |
| 1645. | Robert M'Kean—Skinners. | 1681. | William Borthwick—Surgeons. |
| 1646. | Robert Meiklejohn—Skinners. | 1682. | William Borthwick—Surgeons. |
| 1647. | Robert Meiklejohn—Skinners. | 1683. | William Watson—Cordiners. |
| 1648. | Robert M'Kean—Skinners. | 1684. | William Watson—Cordiners. |
| 1649. | James Borthwick—Surgeons. | 1685. | Thomas Somerville—Tailors. |
| *1650. | | 1686. | Thomas Somerville—Tailors. |
| 1651. | Gilbert Somerville—Tailors. | 1687. | James Cockburn—Goldsmiths. |
| 1652. | Gilbert Somerville—Tailors. | 1688. | James Baillie—Surgeons. |
| 1653. | John Milne—Masons. | 1689. | George Stirling—Surgeons. |
| 1654. | John Milne—Masons. | 1690. | George Stirling—Surgeons. |
| 1655 | Thomas Kincaid—Surgeons. | 1691. | Robert Inglis—Goldsmiths. |
| 1656. | Thomas Kincaid—Surgeons. | 1692. | John Pringle—Bonnetmakers. |
| 1657. | John Milne—Masons. | 1693. | Alexander Thomson—Hammermen. |
| 1658. | John Milne—Masons. | 1694. | Alexander Thomson—Hammermen. |
| 1659. | James Borthwick—Surgeons. | 1695. | Alexander Monteith—Surgeons. |
| 1660. | James Borthwick—Surgeons. | 1696. | Alexander Monteith—Surgeons. |
| 1661. | William Burnet—Surgeons. | 1697. | Alexander Thomson—Hammermen. |

* There was no election this year, in consequence of the English Army, under Cromwell, having entered Scotland.

Year.

1698. Alexander Thomson—Hammermen.
1699. { Alexander Monteith—Surgeons.
{ Gideon Elliot—Surgeons.
1700. Gideon Elliot—Surgeons.
1701. Robert Inglis—Goldsmiths.
1702. William Livingstone—Skinners.
1703. William Livingstone—Skinners.
1704. William Wardrope—Bonnetmakers.
1705. Henry Hamilton—Surgeons.
1706. Gilbert Somerville—Tailors.
1707. John Merrie—Surgeons.
1708. Robert Moubray—Wrights.
1709. Alexander Nisbet—Surgeons.
1710. William Livingstone—Skinners.
1711. William Livingstone—Skinners.
1712. John Monro—Surgeons.
1713. John Monro—Surgeons.
1714. John Dunbar—Skinners.
1715. John Lauder—Surgeons.
1716. William Wightman—Skinners.
1717. Patrick Turnbull—Goldsmiths.
1718. John Lauder—Surgeons.
1719. John Lauder—Surgeons.
1720. William Livingstone—Skinners.
1721. Andrew Wardrop—Masons.
1722. Andrew Wardrop—Masons.
1723. James Mitchelson—Goldsmiths.
1724. John Ker—Baxters.
1725. David M'Lellan—Wrights.
1726. William Cant—Skinners.
1727. David Mitchell—Goldsmiths.
1728. William Keir—Baxters.
1729. John Keir—Baxters.
1730. John Keir—Baxters.
1731. William Ayton—Goldsmiths.
1732. William Clark—Tailors.
1733. John M'Gill—Surgeons.
1734. William Keir—Baxters.
1735. James Syme, Sen.—Wrights.

Year.

1736. John Clarkson—Baxters.
1737. William Sommerville—Skinners.
1738. William Mitchell—Surgeons.
1739. George Cunningham—Surgeons.
1740. Alexander Nisbet—Surgeons.
1741. Alexander Nisbet—Surgeons.
1742. Walter Boswell—Hammermen.
1743. George Langlands—Surgeons.
1744. James Norrie—Wrights.
1745. George Lauder—Surgeons.
1746. James Ker—Goldsmiths.
1747. James Ker, M.P.—Goldsmiths.
1748. Adam Drummond—Surgeons.
1749. Adam Drummond—Surgeons.
1750. James Ker, M.P.—Goldsmiths.
1751. James Ker, M.P.—Goldsmiths.
1752. William Keir—Baxters.
1753. James Russel—Surgeons.
1754. Thomas Clarkson—Baxters.
1755. Thomas Cleland—Hammermen.
1756. Thomas Cleland—Hammermen.
1757. Thomas Simpson—Hammermen.
1758. Thomas Simpson—Hammermen.
1759. Patrick Jameson—Masons.
1760. Patrick Jameson—Masons.
1761. John Balfour—Surgeons.
1762. Alexander Wood—Surgeons.
1763. John Lindsay—Skinners.
1764. John Lindsay—Skinners.
1765. William Milne—Masons.
1766. John Milne—Hammermen.
1767. Thomas Simpson—Hammermen.
1768. Thomas Simpson—Hammermen.
1769. Alexander Smith—Baxters.
1770. William Armstrong—Hammermen.
1771. Orlando Hart—Cordiners.
1772. Thomas Herriot—Wrights.
1773. Thomas Simpson—Hammermen.
1774. Thomas Simpson—Hammermen.

Year.
1775. Orlando Hart—Cordiners.
1776. Francis Brodie—Wrights.
1777. Alexander Hamilton—Surgeons.
1778. John Bonnar—Wrights.
1779. James Craig—Baxters.
1780. James Craig—Baxters.
1781. William Chalmers—Surgeons.
1782. William Fraser—Hammermen.
1783. William Jamieson—Masons.
1784. William Jamieson—Masons.
1785. Orlando Hart—Cordiners.
1786. Robert Dewar—Masons.
1787. William Dempster—Goldsmiths.
1788. Orlando Hart—Cordiners.
1789. Orlando Hart—Cordiners.
1790. Alexander Reid—Masons.
1791. William Inglis—Surgeons.
1792. John Young—Wrights.
1793. Thomas Wood—Surgeons.
1794. Thomas Hay—Surgeons.
1795. Thomas Hay—Surgeons.
1796. Francis Braidwood—Wrights.
1797. Josiah Maxton—Hammermen.
1798. William Ranken—Tailors.
1799. Thomas Kennedy—Furriers.
1800. James Law—Surgeons.
1801. James Law—Surgeons.
1802. William Ranken—Tailors.
1803. John Bennet—Surgeons.
1804. John Young—Wrights.
1805. William White—Hammermen.
1806. James Denholm—Waulkers.
1807. Adam Anderson—Hammermen.
1808. John Auchterlonie—Bonnetmakers.
1809. Andrew Gairdner—Weavers.
1810. James Denholm—Waulkers.
1811. James Innes—Hammermen.
1812. William Fraser, Jun.—Tailors.
1813. James Law—Surgeons.

Year.
1814. James Denholm—Waulkers.
1815. John James—Cordiners.
1816. Thomas Miller—Skinners.
1817. James Thomson—Weavers.
1818. James Denholm—Waulkers.
1819. Alexander Gillespie—Surgeons.
1820. John Crombie—Bonnetmakers.
1821. John H. Wishart—Surgeons.
1822. George Bookless—Masons.
1823. James Burn—Weavers.
1824. David M'Gibbon—Wrights.
1825. James Milne—Hammermen.
1826. Thomas Sawers—Baxters.
1827. David Maclagan—Surgeons.
1828. Gordon Brown—Wrights.
1829. John Chambers—Tailors.
1830. William Marshall—Goldsmiths.
1831. Andrew Wilkie—Hammermen.
1832. Andrew Wilkie—Hammermen.
1833. Henry Banks—Tailors.
1834. William Steven—Waulkers.
1835. William Dick—Hammermen.
1836. William Dick—Hammermen.
1837. William Dick—Hammermen.
1838. John Clark—Wrights.
1839. John Clark—Wrights.
1840. Alexander Scott—Wrights.
1841. Alexander Scott—Wrights.
1842. Frederick MacLagan—Baxters.
1843. John Sheppard—Wrights.
1844. Henry Banks—Tailors.
1845. Robert Sclater—Hammermen.
1846. William Cushnie—Bonnetmakers.
1847. George Copland—Tailors.
1848. Thomas Herriot Weir—Baxters.
1849. Thomas Herriot Weir—Baxters.
1850. William Beattie—Masons.
1851. William Beattie—Masons.
1852. George Crichton—Goldsmiths.

| Year. | | Year. | |
|---|---|---|---|
| 1853. | Henry Banks—Tailors. | 1873. | Daniel Robertson—Wrights. |
| 1854. | Henry Banks—Tailors. | 1874. | Daniel Robertson—Wrights. |
| 1855. | John James—Cordiners. | 1875. | Robert Legget—Skinners. |
| 1856. | John James—Cordiners. | 1876. | Robert Legget—Skinners. |
| 1857. | George Tibbetts—Waulkers. | 1877. | Robert Legget—Skinners. |
| 1858. | George Tibbetts—Waulkers. | 1878. | John Williams—Bonnetmakers. |
| 1859. | George Tibbetts—Waulkers. | 1879. | John Williams—Bonnetmakers. |
| 1860. | John Cox—Skinners. | *1880. | John Smith—Wrights. |
| 1861. | John Cox—Skinners. | 1881. | Alexander Webb—Cordiners. |
| 1862. | John Cox—Skinners. | 1881. | John Masterton—Wrights. |
| 1863. | Adam Beattie—Wrights. | 1882. | John Masterton—Wrights. |
| 1864. | Adam Beattie—Wrights. | 1883. | John Pears Hutton—Goldsmiths. |
| 1865. | Adam Beattie—Wrights. | 1884. | John Pears Hutton—Goldsmiths. |
| 1866. | John Cox—Skinners. | 1885. | John White—Wrights. |
| 1867. | John Cox—Skinners. | 1886. | John White—Wrights. |
| 1868. | Thomas Field—Masons. | 1887. | John White—Wrights. |
| 1869. | Thomas Field—Masons. | 1888. | John White—Wrights. |
| 1870. | Daniel Robertson—Wrights. | †1889. | John White—Wrights. |
| 1871. | Daniel Robertson—Wrights. | 1890. | Alexander Ramage—Baxters. |
| 1872. | Daniel Robertson—Wrights. | 1890. | Alexander Ramage—Baxters. |

* Mr John Smith died during the year 1881, and was succeeded by Mr Alexander Webb.

† Mr John White died during the year 1890, and was succeeded by Mr Alexander Ramage.

## OFFICE-BEARERS AND DEACONS OF THE INCORPORATED TRADES OF EDINBURGH.

*Convener*—Alexander Ramage, Deacon of the Bakers.

*Treasurer*—W. B. Mack.

*Trades Councillors*—Kenneth Scoon and D. W. Beattie.

| | |
|---|---|
| *Wrights*—William Field. | *Tailors*—James Rodger. |
| *Masons*—George Jas. Beattie. | *Fleshers*—John Boyd Morham. |
| *Goldsmiths*—John Crichton. | *Cordiners*—Walter Park. |
| *Skinners*—R. Legget, Sen. | *Websters*—Robert Brown. |
| *Furriers*—A. M'Cullagh. | *Waulkers*—William Bell Mack. |
| *Hammermen*—John James Moir. | *Bonnet-makers*—Andrew M'Donald. |

*Clerk*—William Stuart Fraser, W.S.

# *OTHER INCORPORATED CRAFTS*

## 1. THE CANDLEMAKERS.

THE Candlemakers do not enjoy the privilege of having a voice in the affairs of the Incorporated Crafts. They do not now send a Representative to the Convenery. Nevertheless, they have a Seal of Cause from the Town Council of Edinburgh of a very early date, confirming all their ancient rights and privileges. This Charter is not published in the Burgh Records, and must have been lost or destroyed. At the time Maitland wrote his "History of Edinburgh," the principal Deed was in the possession of the Clerk of the Incorporation.

The occasion on which the Candlemakers would appear to have lost their civic status was in the year 1582, when a difference seems to have arisen between the Merchants and Craftsmen. The question at issue having been referred to Arbitration, the several Incorporations were required to lay their respective Grants or Charters before the two Arbitrators and an Umpire, to show their respective rights and immunities. The Candlemakers, strange to say, failed to do this; and they did not even sign the Minute of Reference along with the Deacons of the other Incorporations. The result of this was—their name was not included in the Decreet-Arbitral, which afterwards was known by *The Sett of The Burgh*. This document constituted the basis upon which all former disputes became adjusted in an amicable manner between the Merchants and Craftsmen at the time.

U

The singular conduct of the Candlemakers did not conduce to their comfort in civic affairs. They imagined that their Rights and Privileges were in danger of being taken away by the Town Council, even although their Charter of Incorporation had been ratified by King James VI. in the thirtieth year of his reign, viz., 1597. They, therefore, made application to Parliament to get their rights secured, against all attacks made upon them. This was effected by an Act passed on the 17th July 1695. The Town Council, however, at a much later period, having been inclined to challenge their rights,— the Incorporation raised an Action of Declarator in the Court of Session, by whose interlocutor of the 4th July 1716, all their Ancient Rights and Privileges (except their having a Representative in the Common Council) were retained to them.

Before the introduction of Gas into the City, in 1819, the Candlemaking Trade was a large and profitable industry. A time of illumination of the Town was a glorious harvest for the Candlemakers. The Lord Provost and Magistrates were in the habit of issuing Proclamations for a General Illumination much more frequently in those days, than their civic successors in office now are. Illuminations were ordered on many occasions when a considerable number of the general public did not quite realise the necessity for such. This led to the old rhyme,

> "There's nae Illumination
>     It's a' big lees;
>  It's naething but the Caunel-makers
>     Makin' bawbees."

The penalty for not lighting up the windows on occasion of an illumination was the breaking of the panes of glass on the part of the mob, with no recourse against the public funds on account of the omission being a gross act of disobedience to the Magistrates' order.

The following is the original Seal of Cause granted to the Candle-makers by the Lord Provost, Magistrates, and Town Council :—

To all and sundrie quhom it effeirs, to quhais knawledge thir present Letters sall cum, the Provest, Baillies and Counsall of the Burgh of Edinburgh, gretin in God evirlasting: Wit zour Universities, that the Day of the Daitt of thir Presentis, comperit before us sittand in the Tolbuith in Jugement, the haill Craftismen of the Candilmakers of the said Burgh; that is to say, Robert Taffintoun, Andrew Galloway, and uthers. The quhilk Persones and Craftismen, producit as their Supplicatioun and Bill of thair Desyres, for the confirming and keeping of thair Statutes and Rules, maid for the common Weill of this Burgh and King's Lieges reparand thairto, according and conformand to the awld Statutes and Previleges that they had of the Provest, Baillies and Counsale of the said Burgh of Edinburgh; the quhilk Supplicatioun and and Bill red before us at Lenth; and we thairat beant ryplie avysit thocht the samyn consonant to Reasoun, and greitt Appearances of Profeit to the said Craftismen to this guid Town and King's Lieges reparand thairto; and thairfoir, it is oure Will, and als we grant and ordain, that the said Craftismen and thair Successors bruik, injoy, and use thair awld Fredom, Statutes, Rowles, Articles and Conditiouns, maid for the guid Rowle of the said Occupatioun and Craft, as efter followis:

1. That zeirlie the hail Craft of the said Candilmakers within this Burgh, sall cheyse ane Deykin amangs them, that is Freman and Burgess of the Toun; quhilk Deykin sall be oblist and sworne to rowle this said Craft in all guid Rowle and Ordinance, for the Honor Worship of the Realme and Toun lyk as uther Craftismen dois within the samyn.

2. That na Maner of Man nor Woman occupy the said Craft, as to be ane Maister, and to set up Buit, bot gif he be ane Freman, or ells ane Freman's Wife of the said Craft allanarlie; and quhan thay set up Buit, they sall pay to *Sainct Geil's Wark*, half a Mark of Sylver, and to the Reparatioun, bylding, and uphalding of the Liebb of ony misterfull Alter within the College Kirk of *Sanct Geil's*, quhar the said Deykins and Craftismen thinks maist neidfull, and half ane Mark by and quhill the said Craftismen be furnist of ane Alter of thair awin.

3. And in lykwayis, ilk Maister and Occupiar of the said Craft, sall in the Honour of Almichtie God, and of his blessit Mother, Sanct Marie, and of our Patroun Sanct Geill, and of all Sanctis of Heaven, sall gif zeirly to the helping and furthering of ony guid Reparatioun, either of Licht or ony other neidful Wark till ony Alter situate within the said College Kirk, maist neidfull, Ten Shillings; and to be gaderit be the

Deykin of the said Craft, ay and quhill they be provydit of ane Alter to thameselffis; and he that disobeis the same the Deykin and the Leif of the Craft sall poynd with ane officiar of the Toun, and gar him pay Walx to oure Lady's Alter, quhill thay get an Alter of thair awin. And that nane of the said Craftismen and ony Lads, Boyis, or Servands, openlie upon the Hie-gait with ony Candill, to roup or to sell in playne streites, under the Payne of escheiting of the Candill, paying ane Pund of Walx; the third Tyme, escheiting of the Candill, and his persoun to be brocht with the Deykin of the Craftismen of the said Craft to the Provest and Baillies of the Toun, and thair to be punist with Avyse of the said Deykin for the Tyme, and the Leif of the said Craft for the breking of thair said Statutes and Rowles. But it sall be leful to ilk Maister of the Craft to haif ane Servand that sall gang honestlie throw the Town with Creills and Stufe, to furneis his Callender with, bot nocht to rowp them oppenlie to sell; and that he beir in his creill his Maister's Mark, to ken him and his stufe. And quha that beis sein gangand otherwayis, the Candill to be escheitt, and the persons punist as said is.

4. That na Man of the said Craft tak ony Prenteis for less Tyme than four Zeir; and that na Man of the said Craft, nor na utheris, tak ane uther Man's Prenteis nor Servand, without Licence and Leif of his Maister, askit and obtenit, quhill the compleit End and Ischeu of thair Termis; and quha sa dois the contrar heirof, the Deykin and the Laif of the said Craft to puneis thame as effeirs; and atour, that all the Maisters of the said Craft mak gude and sufficient Stufe, and honestlie handlit and sufficient wrocht worth the Money; and that all Women be expellit the said Craft, bot Freemenis Wyffes of the said Craft allanerlie, they donand and obeyand to the Deykin and Craftismen, lykeas is contenit in the aforesaid Statutes; but gif it be allanerlie for thair awn Use, and byrning in thair Howss. And quha that will not be maid Freeman, he sall not sett up, nor hald Buit, bot to be ane Servand under a Maister, quhill that he grow and be reddy thairto. And that nane of the said Craftismen, Servands, Boyes, nor Prentes, thair Tymes beand run, mak Service to ony uther Man, except to the Craftismen of the said Craft, unto the Tyme that thay be reddy to wirk thair awin Wark, and to be Freemen of the Toun.

The quhilk Articles, Statutes, Rowles, we the saids Provest, Baillies, and Counsell of the said Burgh, for us and our Successors, approve, ratifye, and confirmis the samyn, in swa far as effeirs till us or his Powar; and this till all and sundrie quhom it effeirs or may effeir in Tyme to cum, we mak it knawin be thir present Letters; and for the mair Confirmation and Strenth of the samyn, we haif to thir present Letters hungin the Common Seill of Cause of the said Burgh of *Edinburgh*, the Fifth day of the Moneth of September, the Zeir of God ane thousand five hundred and seventein Zeirs.

Notwithstanding the introduction of Gas, Candles are still an article of daily use. But the former mode of manufacture is nearly obsolete. The Candlemakers of old made their candles of tallow and cotton wick. There were two kinds of candles sold, viz., "moulds" and "dips." The latter was the candle of the poorer classes—a cheaper kind of candle. The tallow being a substance which was easily melted, the candles of those days were very soon consumed, and the persons making use of them had to be provided with a pair of scissors, or rather "snuffers," for the purpose of taking away from time to time the burnt wick which remained. Of course there were wax candles in those days, to be found in the houses of the more wealthy classes, just as in pre-Reformation times, it was one of the duties laid upon the corporations to provide a suitable supply of wax candles for their respective altars.

At the present time, a superior candle is manufactured. The wax and the tallow candles are still made use of. But the Composite and Paraffin Candles are those generally adopted.

In former days, the chief resort of the Candlemakers in Edinburgh was in the Row which bears their name. Another large manufactory was in the place known as "the Crooked Dykes, Crosscauseway."

## 2. THE BARBERS.

THE Barbers of Edinburgh, as has already been noted, were originally incorporated with the Surgeons on 1st July 1505, by a Charter granted by the Town Council.

Frequent disputes arose between the Surgeons and the Barbers, as to their respective rights and privileges, which continued down to the 23d of February 1722. In an action of Declarator before the Court of Session, at that time, the Barbers were, by decree of the Court, separated from the Surgeons, with this one exception, viz., that their Apprentices should still be registered by the Surgeons' Incorporation, in order to have the fact recorded that they were admitted both by them and the Barbers. The Barbers, by the said decree of the Court, having been constituted into a Society or Company to govern their own affairs, formed a Constitution and Rules for conducting the business of their Craft, and these were placed before the Town Council for the purpose of being approved of.

The following are the Constitution and Rules :—

1. That all those who shall after this be admitted free Barbers within the Burgh of *Edinburgh*, shall be first free Burgesses thereof, and produce their Burgess Tickets with a Petition of the Society; upon which they shall be tried and examined by the Masters of the Trade, and receive their Acts of Admission in terms of, and as is provided by the said Decreet of the Lords of Session, upon payment to the Boxmaster; and that no Freeman shall protect in his Trade or Imployment ane Unfreeman, under the Penalty of Forty Pounds for each Trangression.

2. That none be hereafter admitted a free Barber, but such as is Son, or Son-in-law of, or has served his Apprenticeship to, or discharged of his said Indentures from a free Barber; or is the Son or Son-in-law of a Chirurgeon, in the Terms of that Decreet; reserving still to the Society the Consideration of the Circumstances of such as have been assistant to them in the Prosecution of the foresaid Process, and a Discretion or Power of admitting such as they shall think deserve of the Society.

3. That all Apprentices shall be bound for five Years, and for no less time : That their Indentures be written by the Clerk of the Society, and that they be regularly recorded or booked, as is ordained by the said Decreet, within forty Days after the Date of the Indentures, at the Sight of the Preses or Boxmaister, and two at least of the other Maisters of the Trade ; and that there shall be paid for every such Booking Three Pounds *Scots* Money to the Boxmaister, for the Use of the Society ; besides the common Dues to the Clerk and Officer, and the Crown appointed by the foirmentioned Decreet to be paid therefor to the Society of Surgeons.

4. That no Freeman take Apprentices more than one in three Years for the Freedom.

5. That all hired Servants, who are Strangers, and have not been Apprentices to Freemen, shall be recorded or booked in Manner foirsaid in the Books of the Society, and shall pay for and at such Booking, One Pund ten Shillings *Scots* to the Boxmaister, for the common Use foirsaid : beside Twelve Shillings *Scots* to the Clerk, and Six Shillings *Scots* to the Officer ; and that, on booking of such a Servand, is and shall be sufficient, though they shall afterwards have different Maisters : And that no Freeman recave another Freeman's Apprentice or Servant, until he be discharged from his former Maister.

6. That all free Barbers within the Burgh be obliged punctually to attend the quarterly Meetings of the Society, and all other Meetings lawfully warned thereto, by the Officer, at Command of the Preses, under the Penalty of Six Shillings *Scots* for Absence from each Meeting, and shall pay One Shilling *Scots* for each Meeting that they shall come in after calling the Rolls.

7. That any Barber to be admitted in *Canongate, Leith, Portsburgh, Potterrow, Bristo, Pleasants,* and other suburbs of *Edinburgh,* shall first make Application to the Society of Barbers of *Edinburgh,* and be tryed and examined by the Maisters, and pay an Upsett of Fifty Punds *Scots,* unless he be Son, or Son-in-law of a Freeman in those Places ; in which case he shall pay only Threttie Punds *Scots,* and recave his Admission in the Terms of, and as is appointed by the before mentioned Decreet ; and that all the Barbers in the said Suburbs shall be obliged to obey the Statuts and Acts made, and to be made, by the Society of the Barbers of *Edinburgh ;* and that all their Indentures be written by the Clerk of the Society, and their Apprentices and Servants shall be booked and recorded in Manner foirsaid.

8. That the Barbers, both in *Edinburgh, Canongate, Leith, Portsburgh, Potterrow, Bristo, Pleasants,* and other Suburbs of *Edinburgh,* pay punctually One Merk *Scots* Money to the Boxmaister of the Barbers of *Edinburgh,* at *Whitsunday, Lambas, Mar-*

*tinmass*, and *Candlemass*, in all Tyme comeing; beginning the first Payment at *Lambas* next, for mantening the Poor, and supporting the common Burdens of the Society, under the Pain of Poynding and taking in their Basons, till full Payment of Byegones.

9. That no Barber in Town or Suburbs, by himself, or his Apprentice or Servant, exercise his Imployment on *Sunday*, under the Penalty of Six Punds *Scots* the first, and Twelve Punds *Scots* for each following Transgression.

10. That the Preses and Boxmaister be annually chosen, and that no Man be allowed to continew in one of these Offices for more than two Years together; and that the Boxmaister shall make, and be discharged of his Accompts, before he can be in a Capacity to be chosen Preses: But they inclining to do nothing without the Allowance and Approbation of the Council, they are in Duety bound to demand the same.

11. They, therefore, with all duetyfull Submission, expect the Council would give their Concurrence for the due Execution of the before mentioned Statutes, and such other Rules to be made as shall be necessary for preserving the good Order and Government of the Society, and recovering the quarterly Accompts, and other Money now payable to them, and thereby supporting their own Poor, and curbing all Unfreemen from invading upon their Imployment agreeable to Law; and to their said Constitution, established by the Seal of Cause, and the said Decreet of the Lords of Session: Craving, therefore, the Council to approve of the afore-written Rules and Statuts, and to give their Concurrence for the due Execution thereof, according to, and in Terms of their their said Rights; and as the Council are in use to grant to other Societies within the Burgh, as the Petition signed by the said *John Blair*, and *Alexander Stiven* bears.

The said Petition and Requisition having been received by the Town Council, and remitted to a Committee of their number to consider and report, the following was the Civic Corporation's deliverance. The Report " being considered by the Council, they, with the Extraordinary Deacons, approved, and hereby approve, of the Committee's Report, and of the Articles and Rules before-written, in the whole Tenor and Contents thereof; and do hereby give their Concurrence for the Execution of the said Rules and Articles contained in the said Petition; the Desire of which they granted, and by thir Presents grant, and interponit, and hereby interpone their Authority thereto, for the Punctual Observation of the said Rules and Articles in all Time Coming, as craved in the

Petition. And statute and ordained, and by thir Presents statute and ordain the above Rules and Articles to be inviolably observed in all Time Coming; and granted, and hereby grants, full Power and Warrand to the Petitioners, and their Successors in office to see these Rules and Articles observed accordingly, whereanent thir Presents shall be a Warrand."

Although the Deacon of the Barbers has no seat in the Convenery, he is a Governor *ex officio* of the Trades Maiden Hospital. Mr George R. Dickie, 120 High Street, Portobello, holds the Office at the present time.

# THE INFERIOR TRADES OR CRAFTS.

IT will have been seen, in perusing this Work, that many Members of the Inferior Crafts were at one time associated together as a Company, independent altogether of the chief Incorporation with which they were connected in a civic capacity and otherwise. It is therefore desirable that a List of such should be presented to the Reader to show in which of the fourteen Incorporations each one found his place.

ARMOURERS.—This Craft was united to the Hammermen.

BELT-MAKERS.—This Art or Trade, being in close connection with the Loriners, was united to the Hammermen.

BOWYERS.—This Trade, being annexed to the Masons, formed part of Mary's Chapel.

BLACK-SMITHS.—This Trade was the first of the seventeen Crafts of which the Hammermen was constituted (at the time the Goldsmiths, afterwards separately constituted, were connected with this body).

BRAZIERS.—This Art, being connected with the Loriners, was united to the Hammermen.

COOPERS.—The Fraternity of Coopers, becoming associated with the Wrights, formed part of Mary's Chapel.

COPPER-SMITHS.—This Craft, which was originally part of the Loriners, was united to the Hammermen.

CUTLERS.—This Art obtained a place among the Hammermen.

FOUNDERS.—This Mystery or Art, originally identified with the Loriners, was united to the Hammermen.

GLAZIERS.—This Craft, having united with the Masons, formed part of Mary's Chapel.

GUN-SMITHS.—This Trade was united to the Locksmiths, and like them found a place among the Hammermen.

HAT-MAKERS.—This Art was by a charter of the Town Council associated with the Waulkers.

LISTERS OR DYERS.—This Art was by a Charter of the Town Council united with the Bonnet-makers.

LOCK-SMITHS.—This Trade formed part of the Hammermen.

LORINERS.—This Craft became part of the Hammermen.

PAINTERS.—This Art, having become united with the Wrights, was merged in Mary's Chapel.

PEWTERERS.—This Trade constituted part of the Company of Hammermen.

PIN-MAKERS.—This Mystery, being added to the Locksmiths, was merged in the Hammermen.

PLUMBERS.—This Trade, being annexed to the Masons, formed part of Mary's Chapel.

SADDLERS.—This Craft became part of the Hammermen.

SIEVE-WRIGHTS.—This Art having been united to the Wrights, was merged in Mary's Chapel.

SHEAR-SMITHS.—This Art formed part of the Incorporation of Hammermen.

SLATERS.—The Fraternity, having become associated with the Wrights, formed part of Mary's Chapel.

UPHOLSTERERS.—This Trade, being connected with the furnishing of houses, found a place in Mary's Chapel.

WATCH-MAKERS.—This Mystery, having united with the Locksmiths, became connected with the Hammermen.

WHITE IRON-SMITHS.—The Tinsmiths, having become associated with the Pewterers, found a place among the Hammermen.

# THE TRADES MAIDEN HOSPITAL, EDINBURGH.

POSSIBLY the finest outcome of the Incorporated Trades of Edinburgh, is the existence of the Trades Maiden Hospital, at Rillbank House, Meadows. This Hospital was originally situated near to the subsequently formed Argyle Square, on the West side of the Horse Wynd, and in continuation of what was known as North College Street. All the buildings of these former days have been taken down. Under the City Improvement Scheme of 1871, a broad street has taken the place of the old narrow one, bearing the name of "Chambers Street," in token of his fellow-citizens' approval of the many services rendered to the public during his life-time by Lord Provost William Chambers, LL.D. It was, however, to make room for the building of the Industrial Museum that the Government of the day had previously purchased the house and site of the Trades Maiden Hospital (erected about the year 1740). The Governors were fortunate, however, to secure the more eligible situation to the south of the Meadows, on which the present Hospital stands.

The circumstances under which the Hospital was founded are as follow :—The Merchant Company of Edinburgh, in the year 1695, projected a scheme for the erection of an Hospital for the maintenance and education of poor maidens by charitable benefactions. Considerable contributions flowed in upon them. Their chief benefactor, however, was Mrs Mary Erskine, a widow gentlewoman, of pious memory. Her deceased husband was James Hair, at one time a Druggist in Edinburgh. That good lady purchased a handsome and

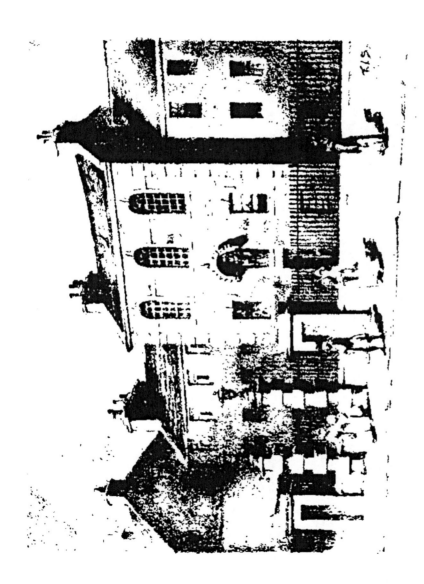

THE TRADES MAIDEN HOSPITAL
(Original Building, after Storer).

convenient building, with large garden attached, and other useful conditions, at an expenditure of Twelve Thousand merks *Scotish*, and bestowed it on the Governors of the Hospital. She likewise left instructions to her executors to pay over a considerable sum of money at the time of her death, which served materially to increase the usefulness of the Institution. The house was opened, under the name of *The Maiden Hospital*, founded by the Company of Merchants of Edinburgh, and Mary Erskine.

The Incorporations of Craftsmen (or Trades) were not long in laudably following in the wake of their brethren of the Merchant Company. During the year 1701 they had formed a design to erect "an Hospital for the Intertainment and Education of the Daughters of their poor members." The various Companies of Arts were not backward in their support. It is recorded that they helped forward the proposal by giving so good and desirable a work their most generous support. The Town Council of the City also expressed its decided approval of their pious and charitable resolution; and, by a minute of 3d May, 1704, they pledged themselves to give the movement all the support in their power.

Having purchased certain Houses and Gardens on the site near Horse Wynd, which has been already referred to, the Incorporation fitted up one of the Houses for the purposes of the Hospital, selected a Governess, Schoolmistress, and Servants for the same; and, having taken sundry poor maidens under their care, they proceeded to make a Constitution and Bye-laws for the proper government of the Institution, with the view of the Constitution being approved of by Parliament.

The terms of the Charter of Foundation, which were ratified by Parliament during the reign of Queen Anne, are as follow :—

"At *Edinburgh*, the twenty-fifth day of *March* One thousand seven hundred and seven Years, Our Sovereign Lady, with Advice and Consent of the Estates of

Parliament, considering that there is a pious and laudable Design now carrying on by the Incorporations of the Craftsmen of *Edinburgh*, and others who join with them, authorised by the Town Council of the said Burgh, by their Act dated the third of *May*, 1704 Years, for founding and erecting an Hospital for the Maintenance and Education of the female children and Grand-children of decayed Craftsmen and others, to be presented by Persons who give Donations thereto; which may be of a general Advantage, and especially to the City of *Edinburgh*. THEREFORE, Her Majesty, with Advice and Consent foresaid, do hereby allow and authorise the said Incorporations of the Craftsmen of *Edinburgh* and others joining, or who shall join with them, to meet as oft as occasion requires, and to make such Rules and Constitutions for the carrying on and supporting of the said Hospital allenarly, as they shall find just and convenient. As ALSO, to settle such Funds as well out of their public Boxes belonging to their respective Administrations as private Estates, as they shall think fit; and to receive Mortifications or Donations from any person who shall be pleased to contribute there-to; the said Rules and Acts to be made by them, being always consistent with the Laws of the Kingdom, and with the Acts and Constitutions of the City of Edinburgh. And STATUTES and ORDAINS the said Rules and Constitutions to be made by them to be as valid and effectual, to all Intents and Purposes, for the ordering and governing of the Hospital above mentioned, as if they were particularly exprest and set down in this Act.

WHEREANENT Her Majesty, with Advice and Consent aforesaid, dispenses for ever. And FURTHER, Her Majesty, with Advice and Consent foresaid, ordains and declares the foresaid Hospital, when set up and settled in its Constitutions and Directors and Overseers, to be a free Hospital for the pious Use foresaid; with power to the said Hospital, and its Overseers and Directors, not only to administrate the Funds and Rents appertaining thereto, but likewise to purchase and acquire Lands, Tenements, and others, for the farther Good and Advantage thereof; and for that End to make, grant, and receive all Manner of Deeds and Writs necessary for that Effect; and to have a Seal, if they shall think needful; and with such Inscription as they shall appoint for the Confirmation of their Deeds. And, generally, to have all such Powers, Liberties, and Immunities of a free Hospital for pious Uses as any other Hospital for the like Uses hath, or by the Law may have, in this Kingdom.—Extracted forth of the Records of Parliament, by me, Sir James Murray of Philiphaugh, one of the Senators of the College of Justice, Clerk to the Parliament, and to her Majesty's Councils, Registers, and Rolls, *sic subscribitur*, JA. MURRAY, *Cls. Reg.*

The Trades Maiden Hospital having received the sanction of Parliament, the same Mary Erskine, who was very considerate to the Merchant Maiden Hospital, contributed so large a sum of money to this new scheme of benevolence, as to cause the Incorporations to come unanimously to the conclusion that she should be named as the Joint Foundress of the Institution. This was done. It was called "The Maiden Hospital, founded by the Craftsmen of Edinburgh and Mary Erskine." It was also agreed that two persons of the name of Erskine, to be named by her, and after her death by the representatives of the Family of Mar, should be Governors of the Hospital in all time coming. After her death, the two persons named by her should have the right of presentation of all those girls that she herself had a right to present, by reason of her generous benefaction. It was also arranged that the senior of her said representatives should preside in all Courts of the Governors (held on account of the Hospital) in the absence of the Preses, viz.—the Deacon Convener of the Trades, and that he should also possess one of the three keys of the Hospital's Charter House.

Mrs Mary Erskine, therefore, nominated and appointed as her two first representatives, Mr James Erskine of Grange, one of the Senators of the College of Justice, and Mr David Erskine, advocate, both for their natural lives. After her death, her powers of appointment were to devolve upon the chief representative of the Family of Mar, under whatever designation it might then happen to be. The successive Earls of Mar and Kellie have for generations taken an intelligent and zealous interest in the affairs of the Institution.

By virtue of the before-recited Act of Parliament, and the contract with Mary Erskine, the Deacon Convener, the Deacons of the various Incorporations of Crafts, the Contributors, the two Trades Councillors, and others, together with the two representatives of the said Foundress, being the Governors of the said Hospital, after divers Meetings, agreed to a Code of Laws or Constitution for the better government of the Hospital. The model adopted by them was that of George Heriot.

The constitution provided that the Deacons of the various Incorporations, the Two Trades Councillors, and two of the name of Erskine (as previously arranged) should be perpetual Governors of the Hospital. And there was a further provision that on the second Monday of October in each year other Governors should be annually elected to make up the Governing body to twenty-seven. The election of the Annual Governors was vested in the other Governors mentioned above, along with every donator to the extent of 2000 merks to the Institution, and such donators were eligible for election as Governors. Vacancies occurring during the year among the elected Governors had to be filled up by the existing body of Governors.

Each Governor was required to take the following Oath :—" I do faithfully swear and promise before God, that, to the best of my knowledge and power, I shall carry and demean myself in all matters which concern the election of the Officers or Scholars, or anything else belonging to the Maiden Hospital, founded by the Craftsmen of Edinburgh and Mary Erskine, truly and honestly : And if I know any going about, at any time, to defraud or prejudge the said pious work, I shall obstruct it to the utmost of my power, and reveal it to the Governors for the time. So help me God."

The Meetings of the Governors usually took place either in the Hospital itself, or in the beautiful little Chapel of *Mary Magdalene*, in the Cowgate. To the Governors belonged generally the management of the affairs of the Hospital, the election of children who were to be admitted, as well as the appointment of all the officials. Chief among these was the Treasurer of the Institution, who was the Receiver-

General of all rents and monies falling to the Hospital as well as the Paymaster of all sums owing, and who was further required to keep a correct account of the same. He had also to look after the buildings, etc., being kept in a thorough state of repair. His appointment might be continued for two or more successive years; and he was entitled to have a vote in the affairs of the Hospital along with the other Governors. He was required to take an oath that he would faithfully, truly, and honestly discharge all the duties of his office.

The Annual Meeting for the election of Governors and the Treasurer used to be held on the second Monday of October. It is now changed to the second and the third Mondays of November. It is the duty of the Treasurer to serve a warning notice on the Members giving intimation of said Meetings. The Accounts are prepared and audited up to the said date, although there is a regular monthly audit throughout the year.

The duty of the Clerk is, "to keep in good order and digest all the evidents and other papers belonging to the Hospital, and make and keep books of a full and particular record thereof, and to attend the Meetings, and form what orders and resolutions are done therein." He has, like the Treasurer, to take the oath *de fideli*, and he can hold his office during life and good behaviour.

The same tenure of office as is given to the Clerk was also granted to the Mistress or Governess; or as she is usually styled "the Matron." She is, by the laws, enjoined to "take care that the scholars and servants be brought up in the fear of God, and shall catechise the scholars in the principles of the Christian reformed religion, and correct them for faults when occasion requires." She must be an unmarried person. When she marries, her situation becomes void. If negligent of duty, she is to be publicly admonished by the Governors, and the fact recorded in the Minutes. She is required, before entering

office, to take the following oath :—" I (A. B.) elected Mistress and
Governess of the Maiden Hospital, founded by the Craftsmen of Edinburgh and Mary Erskine, do swear, and faithfully promise before God,
that, to the best of my power, I shall discharge all which the statutes
of the said Hospital require from me ; and shall do my best to see all
the statutes of the said Hospital observed by others whom they do
concern ; and do promise faithful obedience to the present Governors of
the said Hospital, and their successors in office.   So help me God ! "
The rules enact as follows :—" After which she is to get possession of the
Mistress' lodgings by some of the Governors ; and publicly, in presence
of the children and servants, be declared Mistress and Governess ; " and
the latter are commanded to give her all obedience, under the pain of
being expelled from the Hospital.

There was a schoolmistress, likewise, to be provided whose tenure
of office was " during her life and good behaviour."   Her duties were
thus defined :—To teach the children to read, work stockings, lace,
coloured and white seam, spinning, carding, washing and dressing of
linens, dressing of meat, cleaning of house, and all sorts of needlework,
and other ordinary household thrift.   And, if she can, to teach the
girls also writing, arithmetic, and the common parts of vocal music.
In the event of any one being appointed who was not able to teach the
" whole arts and virtues above mentioned," in such case the Governors
retained the power to themselves, to provide an honest man, for some
part of the day, to come to the Hospital, at such hours as should be
found most convenient, and whose salary should be paid by the
Treasurer.   The same remarks regarding marriage applied equally to
the Schoolmistress as to the Matron.

The Commissariot department was likewise provided for.   It was
ordained that there shall be chosen a woman of good and honest report
to be Cook to the Hospital.   The Cook was charged with the clean and

exact dressing of the victuals; two or three of the children who were educated in the Hospital were appointed by the Matron to be present and assist at the dressing of the victuals, so that they might handle meat neatly. To the Cook was entrusted the custody of all utensils belonging to the kitchen, which were delivered to her by inventory; she had to deliver up her accounts for bread, drink, candle, and other things belonging to her department to the Matron weekly, or as often as she was required. She had, however, no charge in the engagement of the servants of the House, a duty which originally devolved upon the Governors, but has latterly fallen into the hands of the Matron.

Regarding the recipients of the Hospital's benefits, the following law (XIV.) was enacted:—

"There shall be chosen and admitted into the said Hospital, so many children as the revenue of the said Hospital shall be able to maintain *deductus ducendis*. And these girls presented by the Incorporations are to be the children or grandchildren of the Freemen Craftsmen of their own Incorporation; *which failing, any other they please,* of whose poverty and need of the help of the Hospital, the Incorporation who presents them are to be the judges; but the Donators to the Hospital who have a right to present, by giving a donation of 2000 merks, may present any girl they think fit, whether Craftsman's daughter or not; it being made appear to the Governors or their Committee before-mentioned, by a declaration under the hand of the Donator who hath right, and presents a girl, that she is an object of charity; which declaration shall be an instruction of poverty. For each 2000 merks' donation, the person, giver thereof, during his or her life, and after their death any they shall appoint by writ, hath a title to present a girl; and as often as the presentation shall vaick (vacate), they shall have the renewing thereof; and if any two persons shall jointly give in 2000 merks of their own proper means, they shall have the presenting of a child *alternis vicibus,* or as they shall agree. The girls to be admitted to the Hospital must be wholesome and sound of their body at their entry, and capable to learn, and must not be under *seven* years of age, nor above *twelve* when they enter; and are to continue in the Hospital until they be *eighteen* years of age, and no longer; and each of them at their entry must be decently apparelled, at the sight of the Governors and Treasurer; and when that apparel is worn, their apparel afterwards is to be all of one piece, without distinction of persons, and as plain as may be, and all of one colour, and with such mark as the Governors shall appoint; but, when they go out of the Hospital at eighteen years of age, they are to be clad in new apparel, distinct from what they did wear in the Hospital, each girl's apparel not exceeding the sum of 100 merks Scots, which is to be paid by the Treasurer. The ordinary time of receiving in of the girls is to be the first *Monday* of *November* yearly; when it is to be considered by the Governors what vacancies there are, and how many the estate and revenue of the Hospital is able to maintain, that so many qualified, as is before expressed, be then taken in, who shall have a lodging, diet, washing, and common fires allowed to them, besides their being educate and taught in manner aforesaid, and shall be comely and decently apparelled, both in their clothes and linens."

It was provided that one or more rooms should be set apart for sick inmates, and that every sick child should have a bed for herself. Provision was also made for an Annual Meeting of the Governors and Contributors.

These Regulations have been modified from time to time, according to experience and various circumstances which emerged. The age now fixed for a girl leaving the Hospital is seventeen years.

In the year 1748 the Governors of the Hospital purchased the estate of Wrights' Houses, lying to the south-west of Edinburgh, which they subsequently feued out, and which is now represented by the large mass of buildings between Fountainbridge and Bruntsfield Place, including Gillespie's Hospital, part of the Old Lochrin Distillery, the works of the North British Rubber Company, and of the Scottish Vulcanite Company, Gilmore Place, and the villa and other residences in the district of Viewforth. It was probably from their proprietorship of these lands that the girls on the foundation, for whose benefit the lands were held, and who in a beneficial sense therefore were the owners of the estate, came to be known as "the Lassies of Wrights'-houses."

When the Educational Endowments (Scotland) Act 1882 came

into operation, the Commissioners under the Act framed a Draft
Scheme for the administration of the funds of the Hospital on an
altered footing, under which (had it been passed) the Governing Body
would have been materially altered, the Incorporation's Rights of
Presentation would have been taken away and replaced by a reduced
number of mere nominations, and other important alterations on the
existing administration and application of the funds would have been
made. The Governors opposed the scheme, both on its merits, and
also on the ground that the endowment did not come within the
scope of the Act, as it consisted mainly of funds "contributed or paid
by the members" of the Incorporation—*i.e.*, the several Trades Incorporations — which class of funds the Act provided should not be
interfered with, unless with the consent of the Governing Body of the
particular institution proposed to be dealt with by the Commissioners.
Appearance for the objectors was made before the Commissioners by
Counsel, who urged the legal objection to the proposed scheme so
forcibly that it was not proceeded with, the Act being allowed to
expire. The Commissioners probably felt that the legal objection to the
alleged application of the Act to the Hospital was well founded, and
also perhaps came to see that, in respect of the limited number of Girls
housed in the building, and their education being obtained at a Public
Day School along with other Girls, the life of the Foundationers was
not attended with those disadvantages of monastic upbringing which
the Act was passed to remove, and which no doubt did exist in the case
of some of the larger institutions.

At the opening of the Hospital, there were twenty-three inmates.
Now the number resident is more than double the original roll. The
Surgeons' Incorporation had originally the right to present two girls.
They have devolved their functions on the governing board. The
following have now the rights of presentation :—

| | | | |
|---|---|---|---|
| Goldsmiths, . . . . . 3 | Hammermen (White), . . . 2 |
| Hammermen, . . . . . 4 | Skinners (Callender), . . . . 1 |
| Wrights and Masons, . . . 4 | Fleshers (Grant), . . . . 1 |
| Skinners and Furriers, . . . 4 | Bonnet-Makers (Wardrope), . . 1 |
| Bakers, . . . . . . 4 | Learmonth of Parkhill, . . . 1 |
| Tailors, . . . . . . 3 | Earl of Stair, . . . . . 1 |
| Fleshers, . . . . . . 1 | J. W. Murray, . . . . . 1 |
| Cordiners, . . . . . . 1 | C. A. Wilson (late C. H. Wilson), . 1 |
| Websters, . . . . . . 1 | Lady Susan Broun Bourke, . . 1 |
| Waulkers, . . . . . . 1 | Earl of Mar and Kellie, . . . 6 |
| Bonnet-Makers, . . . . . 1 | John Stein of Kirkfield, . . . 1 |
| Barbers, . . . . . . 2 | — |
| Governors, . . . . . 4 | TOTAL NUMBER OF PRESENTATIONS, 50 |

Convener Ramage is at present Chairman of the Governing Body; Mr William Stuart Fraser, W.S., is the Clerk; Mr Edward Sawers is Treasurer; Miss Bonnar, who so faithfully discharged the duties of Matron, having intimated her intention to emigrate, her position has been assumed by Miss MacIntyre, who was recently elected to the position.   Dr James Dunsmure is the Medical Officer.

### LIST OF GOVERNORS.

*Governors,* Convener Alexander Ramage, Earl of Mar and Kellie, Mr Erskine; the Deacons of the thirteen Incorporations, viz., Alexander Ramage (the Convener), William Field, George James Beattie, John Crichton, R. Legget, sen., A. M'Cullagh, John James Moir, Robert Gillespie Muir, John B. Morham, Walter Park, Robert Brown, W. Bell Mack, Bailie Andrew M'Donald.

*Trades-Councillors,* Kenneth Scoon and D. W. Beattie.
*Society of Barbers,* George R. Dickie.
*Additional Governors,* T. L. Sawers, Alexander Webb, Henry B. Kirkwood, Duncan M'Leod, Archibald Pollock, Michael Crichton, Alfred Bryson, Alexander Keir, George Morham, with the Treasurer.

THE TRADES MAIDEN HOSPITAL
(Present Building).

# HISTORICAL ACCOUNT

## OF THE

# BLUE BLANKET.

AN

# Historical Account

OF THE

# Blue Blanket:

OR

## *Crafts-Men's Banner.*

CONTAINING THE

## Fundamental Principles

OF THE

## GOOD-TOWN,

WITH THE

Powers and Prerogatives of the CRAFTS of
Edinburgh, &c.

---

By ALEXANDER PENNECUIK, Burgess and Guild-Brother of Edinburgh.

---

PSAL. lx. 4. *Thou hast given a Banner unto them that fear thee, that it may be displayed because of the Truth.*

GEN. iv. 22. *Tubal Cain was an Instructer of every Artificer in Brass and Iron.*

---

*EDINBURGH:*

Printed by JOHN MOSSMAN and Company, and sold by him and the Author.
M. DCC. XXII.

2 A

To the Worshipful

# The Deacons of Crafts,

And remanent Members of the

## Fourteen Incorporations in the Good Town of Edinburgh.

I PRESENT you with an abridgment of the glorious Actions of your Predecessors; who, by a dutiful Attachment to their Sovereigns, suffering by impious Rebels, shew'd their Hearts flam'd with Loyalty; their Hands were Thunder, and their Deeds Miracles. You enjoy the Honours and Privileges which they procur'd from the Monarchs of SCOTLAND, as Rewards for their Heroic Atchievements. You are, what the greatest Princes and Warriors in Europe, triumphant in the Field of Battle, and press'd down to the Grave with Laurels, have aspired to, Knights of the HOLY GHOST; your Banner being call'd in Original Writs, The Banner of the Holy Ghost. Study then to imitate your worthy Ancestors in their illustrious Virtues, and inviolably maintain the Privileges of your MAGNA CHARTA: 'Tis a sacred Depositum, which you are bound in Conscience, as well as thro' Interest, to defend. If your Enemies should dare to invade your Prerogatives, granted by Kings, the Fountains of Law and Honour, let the Nation's Motto be yours,

*Nemo me impune lacesset.*

Remember King David's Saying, which is very snug to the Purpose, Psal. lx. 4. "He hath given a Banner unto them that fear him; that it may be display'd because of the Truth. *Selah.*"

I have, with unwearied Pains, collected the materials of the ensuing History, from original authentick Manuscripts, and Historians of unquestioned Veracity: And I humbly Dedicate it to you, the Crafts of EDINBURGH; wishing Prosperity to You and the Good Town, whose Pillars and chief Corner-Stones you have always proved. May the Psalmist's Prayer for Zion be granted unto her, "Peace be within her Walls, and Prosperity within her Palaces: May they prosper that love her, and seek her Peace continually." May the inimitable Poet's Lines become a fulfilled Prophecy, to be apply'd to our Sovereign City.

> Now, like a Maiden Queen, she will behold
> From her high Turrets hourly Suiters come :
> The East with Incence, and the West with Gold,
> Will stand like Suppliants to receive her Doom.
> The Silver Forth, her own domestick Flood,
> Shall bear her Vessels, like a sweeping Train,
> And often wish, as of her Mistress proud,
> With longing Eyes to meet her Face again.
> The vent'rous Merchant who design'd more far,
> And touches on our Hospitable Shore,
> Charm'd with the Splendour of this Northern Star,
> Shall here unload him, and depart no more.
>                                         DRYD. Ann. Mirr.

That this may happen, and your Incorporations may flourish with Blessings of the Upper and the Nether Springs, is the ardent prayer of,

Worthy Fellow-Citizens,

Your devoted humble Servant,

ALEXANDER PENNECUIK.

EDINBURGH,
1st *August* 1722.

## Copy of an Epistle, from Two CRAFTS-MEN in Edinburgh, to the Author.

SIR,

      "SINCE you have put an high Respect upon us, to communicate
" in Manuscript your Historical Account of the Blue Blanket, and to ask our
" Advice about its Publication; having carefully and with Pleasure perused
" it, we return you our sincere Thanks, for your elaborate Enquiry into
" the conceal'd Honours of the Trades: But being diffident of our Sufficiency
" to judge of an Historian, we laid it before the ablest of our Brethren, who
" earnestly sollicite you may send it abroad. You have troden in unbeaten
" Paths, the Subject having been overlookt by all Scottish Historians.   As
" we question not you'll oblige the World by publishing the Honours of
" the BLANKET, so assure your self of a Tribute of Praise from all Crafts-
" men, especially from,

                          SIR,

              Your humble Servants,

                            G. H.
                            W. D.

*Edinburgh,*
*1st September* 1722.

# A

# General Preface,

TOUCHING CRAFTS-MEN, AND THE HONORARY OFFICES THEY HAVE ENJOY'D IN
CHURCH AND STATE.

WHEN the Omnipotent Architect had built the glorious Fabrick of this
World; upon a Review of his Works, he pronounced they were
all very good, and rested from his Labours. The Almighty could have spoke
the World into Being in a Moment: but out of the Depths of Infinite Wisdom,
spent six Days in its Creation, that man might learn still to be usefully
imploy'd, copying after the example of his Lord and Lawgiver. Tho' His
Deputy Adam was the first and the greatest of Monarchs, whose Dominions
extended from Pole to Pole, in a state of Innocence, before Sin had blasted
the Beauty of Eden, and Nature spontaneously yielded her Fruits; yet was
he not to eat the Bread of Idleness, having his daily Task assign'd him,
as is inimitably express'd by the matchless Milton, in his beautiful Description
of Adam awaking his charming Eve.

> Awake, the Morning Shines, and the fresh Field
> Calls us; we lose the Prime, to mark how spring
> Our tender Plants, how blows the Citron Groves:
> What drops the Myrrh, and what the Balmy Reed,
> How Nature paints her Colours, how the Bee
> Sits on the Bloom, extracting liquid Sweets.

His eldest Son, by Right of Primogeniture, Fiar of a fair Inheritance,
was educate a Plow-man, and his Brother a Grassier. The fall of Man introduced those liberal Sciences, Divinity, Law and Physick: But tho' we had
continued pure, as when we dropt from the creating Fingers of our Maker

Mechanick Arts had been necessary. In the Infancy of the World, before the Wranglings of Lawyers, the Sophistry of Philosophers, and turbulent Factions of Divines, had debauched Mankind, Artists were in the highest Repute. Adah bare Jabal, the Father of all such as dwell in Tents, and his Brother's name was Jubal, the Father of all such as handle the Harp and the Organ, Gen. iv. Verse 20. and 22. Tubal Cain was an Instructor of every Artificer in Brass and Iron.

'Tis much to the Honour of Crafts-Men, that holy Joseph, Husband to the Blessed Virgin Mary, Mother of the Son of GOD, was a Carpenter, tho' it lessen'd our Lord's Esteem amongst the Populace, who tauntingly cried, (Mat. xiii. 35.) "Is not this the Carpenter's Son?" And if we credit the earliest Ecclesiastick Historians, the Glorious Redeemer of Mankind, before his publick Entrance upon the Ministerial Office, laboured with his hands in the Shop: Tho' he called St. Matthew from the Customs, to evidence the Extent and conquering power of his Grace; yet the most of his Apostles and Disciples, who spread the everlasting Gospel, and supplanted the Government of Satan, purchased Food with the Sweat of their Brows.

GOD seems to have put a distinguishing Honour upon Trades-men, that in all Ages, Men of the greatest Learning, and the Noblest Heroes, have sprung from their Loins; Porus, Monarch of the Indies, was the Son of a Barber, and wrought himself as a Tinker; Braydillus, Prince of the Sclavonians, Son of a Coallier; Artagorus, Governor of the Cyconians, Son of a Cook; Agathocles, King of Sicily, Son of a Potter. The good Arch-Bishop Villagesius, Son of a Carter, for which Reason he took Wheels for his Armorial-bearing. Cardinal Woolsey, Chancellor of England, was begot by a Butcher. One of the greatest States-Men of this Age, Cardinal Julius Alberoni, by a Gardener; and our famous Countryman Mr Law, by a Goldsmith of Edinburgh.

As the Seed of Mechanicks have risen to the highest Dignities, so Mechanicks themselves have sway'd Scepters, proven the bravest Generals, the wisest States-Men, and the greatest Monarchs: Tho' the unthinking mass of Mankind may despise a person for low Birth; the first Circumstance of Life ought to have no Influence in our Judgment of a great Man; because we cannot pretend to be the Children of whom we please; and that a man may owe his birth to a

Prince, whose natural Temper and Inclinations discover more Meanness of Birth, than if he were the Son of a Weaver: Whereas nothing is more glorious, than when, notwithstanding of the Defect of Education, a Man knows how to rectify and elevate the Inclinations, which an obscure Birth naturally inclines to be servile.

Quintus Cincinnatus, when called to the Government of Rome, was found hard at Plow; being saluted by the Name of Dictator, invested with Purple, honour'd with the Fasces, and other Ensigns of Magistracy, was desired to take Journey; after a little Pause, he answered with Tears in his Eyes, *Then for this year, my poor Farm must be unsown:* Taking Leave of his Family, perform'd his Office with that Prudence and Justice, that he prov'd the Admiration of the World: And having finished his Dictatorship, return'd again to his Plow. Arsaces, from being a private Mechanick, was call'd to found the Parthian Empire: And such an one was Tamberlane, the Vanquisher of Asia. Peter du Brosse, Chirurgeon, was high Chamberlain of France, and Secretary to King Philip III. Massianello, a Neapolitan Fisher-Man, raised an Army of 50,000, 7th July 1647, and trampled on the Government of Naples, till they were oblig'd to yield to the Demands of the People groaning under the Burden of exorbitant Taxes. The Anabaptists in Munster, choos'd John of Leyden, a Taylor, for their King, A. D. 1535. Zeno, the famous Bishop of Constantia, was a Weaver, who liv'd till he was past an Hundred Years of Age; and tho' he was the most eminent Bishop, and had the largest Diocese in that Country, kept a Weaver's Shop, and wrought himself daily at the Loom, to clothe the Naked. When the Peasants of Upper Austria rose up against P. Maximilian, Elector of Bavaria, A. D. 1627, their Army consisted of 60,000; it was commanded by Stephen Tudiner, a Hatter; and after his Death, by Walmer, a Shoe-Maker, kill'd by Count Papenheim. And I cann't omit to hint at the beautiful Story of Mr Edmond, a Baxter, and Son of a Baxter in Stirling, who shew'd such unparallel'd Valour in the Swedish Wars, under the Command of that Immortal Thunderbolt of War, Gustavus Adolphus, that he became a General. His swimming the Danube, and, by an artful Stratagem, carrying off the General of the Imperialists, and other marvellous Actions of his Life, are recorded in the Chronicles of Sweden. In his old Age, he returned to his native Country Scotland, and built a stately Manse at Stirling, which he doted to the Church.

Historians, Ancient and Modern, not only record the Martial Atchievements, but the singular Sanctity of Mechanicks, not to mention the Faith of a Shoe-Maker, under the Reign of a King of Persia, who removed a Mountain by a holy Harangue, related by Paulus Venetus, de Rebus Orientalibus, and Nazian-zen Causen in his holy Court, as savouring too much of a Monkish Fable, nor the known Story of Crispianus, who suffered by the Cruelty of Maximilian. The Church records a noble Army of Martyrs, who died for the Protestant Faith in the Reign of Henry VIII. and Mary, Sovereigns of England.

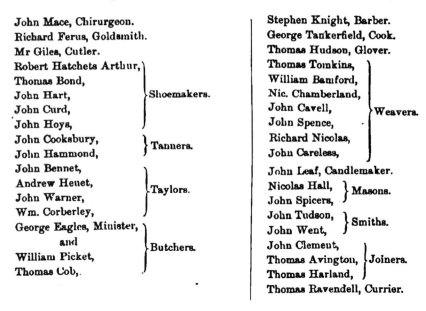

John Mace, Chirurgeon.
Richard Ferus, Goldsmith.
Mr Giles, Cutler.
Robert Hatchets Arthur,  ⎫
Thomas Bond,             ⎪
John Hart,               ⎬ Shoemakers.
John Curd,               ⎪
John Hoys,               ⎭
John Cooksbury,          ⎫ Tanners.
John Hammond,            ⎭
John Bennet,             ⎫
Andrew Heuet,            ⎪
John Warner,             ⎬ Taylors.
Wm. Corberley,           ⎭
George Eagles, Minister, ⎫
and                      ⎪
William Picket,          ⎬ Butchers.
Thomas Cob,              ⎭

Stephen Knight, Barber.
George Tankerfield, Cook.
Thomas Hudson, Glover.
Thomas Tomkins,      ⎫
William Bamford,     ⎪
Nic. Chamberland,    ⎪
John Cavell,         ⎬ Weavers.
John Spence,         ⎪
Richard Nicolas,     ⎪
John Careless,       ⎭
John Leaf, Candlemaker.
Nicolas Hall,     ⎫ Masons.
John Spicers,     ⎭
John Tudson,      ⎫ Smiths.
John Went,        ⎭
John Clement,        ⎫
Thomas Avington,     ⎬ Joiners.
Thomas Harland,      ⎭
Thomas Ravendell, Currier.

*Sanctitatis radiis, in Orbe refulsit.*

Behold the Martyrs who for Truth have died.
Heaven's Glory now, and Britain's greatest pride.
No Popish Flames to them a Period give,
Their Memories eternally shall live.

Wise Princes and States have always had Mechanicks in highest Estimation. The grand Seignior, tho' one of the greatest Princes in Europe, is always educate in some Hand-craft. The Dutch, and the Czar of Muscovy, by encouraging Crafts-Men, have made their Countries flourish, and are become the Terror and Envy of their Neighbours. King Charles II. was an excellent Worker in Ivory: Neither the Affairs of State, nor Pleasures of his Court, could divert him from his Morning Task at the Turner's Loom. Lewis the XIV. of France, was so exquisitely good at making of Watches, that he was equall'd by few in his Reign.

What Respect the Kings of Scotland have put upon Tradesmen, the following History of the Blue Blanket, or Crafts-Mens Banner, will declare. They have had the Happiness to taste the Bounty of our Princes in the Highest Honours: For this Order of the Blanket, originally of Ecclesiastick Institution, is confirmed by the Royal Sanction. It had its Rise about the 1200 Year of GOD, when the Croisade was carried on by Pope Urban the Second; and so is older than any of the Orders of Knighthood in Europe, save that of St. Andrew, or the Thistle, which had its Original about the 800, when the King of Scots and Picts made War against Athelston King of the West Saxons; and that of the Star, or Blessed Virgin, which, as Selden, in his Titles of Honour, remarks, had its Rise in the Year 1022: For that Order of St. George, or the Garter, was not institute till the year 1345, that of St. Michael, not till 1448, and that of the Golden Fleece 1429. So that I may say the Words of Doctor Hellen in His Preface to his History of the English Nobility, "Kings have so much of GOD in them, whose Deputies they are on Earth, as many Times, where they find Merit and Desert, they raise the Poor out of the Dust, that they may set them with Princes, even with the Princes of the People."

AN

## HISTORICAL ACCOUNT

OF THE

# BLUE BLANKET,

OR

*Crafts-Men's Banner.*

CONTAINING THE

FUNDAMENTAL PRINCIPLES OF THE GOVERNMENT OF THE GOOD TOWN,
POWERS AND PREROGATIVES OF THE CRAFTS OF EDINBURGH.

THE Metropolitan City of Scotland, by some Historians, (as Buchanan observes) either thro' Ignorance, or ill Will, call'd, *Valla Dolorosa,* The doleful Valley ; by the Pictish Records, *Castrum Puellarum,* the Maiden Castle, from its Royal and Impregnable Castle, built by Cruthenus Camelon, King of the Picts, where the Daughters of the Pictish Kings were kept working at their Needles, till married ; which, for Strength, and Command of Prospect, may challenge Precedency of the Best in Britain. Some of the Ancient Scots call'd it, *Castrum Allatum,* others *Dunedinum ;* and the latter *Edinum,* which we render, *Edinburgh.* 'Tis situated on the declining of an Hill ; from whence she views her tributary River Forth, encompassed about with fertile Fields, spacious Pastures, and goodly Gardens, grown by Degrees, in such Magnificence of Buildings, as to stand in Competition, almost, with any in Europe; and justly merits the Encomium Dr Arthur Johnston bestowed upon her.

> That Edinburgh may view the Heavens at will,
> 'Tis built upon a lofty rising Hill.
> The Fields and Rivers, which her Hand-Maids be,
> She thence views, and the tributary Sea:
> And when the Sun displays his Morning Light,
> The Palace doth present it self to Sight.
> That Princely Dwelling under Arthur Seat,
> Adorn'd by most ingenious Art of late;
> Towards the West the glorious Castle stands;
> Which with its Thunder giveth loud Commands.
> Each Citizen hath such a House, that it
> May Peers of greatest Quality well fit.
> The Threats of Foes do not make them dismay'd,
> Nor need they be of their Assaults afraid.
> Sure, for a Kingly City, none can wish
> A Seat that's more convenient than this.

'Tis not only beautiful, but ancient, tho' the Time when it was founded is not easily discovered. The Magistrates of Edinburgh, in their congratulatory Harangue to King James VI. of Scotland, and I. of England, recorded in the Muses Welcome to that Prince, assert, it was builded by Fergusius, the first Builder of this Kingdom, Three hundred and thirty Years before the Incarnation of Christ.

In our fierce and frequent Wars with the Picts, Danes, Romans, and English, this City was so often destroyed, her Monuments and Charters lost, that her Original cannot well be documented. The first Charter I find in her Favours, is granted by King Alexander I. sirnamed the Good, and the Second by his Successor St. David. 'Tis generally agreed upon, that it was made a Burgh Royal by King William I. in whose Reign a Ferveur of Devotion, encourag'd by Pope Urban II. seis'd the Spirits of the Princes and Cavaliers of Europe, under the Command of Godfrey of Bulloign, to rescue Palestine and the City of Jerusalem out of the Hands of Saladine, and to pluck the Sepulchre of Jesus from the Possession of the Infidels.

The zealous Pontiff was afflicted, that the Holy Land, the City of God, the Inheritance of Jesus, should be sully'd by Infidels, Saracens and Turks; who, in some Measure, might be said to have driven our Lord from his Capital, that the Cross, the Glory and Ornament of Crown'd Heads, should be trampled upon by the vilest of Adam's Posterity. Therefore he inculcated the Necessity of taking Arms, and united all the Powers of Christendom; and to whet their Courage, promis'd to those that would join in this holy Service, a plenary Indulgence, that is, A Remission of all Penances impos'd by Confessors.

Vast Numbers of Scots Mechanicks having followed this holy War, taking with them a Banner bearing this Inscription out of the li. Psalm, *In bona voluntate tua edificenter muri Jerusalem.* Upon their returning Home, glorying, that they were amongst the fortunate who placed the Christian Standard of the Cross in the Place that Jesus Christ had consecrated with his Blood, they dedicated this Banner, which they stil'd, The Banner of the Holy Ghost, to St. Eloi's Altar in St. Giles' Church in Edinburgh; which, from its Colour, was called, The Blue Blanket.

Tho' none of our Historians mention the Original Institution of the Blue Blanket, nor is there any Vouchers for it, saving old imperfect Manuscripts; yet 'tis highly probable, it had its Rise from the Croisade, or Holy War: For Monsieur Chevereau, in his History of the World, tells us, That Scotland was engaged in that War, and sold or mortgaged their Estates for that Expedition; and that she was amongst the most forward Nations in it. Pére Maimbourg, *Histoire des Croisades,* informs us, That the Knights of St. Lazarus, an Order of Men educate to the holy War, were numerous everywhere, but especially in Scotland and France; as appears by the Charters and Grants of Princes in their Favours; and the distinctive Crosses they wore, evince, that the Scots were as forward, gallant, and zealous in the Service, as any of their Neighbours.

Our Histories bear, That a great many of the Scots went to that War, under the Command of Allan, Lord great Steward of Scotland; and they, with their Confederates, got Possession of Jerusalem in 1099.

When Saladine prevail'd against the Christian Arms, William King of Scotland assisted the War with Money, and sent Supplies of Men to the meritorious Action, under the Command of David his Brother, and that Five thousand Scots had their Share in the Mallheurs and Successes of that unfortunate Enterprise. And if we may believe Boethius, *in Vita Gull.* the renown'd City Ptolomais was taken by the good Conduct of Earl David, Brother to the King of Scots, Anno 1091, and that the Christian Intelligencer was one Oliver, a Scots Man.

This Blue Blanket, whose Original I have endeavour'd to discover, was, in the dark Times of Popery, held in such religious Veneration, that whenever Mechanicks were artfully wrought upon by the Clergy, to display their holy Colours, it served for many Uses, and they never fail'd of Success in their Attempts. Which is not to be wondered at; for, as the learned and judicious Doctor Abercromby observes in the Life of St. David, King of Scotland, speaking of the Battle of the Standard, "So good a Use have Churchmen " in all Ages been known to make of Religious Pageantries, and so much have " the Vulgar been misled into the Belief of Heavenly Protection, by the Legerde- " main Tricks of spiritual Guides, who, while they have no other View but to " gratify their private Passions, muster the deluded People into Rebellion."

Having thus accounted for the Original of the Order of the Blue Blanket, I may fairly infer, That 'tis as Ancient, and more Honourable than the English Order of the Garter, the Institution whereof some ascribe to a Garter falling occasionally from the Countess of Salisbury, tho' others affirm, the Garter was given in Testimony of that Bond of Love whereof the Knights and Fellows of it were to be tied to one another, and all of them to the King. And others made it yet more Ancient, giving it the same Original with the Blue Blanket, relating, That when King Richard I. of England was at War against the Turks and Saracens in the Holy Land, the Tediousness whereof began to discourage his Souldiers, he, to quicken their Courage, tied about the Legs of several choice Knights a Garter, or small Thong of Leather, the only Stuff he had at Hand, that as the Romans used to bestow Crowns and Garlands for Encouragement, so this might provoke them to stand together, and fight valiantly for their King.

The Crafts of Edinburgh having this Order of the Blanket to glory in,

may justly take upon them the Title of Knights of the Blanket, or, Chevaliers
of Arms: For, as the learned Skene, *De Verborum Significatione*, in his Title,
*Banrents*, observes, That Banrents are called, Chevaliers of Arms, or Knights,
who, obtaining great Honours and Dignities, have power and Privileges granted
to them by the King, to raise and lift up a Banner, with a Company of Men of
Weir, either Horse or Foot; which cannot be done by any save Banrents, without the King's special Licence, as *Pasquiers*, Lib. 2. *des Rechercheres de la France*,
Ch. 9. Fol. 100. by sundry Arguments proves, and Dr. Smith, in his Treatise
of the Common Wealth of England, Lib. 1. Ch. 17. informs us, That Knights
Banrents are allow'd to display their Arms on a Banner in the King's Host.

As the Knights of St. George have their Meeting at Windsor-Castle, and
those of the Thistle in the Royal Palace of Holyrood-House, so the Knights of the
Blanket have theirs at St. Eloi, who was a French Bishop and their Guardian,
his Altar, to which they mortify considerable Sums for the maintenance of a
Chaplain, and Reparation of the Ornaments of the Chapel; as appears from
the Craftsmen's Seal of Cause.*

The Trades having been confirmed in their Privileges by the Royal Sanction,
gave such extraordinary Proofs of Loyalty, that they established themselves in
the Grace and Favour of their Princes; and their loyal Actions I shall trace,
beginning with the Reign of

### KING ROBERT BRUCE.

For many eminent Services performed by the Crafts, and other Citizens
of Edinburgh, contained in an Charter granted by the said King Robert, dated
at Cardross, in the 24th Year of his Reign: He Dispones to the Provost, Baillies,
Council and communities of the said Burgh, and their Successors, the Haven
of Leith, Mills, and other Pertinents thereof, to be holden of His Majesty, and
Successors, als freely, and with the same Liberties and Commodities, as the
same were enjoyed in the Time of King Alexander his Predecessor, of happy
Memory, for Payment of 52 Merks. Nor was Edinburgh, by her loyal Deport-
ment, less in Favour with his Successor,

---

* Here is quoted the original Seal of Cause to the Hammerman, etc., *vide* pages 11, 12.

## KING ROBERT II.

In the Beginning of his Reign, Edinburgh, to speak properly, was not the Capital City of Scotland, being only a small Burgh (which made Walsinghame, and other Historians of these Times, call it a Village) the Houses of which, because they were so often expos'd to Incursions from England, being thatch'd for the most Part, with Straw and Turf; and then burnt, or demolish'd, were with no great Difficulty repair'd: For in ancient Times, the Highlands was properly the Scots Kings Territories, till the Picts were expell'd, who had Edinburgh, and the Lothians in Possession, in the Reign of King Kenneth II. Anno 839: But the Loyalty of the Citizens, impregnable Strength of the Castle, and the Conveniency of the Abbay of Holy Rood-House, in the Royal Chappel whereof his Corps is interr'd, invited the King to dwell, and hold his Parliament there. From this proceeded a great Concourse of People, who were of Course obliged to resort to it, and occasioned these magnificent, but too costly Structures, with which it is since crowded. But the Loyalty of this City of Edinburgh, was more remarkable in the Reign of

## KING JAMES III.

who having offended his Nobles, for advancing Robert Cochran, a Mason, to the Dignity of Secretary of State, and creating him Earl of Mar, James Hommel, a Taylor, and one Leonard, a Smith, to extraordinary Favour, and Places of Trust, so incens'd the ancient Peerage, for ennobling these Mushrooms, sprung from the Dreg of the People, quarrelling the King's arbitrary Power, in dispensing these Honours, and marshalling those Persons whom he had advanced to these high Dignities, that in an impetus of Passion, they hang'd Cochran, Earl of Mar, over the bridge of Lauder, and rais'd such violent Emotions in the State, that His Majesty, for Security of his Royal Person, was forc'd to shelter himself in Edinburgh Castle. During his Confinement there, the English, with whom he was at War, having march'd to Edinburgh; and there being a Treaty betwixt the Scots and them, of the 2d August 1482; the next Day after this Cessation,

Alexander Duke of Albany, the King's Brother, importun'd by the Prayers and Tears of the 'Queen, for the King's Liberty, by the Assistance of William Bartrem, Provost of Edinburgh,* and with him the whole community, and Incorporations of Crafts-Men, intirely loving their King, and devoted to his Service, loyally, and generously oblig'd themselves to repay to the King the Sums of Money depurs'd by him in View of the Marriage betwixt the Duke of Rothesay and his Daughter the Lady Cecil: Or if the King did yet incline that the Marriage should be completed, they undertook for their Sovereign Lord, the King of Scotland, that he should concur, conform to his former Obligation, providing that their said Sovereign Lord, or the Lords of his Council, or the said Provost and Burghers, were informed of the King of England's Pleasure and Election upon the Matter, by the First of *All Saints* next to come. And the saids Citizens surpriz'd and storm'd the Castle of Edinburgh; and to the great Dissatisfaction of the rebellious Nobles, set their Sovereign at Liberty. These surprizing Instances of Loyalty and Valour, for which they shall be had in everlasting Remembrance, procur'd from the King a Grant of many new Privileges, contain'd in a Patent, which they call their Golden Charter, dated 1482; particularly, the Magistrates are made heretable Sheriffs within the said Burgh, and Liberties of the same. And another Charter from their said Sovereign Lord, in Favours of the said Provost, Baillies, Council and Communities of the said Burgh, and their Successors for ever, of all the Customs of the Haven of Leith, and Road of the same, dated 16th November 1482; and a confirmation of a Charter and Infeftment granted by Sir Robert Logan of Restalrig, to them, of all the Passages and Ways leading to the Haven and Harbour of Leith, and from the same; containing divers Liberties and Immunities.

Indeed they very well deserved the Favours bestowed on them: For 'tis certain, that upon the King of England's sending his Servant, the Garter King at Arms, to let them know, that for several great Causes and Considerations,

---

* Fœd. Aug. tom. xii. p. 161.  Godscraft's History of the Douglasses.  Abercromby's Martial Atchievements.  Hauthernden's Hist.

he had intirely refus'd to comply with the Marriage betwixt the Duke of Rothesay and his Daughter, they repaid all the Money, amounting to 6000 Merks, which he depurs'd on that Account.

Having trac'd the Blue Blanket to the Origine of the Croisade, from whence it undoubtedly had its Rise, I cannot pass over in Silence the Honour put upon it by this Monarch, who was the first that gave it the Civil Sanction, not thinking the above Donatives a sufficient Reward to the Loyal Crafts, confirmed to them all the Privileges of the Blue Blanket, which they claim'd by Prescription, or an immemorial Possession, and ordain'd it to be call'd in all Time coming, *The Standard of the Crafts within Burgh :* For that King, full of the Spirit that warms the Blood of absolute Monarchs, highly resented the Treatment Robert Cochran, Mason, by him created Earl of Mar, had met with by his factious Nobles, would needs confer this Dignity upon the Trades, in whom he plac'd his special Confidence. The Trades thus honour'd, renewed their Banner; or, to speak in the Language of Heraulds, their Ensign, by Way of Pennon, and the Queen with her own Hands painted upon it a Saltire, or St. Andrew's Cross, a Thistle, an Imperial Crown, and an Hammer, with the following Inscription :

> " Fear GOD, and honour the King,
>     With a long Life, and prosperous Reign,
>     And we the Trades shall ever pray."

The Crafts having now not only the Cross, but the Crown on their Ensign, were as firmly perswaded of Success in all their publick Actings, as Constantine the Great, the first Christian Emperor, in the Year 306, of defeating the Tyrant Maxentius, when at Noon-Day he saw a luminous Cross in the Air, with these Words in Greek,

> " In hoc Signo vinces."

The old Nobility and Gentry were exceedingly nettled at the Proceedings of the King to re-establish his Authority, but in the Judgment of wise and loyal Men, very unjustly ; for the Foundation of all Obedience to Superiors, are Rewards and Punishments, and Royalty is an Invention of Divine Wisdom, for the Happiness of Subjects ; and Kings being common Fathers to their

People, are to reward Virtue wherever they find it; 'tis their Duty to do it, and the Promise of the KING of Kings that they shall do it. "He will take " their Daughters, and make them Apothecaries, Cooks, and Bakers; and he " will take their Sons, and appoint them to his Chariots, and to be his " Horsemen, and he will make them Captains over Thousands. As the Wrath " of a King is like the Roaring of a Lion : So in the light of his Countenance " is Life, and his Favour as the latter Rain."

As the Crafts of Edinburgh, in the Reign of his Successors, made a very grateful and prudent Use of the Blue Blanket, with respect to Government; so they never failed, with this Standard, to chastise all who in the least infringed their Rights and Privileges, which King James VI. takes notice of in his *Basilicon Doron*, or, Advice to his Son and apparent Successor, Henry Prince of Wales, Page 164. "The Crafts-men think we should be content " with their Work, how bad soever it be; and if in any Thing they be controul'd, " up goes the Blew Blanket."

As they flourished in the Favours of their Sovereign King James III. so did they in the Reign of that couragious and pious Prince his Successor,

## KING JAMES IV.

Crown'd at Edinburgh 1489; who, for singular Acts of Loyalty perform'd by the City of Edinburgh, by his Charter of Confirmation under the great Seal, to the said Provost, Baillies, Council, and Communities of the said Burgh, ratified and confirmed the two above Charters granted by King James III. and Charter granted by Sir Robert Logan of Restalrig; which Charter of Confirmation is dated at Stirling the 9th day of March 1510. And, by another Charter, disponed to them the Lands and Haven of Newhaven, with the Haven, Silver, and all other Profits, Duties, Liberties, and Immunities pertaining thereto, dated at Stirling the said 9th March 1510. Thus far was the City of Edinburgh honoured and privileged in the Reign of King James the IV. and were no less so, during the Government of his Son and Successor,

## KING JAMES the V.

For during the Wars 'twixt him and the Earl of Northumberland, John Armstrang, Chief of a Gang of Thieves, was entic'd by the King's Officers to have recourse to the King, who had written a Letter to him with his Royal Hand, to attend him at his Palace of Hally Rood-House. The King hearing a distinct Account of the Crimes he was guilty of, ordained him to be committed to Goal, and suffer, with his Accomplices, according to Law. This notorious Highwayman, with the Assistance of his Followers, drew upon the King in his Chamber of Audience, who was, with much Difficulty, rescued by the Courtiers and their Attendants, and continued in their Hostilities, designing to have murdered every Soul in the Royal Palace, till it was nois'd in the City of Edinburgh that the King was in eminent Danger of being cut off by the Hands of bloody Ruffians, the Crafts of the City rose, and slew every one of the Assassins. The Story is preserv'd in Memory, not so much by our Historians, who gave but a faint Account of it, as a Balland compil'd by one of the greatest Poets of that Age.

> " There dwelt a Man in fair Westmorland,
> John Armstrang Men did him call,
> He had neither Lands nor Rents coming in,
> Yet he kept eightscore Men in his Hall, &c.
> The King he wrote an a Letter then,
> A Letter which was large and long,
> He sign'd it with his own Hand,
> And he promised to do him no Wrong.
> When this Letter came John him till,
> His Heart was as blyth as Birds on a Tree ;
> Never was I sent for before any King,
> My Father, my Grandfather, nor none but me, &c.
> By the Morrow Morning at ten of the Clock,
> Toward Edinborrow gone was he,
> And with him all his eightscore of Men,
> Good Lord, an it was a goodly Sight to see.
> When John came before the King,
> He fell down low upon his Knee,
> O pardon, my Sovereign Liege, he said,
> O pardon my eightscore Men and me.
> Thou shalt have no pardon thou Traytor strong,

Nae for thy eightscore Men and thee ;
For to Morrow Morning by ten of the Clock,
Both thou and them shall hang on the Gallow Tree.
    Then John looked over his left Shoulder,
Good Lord what a grievous Look looked he !
Said, " I have asked Grace at a graceless Face,
Why, there is nane for ye nor me."
But John had a bright Sword by his Side,
And it was made of Mettal so free,
That had not the King stept his foot aside,
He had smitten his Head from his fair Bodie,
Saying, " Fight on my merry Men all,
And see that none of you be tane ;
For rather than Men should say we were hang'd,
Let them report that we were slain."
God wot, the Trades of Edinburgh rose,
And so beset poor John round,
That Fourscore and and ten of John's best Men,
Lay gasping all upon the ground," &c.

Having trac'd the loyal Actions of the Citizens, especially the Crafts of
Edinburgh, thro' the Reigns of several Sovereigns, before I proceed to the
Reign of Queen Mary, I must take notice of the pious donations of an eminent
Citizen of Edinburgh, Michael Macquhan and his Spouse, in favours of the
Hammermen, (who dedicated and consecrated the Blue Blanket to St Eloi's
Altar in St Giles' Church) for founding of the Magdalen Chapel, where they
now meet, which is contain'd in the following Charter.

'TO all and sundry, to whois Knowledge thir Presents sall come, and be seen, I, Jonet
' Ryne, Relict, Executrix, and only Intromissatrix with the Goods and Gear of umquhil
' Michael M'Quhan, Burges of Edinburgh, wishing Peace in our Lord, makes known by thir
' Presents, That when the said Michael was greatly troubled with an heavy disease, and
' oppressed with Age, zit mindful of Eternal Life, he esteemed it ane good Way to obtain
' Eternal Life, to erect some Christian Work, for ever to remain and endure, he left Seven
' hundred Pound, to be employed for the Supplement of the Edifice of the Magdalen Chapell,
' and to the other Edifices for Foundation of the Chapell, and Sustentation of several poor
' Men, who should continually there put furth their Prayers to God Almighty ; for there was
' many others that had promised to mortifye some Portion of their Goods for perfeiting and

' absolveing of the said Wark, but they failzied, and withdrew from such ane holly and
' religious Work, and altogether refused thereupon to confer the samen. Quhilk Thing I
' taking heavyly, and pondering it in my Heart, what in such ane deficle Business sould be
' done ; at last, I thought Night and Day upon the fulfilling of my Husband's Will, and took
' upon me the Burden of the haill Wark, and added two thousand Pound to the 700*l.* left
' be my Husband : And I did put furth these Soumes wholly, after his Death, upon the
' Edification of that Chapell, Ornaments thereof, and Building of the Edifice for the Habit-
' ation of the Chaplane, and seven poor Men, and for buying of Land, as well Field Land as
' Burgh Land, and yearly Annualrents, for the Nourishment, Sustentation, and cloathing of
' them as hereafter mair largely set down. Therefore wit ye me, To the Praise and honour
' of Almighty God, and of his Mother the Blissed Virgine Mary, and of Mary Magdallen, and
' of the haill Celestial Court, to have erected and edified ane certan Chapell and Hospital
' House, lyeing in the Burgh of Edinburgh, upon the South Side of the King's high Street,
' called the Cowgate, for Habitation of the foresaid Chaplain and Poor, and that from the
' Foundation thereof ; and has dedicate the samen to the Name of Mary Magdallen, and has
' foundit the said Chaplain, and seven Poor, for to give furth their continual Prayers unto
' God for the Salvation of the Soul of our most illustrious Mary Queen of Scots, and for the
' Salvation of my said umquhil Husband's Soul and mine : And also, for the Salvation of the
' Souls of my Fathers and Mothers, and for the Salvation of all the Souls of those that shall
' put to their helping Hand, or sall give any Thing to this Work : As also, for the Patrons
' of the said Chaple : And also, for the Souls of all those of whom we have had any Thing
' whilk we have not restor'd, and for the whilk we have not given Satisfaction ; to have
' given and granted, and by this my present Charter in poor and perpetual Alms, and to have
' confirm'd in Mortification : As also, to give and grant, and by this present Charter, gives
' in poor Alms and Mortification, to confirm to Almighty God, with the Blessed Virgin Mary,
' the said Chapell and Chapell House, for the Sustentation of ane secular Chaplain, and seven
' poor Men, and for Chaplain, and four poor Brethren, to have their Food, and perpetual
' Sustentation within the said Hospital, and for buying of their Habits every twa Year once,
' I mortify these Annualrents under-written ; to wit, Ane yearly Annualrent of aughtscore
' and aught Merks Money of Scotland, out of that Annualrent of threescore Pounds yearly,
' to be uplifted and tane at twa Terms yearly, Whitsunday and Martinmass in Winter, be
' equall Portions, out of all and haill the Barony of Carnwath Miln, and Pertinents thereof,
' and the other two Merks of the said Annualrent of threescore Pound, to be apply'd and used
' for my Use, during my Lifetime, and after my Decease, to the poor Brethren under-written :
' As also, for the Dyet and Sustentation of other three poor ones, and buying of their Habites
' ilk twa Year, after the Decease of me the said Jonet, reserving to me my Liferent during
' my Lifetime, viz. The foresaid Annualrent of twa Merks of the said Annualrent of three-
' score Pounds yearly, to be uplifted out of the Lands of Carnwath : As also, another yearly
' Annualrent of twenty Merks Money of Scotland, yearly to be uplifted, as said is, out of all

' and haill the Lands pertaining to Kathrine Gillespie and John Cockburn her Spouse, lyand
' in the Burgh of Edinburgh, upon the south side of the High Street thereof, betwixt the
' Trans of the Vennel called Hair's Closs, and the Trans of the Vennel called Borthwick's
' Closs : As also, ane other yearly Annualrent of ten Merks, out of the Tenement of umquhile
' Andrew Harly, lying upon the North part of the King's High Street : And alse, ane other
' Annualrent of 12 Merks, out of the Tenement of Land pertaining to umwhile James Young :
' And als, another Annualrent of xiii sh. iiii. d. out of the Tenement of Land pertaining to
' Edward Thomson Baxter, lyeing in the said Burgh in Peebles-Wynd.  Whilk Chaplain and
' his Successors, shall have for their yearly Sustentation Twenty Four Merks Money of
' Scotland, out of the foresaid yearly Annualrent of aughtscore and aught Merks, dureing
' Jonet Rynd's Lifetime, and after her Decease, out of all the foresaid yearly Annualrents,
' to be taken up be himself at Whitsunday, and Martinmass in Winter, evry Year in all
' Time comeing, be equal Portions.  Whilk Chaplain shall have the Care, Government and
' Administration of the foresaid Hospital, and of the foresaid poor Brethren, and of all other
' poor Brethren that shall, in any Time thereafter, be put thereintill, and shall, three Times
' in the Year, provide to them the Ecclesiastical Sacraments, provideing they be found meet
' and apt for receaving thereof ; to wit, the Feast of Pasch, Pentecost, and Nativity of our
' Lord Jesus Christ.  Whilk Chaplane alse shall see, that in the foresaids Feasts, and other
' convenient Times, chiefly when they shall be sick of any heavie Infirmity, how the foresaid
' Poor shall be worthyly disposed for receaving of the Sacrament ; and for that Effect, he
' shall exhort them, and shall charitably move them, and shall hear their confessions.  And
' the said Chaplain shall be obliged every Feriat Time of the week, if it be not ane Feast Day,
' to make ane Mess of Rest, with ane Psalm direct to the LORD, for the foresaid Souls.
' Neither shall it be leisome to the said Chaplain to have any Substitute under him, to serve
' in the said Hospital for him, except in the Time of Infirmity and weakness allenerly ; to the
' whilk Mess the foresaid seven Poor, and any others to be found thereintil to be present, and to
' interceed at God for the foresaid Souls, and he sall have ane Care, that the foresaid Poor shall
' diligently observe the whole Foundation and Articles as is herein sett down.  And farder,
' We will and ordain, that the said Chaplane and his Successors for the Time, at the first
' term of their Entry and Admission in the said Hospital, shall find sufficient Caution to
' the Patrons of the said Hospital, for the well Preservation of all the Jewells, Ornaments,
' and others whatsomever, whilk sall belong to the said Hospital, to be delivered be them to
' the Patrons under an Inventar ; and that he shall not sell, nor put away any of the said
' Ornaments, neither shall it be leisume to the said Chaplane to embrace any other Chaplanrie
' or Ecclesiastick Office ; whilk if he doe, his Chaplanrie shall Vaik without any Declarator
' of any Judge, and it shall be leisume to the Patrons to confer the samen upon ane other.
' And if he be found incontinent of his Body, either be Lunury, Adultery, Incest, Drunken-
' ness, Dissentions, or of any other nottor or manifest Crimes, and found culpable by the
' Patrones, or most Pairt of them, before ane Nottar and faithfull Witnesses, shall be three

' Times admonisht to desist frae them, and after ane full Year outrun, he be found incor-
' rigible, it shall be conferr'd be the Patrons upon ane able Chaplane.  And farder, the said
' Chaplain, every Year, once in the Year, for the said Michael and Jonet, sall make Suffrages,
' which is, " *I am pleased, and direct me O LORD, with an Mess of Rest, being naked, he
' cloathed me:* " with two Wax Candles burning on the Altar.  To the whilk Suffrages and
' Mess, he shall cause ring the Chappell Bell the space of ane Quarter of ane Hour, and that
' all the foresaid Poor, and others that shall be thereintil, shall be present at the foresaid
' Mess with their Habites, requesting all these that shall come in to hear the said Mess to
' pray for the said Souls.  And farder, Every Day of the blessed Mary Magdallen, Patron of
' the foresaid Hospital, and the Day of the Indulgences of the said Hospital, and every other
' Day of the Year, the said Chaplane shall offer up all the Oblations, and for every Oblation
' shall have twa Wax Candles upon the Altar, and twa at the Foot of the Images of the
' Patron in twa Brazen Candlesticka, and twa Wax Torches on the Feast of the Nativity of
' our Saviour, Pasch, and Whitsunday, of the Days of Mary Magdallen, and of the Days of
' the Indulgences granted to the said Hospital, and doubleing at other great Feasts, with
' twa Wax Candles allenerly.  And likewayes, he sall preserve the Alter in the Ornaments
' thereof, and he sall preserve the Jewells and Ornaments of the said Alter clean and tight,
' and he sall be obliged and resticted to furnish Bread, Wine and Wax to the said Hospital,
' for the haill Year.  As also, the said Chaplain shall be obliged, at his entry, before he be
' admitted to the said Hospital, to give his great Oath, by touching the sacred Evangile, That
' he shall neither, directly nor indirectly, by whatsomever Pretence or Collor, seek the De-
' rogation of this Foundation, in haill or in Part, neither be himself, nor be any other Party ;
' neither shall he have any Dispensation or Derogation from ony other the Time of his
' Admission ; neither shall he be put into the said Chaplanry be any other, but shall only
' have his Admission from the said Patrons, to the Effect, that if he derogate any Thing from
' the said Hospital, and sall not fulfil the haill Articles and Clauses thereof, he sall be the
' same Patrons be removed, and another able Chaplain put in his Place.  And also, We will and
' declare, That the foresaid Seven poor Men, and likewise any other of that Kind that shall
' be foundit or put thereintill be any others, that they shall give Obedience to the said
' Chaplain in all honest and leisome Things, as their undoubted and lawful Master of the
' said Hospital ; and that none be admitted amongst the said poor Brethren of the said
' Hospital, but such as are not married, and not stained with an Concubine, or with any
' other notorious Crime, and that none be admitted, except he be passed, before his Admission,
' Threescore Years, except they be impotent and miserable Persons, who otherwise are not
' able to get their daily Bread.  And that no Woman, howsoever miserable or impotent, be
' any ways received or admitted in the said Hospital ; and that no Woman shall frequent
' this House of Hospital at no Time, and chiefly in the Night-time ; and that one of the said
' seven poor Men, Weekly, in his own Turn, shall be Janitor, who shall open and steik the
' Gates thereof, and shall make clean the said Chapel and common House thereof every Day,

' and keep it honest from all Filth.  And if it chance that the said Janitor be sick for the Time,
' that he cannot do it, then ane other of the said poor Brethren, in his Turn, most able and
' meet, by the Discretion of the said Chaplain, shall be appointed.  And the said Janitor,
' every Day from Pasch to the Feast of St. Jude, from Half Six in the Morning, he shall open
' the Gates, and Close them again at Aught Hours at Night : and the rest of the Year he
' shall open at Seven Hours in the Morning, and close them again at Seven at Night, and
' shall ring the Bell of the said Chapel for the space of a Quarter of an Hour, immediately
' after the opening, and a little before the Closing : And that the said seven Poor, and every
' one of them, shall immediately, after ringing of the Bell, repeat the Lord's Prayer Five Times,
' and the Angelical Salutation Fifty Times, and the Belief of the Apostles once in the Day :
' and they shall repeat the twa Psalms that are called the blessed Virgin's, before the compleat-
' ing of their Dinner, and Reflection at Twelve Hours.  And the Dinner being done, the fore-
' said haill Poor, within the said Hospital for the Time, shall conveen before the great Altar,
' and there, with their bowed Knees, give Five *Pater Nosters*, Fifty *Ave Maria's*, and ane
' *Creed*,' &c.

The Hospital was Founded by Michael M'Quhan, Anno 1503; but the
Charter by the Relict, Anno 1545.

This Chapel is adorned with the Arms of the Good Town of Edinburgh, being Argent, a Castle triple Tower'd Sable, marshalled of the first,
surmounted with Thanes Gules, supported on the Dexter by a Virgen Lady,
on the Sinister with a Deer, and Accolee: Behind the Shield the Sword of
Honour, and Mace Ensigned with an Imperial Crown ; Below in a Compartment, *NISI DOMINUS FRUSTRA.*

Round this Atchievement are the Armorial Ensigns * of the following Incorporations, according to their Precedency.

---

* The Armorial Ensigns of the Incorporations will be found at the end of each Chapter.

## In the first Oval

I. CHIRURGEONS.—*Az.* on a Fess. *Ar.* a naked Man Fess-Ways proper, 'twixt a dexter Hand palmed, and in its Palm an Eye proper, issuing from the Chief. In the dexter Canton a Saltire *Ar.* under an Imperial Crown *Or,* or proper, surmounted of a Thistle proper, or Vert. and in Base a Castle *Ar.* masoned Sab. all within a Border *Or,* charged with the several Instruments suitable to the Society.

II.—GOLD-SMITHS.—Quarterly *Gu.* and *Az.* on the 1. a Leopard's Head *Or,* 2d, a cover'd Cup, and in Chief 2 Annulets *Or,* 3 as 2, and 4 as 1.

III. SKINNERS.—*Parted per cheveron.* Gu. and Arg. 3 Stags passant, mantled proper.

IV. FURRIERS.—*Ermine on a chief* Gu. 3 Imperial Crowns Or.

V. HAMMER-MEN.—Az. a *Hammer proper,* ensign'd with an Imperial Crown.

VI. WRIGHTS.—Az. a *Square* and *Compass* Or.

VII. MASONS.—Az. on a *Cheveron* betwixt 3 *Towers* embattelled Sab. a *Compass* Or.

VIII. TAYLORS.—Az. *Scissars* expanded Or.

IX. BAXTERS.—Az. 3 *Garbs* Or. from the *Chief* waved, a Hand issuing, holding a pair of Ballances extending to the Base.

X. FLESHERS.—Ar. 3 *Slaughter Axes proper* Saltire-ways, accompanied with 3 *Cow's Heads* couped Sab. 2 *in Flank,* and 1 *in Base,* and on a Chief Az. a *Boar's Head* couped 'twixt 2 *Garbs* Or.

XI. CORDINERS.—Az. their *Cutting-Knife* in Pale, and in Chief, a *Ducal Crown* Or.

XII. WEBSTERS.—Ar. on a *Chev.* Az. 'twixt 3 *Leopards' Heads* of the same, holding in their Mouths a *Spool* or *Shuttle* of Yarn Or, as many Roses Gu.

XIII. HATTERS and WAKERS.—*Parted per Pale* Gu, and Ar. on the 1st, a *Chev.* of the last, 'twixt 2 *Hat-string Bands* in Chief, and in Base a *Thistle* Or, on the 2d, a *sinister Hand* palmed proper, erected in Pale 'twixt 2 *Hat-Strings* Sab. and in Chief a Hat of the last.

XIV. BONNET-MAKERS and LITSTERS.—Ar. a Fess 'twixt 2 *Bonnets* Az. or proper, tufted Gu. impal'd with Or, a Chev. Gu. betwixt 3 Cushions Az.

2 D

*And round the Hammer-Men's Arms, in a second Oval, the Ensigns
of the following Arts.*

XV. BLACK-SMITHS.—Az. a *Chev.* betwixt 3 *Hammers*, each ensigned with
*Ducal Crowns* Or.

XVI. CUTLERS.—Gu. 6 *Daggers* plac'd Saltire-ways, 2 and 2, proper,
handled Or.

XVII. SADDLERS.—Az. a Chev. betwixt 3 *Saddles* Or.

XVIII. LOCK-SMITHS.—Az. a *Key impaled* Or.

XIX. LORIMERS.—Az. a *Cheveron* betwixt 3 *Horse-Bridle Bitts* Ar.

XX. ARMOURERS.—Arg. on a *Chev.* Gu. 4 *Swords* Saltire-ways, *proper,
handled* Or, and on a *Chief* of the second, 2 *Helmets* of the same.

XXI. PEUTHERERS.—Az. on a *Chev.* Ar. betwixt 3 *Porcullices* Or, as many
*Thistles vert*, and flowered Gules.

XXII. SHEAR-SMITHS.—Gu. *Wool-shears impaled* Az.

*Placed above these Arms, are the imperial Arms of Scotland, thus
blazoned, viz.*

Or, a *Lion ramp.* Gu. arm'd and lingued Az. within a *double Tressure*,
flower'd and counter-flower'd, with *Flower de Lisses* of the 2d, encircled with
the Order of *Scotland*, the same being composed of Rue and Thistles, having
the Image of St *Andrew*, with his Cross on his Breast, above the Shield a
*Helmet*, answerable to His Majesty's high Quality and Jurisdiction, with a
*Mantle* Or, *doubled Ermine*, adorned with an Imperial Crown, beautified with
*Crosses Pattee*, and *Flower de Lisses*, surmounted on the Top, for His Majesty's
Crest, with a *Lion Sejeant*, full-faced, Gu. crown'd Or, holding in his dexter
Paw a naked Sword proper, and in the sinister, a Scepter, both erected pale-
ways, supported by two *Unicorns* Argent, crowned with *Imperial*, and gorged
with open Crowns, to the last Chains affix'd, passing 'twixt their Fore-legs, and
reflexed over their Backs Or, He on the Dexter imbracing and bearing up a
Banner of Cloth of Gold, charg'd with the Royal Arms of *Scotland;* on the
*Sinister*, another Banner Azure, charged with the St *Andrew's* Cross Argent, both
standing on a Copartment placed on a Copartment placed underneath, from

which Issues two Thistles, one towards each Side of the Escutcheon: and for Motto in an *Escrol* above all, *In Defence;* under the Table of the Compartment, *Nemo me impune lacesset.*

The Hammermen's Seal, is the Effigies of St Eloi in his Apostolical Vestments proper, standing in a Church Porch, a Porch adorn'd with five Pyramid Steeples engraven, each surmounted with a plain Cross, holding in his Dexter a Hammer Bar-ways, and in the Sinister a key bend-ways. Round the Effigies, are these Words, *Sigillum commune Artis Tudiatorum.*

The above fundamental Charter, in Favours of the Magdalen Hospital, is swell'd with the Popish Doctrine of Merit, and gives us a true Representation of the Chicanry of Romish Priests, who, to fill their Coffers, and make their Kitchen smoak, set Heaven it self to Sale. The Avarice of Church-men, in these dark Times, as the learned Sir George M'Kenzie in his printed Pleadings observes, was so extravagant, that the Legislature in Germany, Denmark, and other Countries, tax'd the Quotas of pious Donations, lest the People, decoy'd by their Priests to purchase Heaven, should have starved themselves upon Earth.

The Crafts, who behav'd so loyally before they were incorporate, and form'd into Societies, continued to flourish in their Sovereign's Favours, and were warm'd with Beams from the Throne; a signal instance of their Fidelity to King James V., I cannot miss to relate. The Crown being Debitor to the Town of Edinburgh in vast Sums, for which she had not only the Security of the Government, but the Personal Obligations of the Monarch; wearied with Disappointments, and the Merchants murmuring for want of Payment from the Town, to whom they had given considerable Loans, for the Behoof of the Publick; the Magistrates, and Merchants in Concert, raised a Mob, and gave Directions to the Ring-leaders, what, and how far to act, to insult the King as he was passing the Streets to the Parliament House; who, after a Scuffle with his Guards, violently seiz'd upon his Sacred Majesty; and thrust him within the Walls of their common Goal: Some of His Majesty's Retinue having alarm'd the Deacons of Crafts with what had happen'd, the Trades instantly conveen'd, and unanimously agreed, that their

Ensign should be displayed, for convocating the Lieges, to rescue their captive Monarch; which was accordingly done, and soon procur'd him to be liberate, and safely convey'd to His Royal Palace of Holy Rood-House. The Magistrates, who had hounded out the Mob, dreading the Consequence of their trayterous Actings, and knowing the weak Side of Cuthbert the Deacon Conveener, who headed the Trades, brib'd him by a lusty Purse of Gold, to betray his Trust.

The King next Morning sent for Cuthbert, (whom he call'd his faithful General) and told him, He had a grateful Remembrance of the Loyalty and Valour of his faithful Subjects the Trades of Edinburgh, and was resolv'd to confer some remarkable token of Favour upon them.

Cuthbert, well instructed by the Magistracy and Merchant Council how to behave, *Answered*,

*May it please your Excellent Majesty, We your obliged and devoted Servants the Trades of Edinburgh, did nothing but what was our bounden Duty: But since your Majesty is graciously pleas'd not only to remember but reward our dutiful Behaviour, I presume in name of my Brethren to beseech your Sacred Majesty, to make your most faithful and loyal Servants the Trades of Edinburgh, in all Time coming free of that toilsome Affair of being Magistrates of the Burgh, and let the disloyal Merchants be henceforth loaded with the Office.*

The King surpriz'd with the Supplication, gave a Smile, and said, Cuthbert, It shall be done.

The Man's Treachery was soon blown about, to the Amazement of the Incorporations, who found, that their Loyalty, which they justly expected would have advanced their Interest, as it did their Honour, had turn'd to their real Detriment: And therefore they applied to the Courtiers, to represent to His Majesty, how villainously they had been betray'd. As soon as the King was inform'd, he commanded the Crafts to lay their Demands before him, which they accordingly did in a short Memorial, craving His Majesty would be pleased to confirm all their ancient Privileges of the Blue Blanket. His Majesty graciously received their Petition; and not only granted their Request, corroborating all former grants, and Privileges by immemorial Possession ; but considerably enlarged its Authority, declaring, That whenever they display'd their Ensign of the Blue Blanket, either in Defence of the Crown, or Crafts, all Crafts-men in Scotland, and Souldiers in the King's Pay, who had been educate in a Trade, should repair to that Standard, and fight under the Command of their General. Thus did that excellent Monarch reward Loyalty, and the treacherous Conveener was murder'd at the North Loch near a Well, yet known by the Name of Cuthbert's Well.

This was certainly the highest Honour the King could put upon the Crafts : For a Standard hath been esteemed so in all Ages. Hence the Scripture expresses the Strength and Power of the Church by a Standard, Cant. 6. 4. "Thou art beautiful, O my Love, as Tirzah, comely as Jerusalem, " terrible as an Army with Banners," and the Love and Favour of God, Cant. 2. 4. "He brought me into the Banquetting-House, and his Banner " over me was Love." Cant. v. 10. According to the Hebrew Text, "My " Beloved is the Standard-Bearer among Ten thousand," which our Translators very defectively render, "The Chief among Ten thousand." And the Antiquity and Honour of the Standard is more plainly express'd in the Book of Numbers ii. 2, &c. "Every Man of the Tribe of Israel shall pitch " by his own Standard, with the Ensign of their Father's House, far off, " about the Tabernacle of the Congregation shall they pitch, and on the " East Side, toward the rising of the Sun shall they of the Standard of " the Camp of Judah pitch throughout their Armies, and Naashon the Son " of Amminadab shall be Captain of the Children of Judah. On the West " Side shall be the Standard of the Camp of Ephraim according to their " Armies, and the Captain of the Sons of Ephraim shall be Elishama the " Son of Ammihud. The Standard of the Camp of Dan shall be on the " North Side, by their Armies," &c.

As the Almighty has compar'd the Power of his Church to, and honoured his Saints with a Standard ; so hath it been the Custom in all ages of the World, for generous Princes, in rewarding Valour and Noble Atchievements, to confer a Standard, as Guillim in his display of Herauldry observes, Hungus King of Picts gave to his Warriors, an Ensign, bearing the Figure of a Cross, in the Fashion of a Saltire. Philip King of France (or as Favin would have it) Baldwin the First, King of Jerusalem, gave to his Followers an Ensign, with two red Crosses united unto one: and to the Christian Merchants of Naples, who fought against the Saracens for the Christian Religion, whom he made Knights of Rhodes, now of Malta, a white Cross, to be worn on their left Shoulder. Reme Duke of Anjou, King of Jerusalem and Sicily, gave to his Warriors an Ensign of Crimson Velvet, with a Golden Crescent, and enamell'd red, because they had been long dy'd in Blood. Arthur King of the Britains (as Segur remarks) Founder of the Order of the round Table, instituted the Fraternity of the Knights of the Table, in token of brotherly Love, gave them a round Table, which yet hangs in their Castle: And to give no more Instances, Sir John Smith got from King Charles I. the Royal Standard which he carried off at the Battle of Edgehill, and was knighted under it.

Since Kings in all ages have bestowed the Ensign upon well deserving Persons, we need not wonder that the Kings of Scotland, to whose Blood Generosity is congenial, bestowed this standard of the Blue Blanket upon Tradesmen, who rendered themselves noble by their Actions. As Diogenes says, Nobleness of Blood is a Cloak of Sloath, and a Vizard of Cowardice, but immortal is their Fame upon whom Princes confer Honours, according to their Deserts, for defending the Holy Church, King or Country. And what Reason can be assign'd, why Tradesmen should not be advanc'd as well as others, since the greatest Princes on Earth have been Artists. Henry Peacham tells, That Solyman the Magnificent, his Trade was making of Arrows. In Venice, every Artificer is a Magnifico. In the low Countries, Mechanicks are declared Gentlemen, by a Grant from King Charles V. in Consideration of their Services, during his Wars. And to all those who contemn Mechanicks, who raise themselves by their Valour, I must give the memorable Answer of Verduge a Spaniard, and a General in Friezland, to some Persons of Quality, who resented his taking the Head of the Table at a Publick Entertainment. Gentlemen, question not my Birth, (tho' I be the Son of a Hangman) for I am the Son of my own Desert and Fortune. If any Man do as much as I have done, let him take the Table Head with all my heart,

Thus far have I trac'd the Loyalty of the Crafts of Edinburgh, and shall now proceed to the Reign of

## Mary Queen of Scots,

During whose Minority, a Controversy being betwixt the Magistrates of Edinburgh and the Deacons of Crafts, for breaking in upon the Legal Privileges of the Incorporations; which so inflam'd the Deacons of the Trades with a keen Resentment, that in the Tolbooth of Edinburgh, where the Courts of Justice then sat, they drew their Swords, demanding Justice; and if they had not been restrained by the King's Forces then in the City, whom the Magistrates call'd to their Assistance, they had been kill'd on the Bench.

Being thus reliev'd, they committed the Assassines, as they termed them, Prisoners to the Castle of Edinburgh, where they remain'd in close Confinement, till the several Incorporations having met in the Absence of their Deacons, and concluded to relieve them, after the never failing Method of displaying the Blue Blanket, which they did, and thereby convocated Thousands of the King's Lieges in a very few Hours.

The extraordinary Concourse of People alarm'd the Government so, that the King's Privy Council met upon the extraordinary Emergent, and resolved, That the Earl of Arran should interpose his Royal Authority, and stop Procedure of the Lords of Justiciary, before whom was a Criminal Process intented at the Instance of the saids Magistrates of Edinburgh, against the Deacons of Crafts, and to importune the Differences betwixt them to be submitted to him. The wise Regent comply'd with the Advice, and publish'd the following Edict.

Gubernator,

' Justice and Justice-Clerk, and zour Deputis, We greit zow weille, FORSAEMEIKLLEAS,
'     William Smebert, Robert Hutchiesoune, James Forres, Thomas Schort, Archibald
' Dewar, Andro Edgar, George Richardsone, Thomas Ramsay, James Downwieke, William
' Purdie, William Quhite
'
'         being in Warde within the Castle of Edinburgh, for alleadged drawing of Quhin-
' zearis in the Tolbuith of Edinburgh, in Presence of the Provost and Baillies thairof, the xi.
' Day of August instant, and furth-bringing in the Blew Banner of the Blew Blankett in our

'Presence, callit, the *Hally Guist*, has fundin Suretie to underlye the Law for the Samyne, and
'for all otheris Crymes that can be impute to them the x. Day of October nixt to cum, as the
'Act of Adjournal maid thairupon beirs : Howbeit, as we are informit, the saidis Persouis are
'innocent of the saidis alleagit Crimis.  OUR WILL IS HEREFORE, and for certain uthiris
'reasonable Causes and Considerationis moveing us, We charge zow strictly and commandis,
'That incoutinent, efter the sicht hereof, ze desist and seiss frae all Preceeding against the
'saids Persons, or ony othiris Craftismen of the said Burgh, for the saidis allegett Crymes,
'till the Day above-written ; or for ony othiris Actionis, Transgressionis, Crymis, or Offeucess
'quhatsomever, comitit or done be thame, or ony of thame, in ony Time bygane unto the Day
'of the Date hereof; but continowe the samyn to the third Day of the Air.  Dischargeing
'zow othirwayes theirof, and of zour Offices in that Parte in the meue Tyme be thir Presentis,
'Notwithstanding ony Writtingis gevin, or to be givene in the contraire, or ony Pains con-
'tenit therein, as ze will answer to us theirupon.  Subscrivit with our Hand, and geven under
'our Signet at Halyrudehouse, the first Day of September, the Zeir of God One thousand five
'hundred and forty three Zeirs.                                    JAMIS G.'

Thus, the Crafts defended the Rights and Liberties of the Blanket to
the exposing of their Lives; for they could not bruik the unjust Proceedings of the Magistrates, and therefore determined to keep them intire, which
they had obtained by an infinite Multitude of Great Actions.

I must here take Occasion to remove a common Objection against the
Authority of the Blue Blanket, That it never had any legal privileges:  For,
had not the Regent known that the Crafts were warranted to display their
Colours when the Privileges of their Incorporations were violate, he would
surely have done Justice to the Magistrates in punishing these Crafts as a
seditious Rabble, and with the Power of the Queen's Forces reduced them to
Obedience, especially the Deacons, by whose Authority the Lieges were con-
vocate, who were Prisoners within the King's Garrison:  But it is remarkable
tho' the Banner was displayed in his own Presence, as his Edict relates, he did
not punish them for a Trespass against Law, but was forc'd to have a Recourse
to Policy, to stop the Effusion of Christian Blood, by interpelling the Judges of
Justiciary from proceeding against them for their Riot, in assaulting the
Magistracy in their Court of Justice with Weapons; for doing of which they
were certainly culpable, and therefore he obliged them to find Baill as to that.
We must undoubtedly conclude they justified their Actings in displaying the

Blanket, otherwise there had certainly been a Law enacted prohibiting them from that Practice for the Future, under the Pain of High Treason.

Tho' the Crafts and other Citizens of Edinburgh made a bold Stand for the Glorious Reformation (which was carried on in the Reign of this beautiful, learn'd, but unfortunate Lady, Queen Mary, who tenaciously adhear'd to the Interest of the Romish Church) in a more tumultuary way than in England, and other Reformed Countries: Yet had they a just Sense of their Obedience to Cæsar, and acted under the Influence of that Christian Maxim,* 'That it is ' the Duty of the people to pray for Magistrates, to honour their Persons, pay ' them Tribute, obey their lawful Commands, to be subject to their Authority ' for Conscience sake; and that Infidelity and Difference in Religion doth not ' make void the Magistrates' just and legal Right, nor free the People from due ' Obedience to them.' So that their Actions during this Reign, when turbulent Factions were bandying one another, show'd a venerable Decorum. And the Queen was sensible of their Loyalty, as is evident from the Preamble of a Charter granted by her, and Henry her Husband, under her Great-Seal, to the Provost, Council, and Communities of the said Burgh and their Successors, ' Of all and haill the Superiority of the Village of Leith, with the ' Pertinents and Superiority of the Inhabitants and Indwellers of the samen, ' as of the Houses, Tenements, Annual rents, Links, Orchards, Profits, Duties, ' Services, Tenants, Tenandries, Services of Free-Tenants, &c.' As is at more Length exprest in the said Infeftment, dated the 4th Day of October 1565, and the 1st and 23d Years of their Reign. Which Superiority of Leith the Magistrates of Edinburgh, by a Letter of Reversion, dispon'd back to the said Queen Mary, under Reversion of 10,000 Merks usual Money of Scotland. This Superiority of Leith was thereafter, by her Son and Successor King James VI., assigned to his beloved Counsellor Sir John Maitland of Thirleston, his Chancellor and Secretary, his Heirs and Assignies, dated the 7th of July 1587, ratified and approven by the States of Parliament, the 29th Day of the Month and Year foresaid; which Reversion, is renounc'd by John Lord Thirleston, Son and Heir to the said Sir John Maitland, with Advice and Consent of Sir

---

* Westminster Confession of Faith, Chap. 23, Sect. 4.

2 E

John Cockburn of Clairingtoun, his Tutor-Testamentor, in Favours of the
Provost, Baillies, Council, Deacons of Crafts, and Community of the said
Burgh of Edinburgh, as is at length contain'd in the saids Letters of Renun-
ciation of the Date the 28th of December 1607, and ratified by the said John,
Lord Thirleston, to the saids Provost, Baillies, Council, Deacons of Crafts, and
Community of the said Burgh, the 24th of November 1614.

The loyal Crafts of Edinburgh gave surprising Evidences of their Loyalty
to their King, and Gratitude for the Privileges of the Blue Blanket during the
long and peaceful Reign of the first Protestant King of Scotland (who with
Learning and Eloquence defended the Reformation against Cardinal Robert
Bellarmine, one of the stoutest Pillars of the Romish Hierarchy, and show'd
how well he merited the Royal Title, Defender of the Faith).

But before I proceed to this Reign, I must relate two remarkable Passages
relating to the Crafts, which I had almost omitted.

When Faction and Tumult possessed an absolute and unlimited Sway,
during this Queen's Reign, the Loyalty of the Crafts was not at all diminish'd :
For when the Queen had Recourse to Arms to oppose the Earl of Murray and
his Associates, who, under Pretence of bringing the Earl of Bothwel, her
husband, to a fair Trial, as accessory to the late King Henry's Murder, had,
Anno 1567, raised an Army against her, and made her Prisoner at Carberry
Hill ; she was brought to Edinburgh, where, in stead of allowing her the Use
of her Palace, she was shut up in the Provost's House. As she enter'd the
City, cover'd with Tears and Dust, and in a Garb far below her Birth and
Merit, and insulted by the Mob, who cried, " Burn the Whore, Burn the
" Parricide." * This she bore with Fortitude of Mind, becoming a Christian
and a Queen ; but next Morning, when she open'd the Windows, and beheld
not only strong Guards plac'd before the Entry to the House, but a Banner
display'd on the Street, on which was painted her dead Husband, King Henry,
beneath the shade of a Tree, with the young Prince by his side, and the Motto,
" Judge and revenge my Cause, O LORD," she burst into Tears, and complain'd
against the Affronts she received, begging the People to compassionate her,

---

* Crawford's Memoirs, p. 38, and Melvill's Memoirs, p. 84.

now become a Captive. The honest Crafts, join'd with other loyal Citizens, pierc'd with Pity to see their Sovereign thus us'd, and their Ensign display'd, where the Ensign of the Blue Blanket us'd to be erected in the Cause of Loyalty, crowded to the Place, and compell'd the Conspirators to restore her to the Palace of Holy Rood-house.

I must indeed, as a faithful Historiographer, relate that, Anno 1571, when the Associators against the Queen held a Parliament in the Canongate, the City of Edinburgh being possess'd by the Loyalists Troops, the Crafts, who believ'd their Religion to be in eminent danger, display'd the Blue Blanket (which, in ancient Times, they were in Use to do, for Defence of Religion) at the Town of Leith, as Mr Crawford, Historiographer to Queen Anne, relates it in his Memoirs of the Affairs of Scotland, during the Reign of Queen Mary, P. 210. ‘ The Citizens, who either lik'd not the Queen or the new Magistrates, ‘ went off in an intire Body to Leith, and set up their own Standard, upon ‘ which was written in Golden Letters, “ For GOD and the King,” and ‘ vanquished the Loyalists.’

I now proceed to the Reign of King JAMES VI. of Scotland and I. of England.

The City of Edinburgh gave the highest Testimonies of their Love and Loyalty to their Infant Sovereign that they were capable of, and oppos'd the Earl of Morton, Regent, who rul'd the Roast, and overaw'd the young King's Inclinations to Mercy. Morton, to gain the Affections of the Citizens of Edinburgh, Anno 1579, caused summon a Parliament to meet at Edinburgh, and the King to leave Stirling, where formerly Parliaments were held. When his Majesty, upon his Journey to the Capital City, came near the West-Port, he alighted from his Horse and a stately Conopy of Purple coloured Velvet being held over his Head, he received the Magistrates of the City, who came Bareheaded all the Way without the Gate ; within the Gate stood Solomon, with a numerous Train in Jewish Habits, with the two Women contending for the Child, as is recorded, 1 Kings iii.

As his Majesty ascended the West Bow, there hung down from the Arch of the old Port, a large Globe of polished Brass, out of which a little Boy, cloathed like a Cupid, descended in a Machine, and presented him with the Keys of the City, all made of massy Silver, and very artificially wrought, an excellent Consort of Musick all the while accompanying the Action.

When he came down the High Street as far as the Tolbooth, Peace, Plenty, and Justice, met him, and Harangu'd him in the Greek, Latin, and Scottish Languages. Opposite to the Great Church stood Religion, who addressed him in the Hebrew Tongue : Upon which he was pleased to enter the Church, where Mr Lawson, a Presbyterian Divine, made a Learn'd Discourse in behalf of these of the Reformed Religion.

When his Majesty came out, Bacchus sat mounted on a gilded Hogshead at the Market-Cross, distributing Wine in large Bumpers, the Trumpets all the while sounding, and the People crying, "GOD save the King." At the East Gate was erected his Majesty's Nativity, and above that the Genealogies of all the Scots Kings from Fergus I. All the Windows were hung with Pictures and rich Tapestry, the Streets strowed with Flowers, and the Cannon firing from the Castle, till his Majesty reached his Palace.

Nothwithstanding all this Pomp and Ceremony, which exprest the Love and Reverence both clergy and Laity bore to his sacred Majesty, there was a sudden Change of Affairs. For,

Presbyterian Government being establish'd in the Church of Scotland, Anno 1592,* which, 'tis probable, the wise King would not have altered, had not the English Clergy influenced him to admit Thoughts of Episcopacy, which the Scotch Clergy perceiving, strove to oppose his Purpose, and strengthen their own Interest. New Debates arising grew to that Height, that in the Year 1596, some Noblemen, Barons, and Ministers, being assembled at Edinburgh, and perceiving that the Process laid against Mr David Black, who was prosecute before the Privy Council for seditious Sermons, as stirring the People up to Rebellion, wrong'd the Privileges of their Ecclesiastick Discipline, and withal, being displeased at the Clemency shown to the Popish Lords, plotted Resentment.

The King having dissolv'd the Commission of the General Assembly by his Royal Proclamation,† declaring it an unlawful convocation. The Commission

---

* Bishop Guthry's Memoirs.                    † Spotiswood's Church History.

resolved, "That since they were conven'd by CHRIST'S Warrant to see into
" the Good of the Church, *Et ne quid Ecclesia detrimenti caperet,* they should
" continue." And sent some of their Number to the Octavians, (that was the
Title commonly given to the Eight Counsellors that were trusted with the
King's Affairs), to advertise them of the Church's Troubles, proceeding from
their Counsels, and thereafter petition'd the King himself, which was rejected
and a Protestation enter'd against the Refusal; but some Noblemen, with Mr
Robert Bruce, having procur'd Access to his Majesty, Mr Robert said, " They
" were sent by the Noblemen and Barons to bemoan the Dangers threatened
" to Religion, by the King's Dealings against the true Professors." " What
" Dangers do you discover ? " said the King. " Undercomoning," said the other,
" our best affected People, that tender Religion, are discharg'd the Town." The
King ask'd, " Who they were that durst conveen against his Proclamation ? "
The Lord Lindsay reply'd, " They durst do more than so, and that they would
" not suffer Religion to be overthrown." Numbers of People were, by this Time,
thronging unmannerly into the Room; whereupon the King, not making any
answer, arose, and went where the Judges sate, commanding the Doors to be
shut. They that were sent to the King, returning to the Church, told, " That
" they were not heard ; and that therefore they were to think of some other
" Course." " No Course," said the Lord Lindsay, " but let us stay together who
" are here, to stand fast to one another, and advertise our Friends and Favourers
" of Religion to come into us ; for it shall be either theirs or ours." In
Consequence of this Concert, they pitched upon the Lord Claud Hamilton
to be their Head, and dispatch'd a Letter to him by Mr Robert Bruce, and Mr
Walter Balcanqual, to come with Diligence and accept the Charge. But the
Fury of the Multitude who attended that Meeting, heated by the Lord
Lindsay's unhappy Expression, did not suffer them to wait upon the General's
coming, but presently they leapt to Arms. Some cry'd, " Bring out Haman ; "
others cry'd, " The Sword of the LORD and of Gideon, the Day shall be theirs
" or ours." And so great was the Zeal of the unwary Populace, that taking their
March, they went straight towards the Tolbooth of Edinburgh, where the
King and his Council were sitting, and would have forc'd open the Doors,
which, upon the Noise of the Tumult, were shut, had not his Majesty's

Standard-Bearer, John Wat, Deacon-Conveener of the Trades, drawn up his Lads the Souldiers of the Blue Blanket, and kept the Rabble back till their fever cool'd, and the Earl of Mar, from the Castle, sent a Company of Musqueteers to guard the King, which his Lieutenant quickly brought down the Castle-Bank to the Grass-Market, and from thence march'd to the Foot of Forrester's-Wynd, and entering by the Back-Stairs, came where the King was; then the King commanded to open the Doors, and advanced to the Street. Upon Notice whereof, Sir Alexander Home of North-Berwick Provost of Edinburgh, with the Crafts, convoy'd the King to his Royal Palace at Holy Rood-House; from whence, next Morning, he went to Linlithgow, where he swore, 'Had it not ' been for the Loyalty of the Crafts, he would have burnt the Town of ' Edinburgh, and salted it with Salt.'

By the stedfast Adherence of the Crafts to their Sovereign, even when they did not approve of, but were sorry for his Actings, our Capital City was preserv'd from Destruction, as by their Behaviour afterwards, it flourished in his Favours.

On the last of that Month of December, the King came to Leith, and staid there all Night, giving Orders for his Entry into the Town of Edinburgh next Morning, which he did, and call'd for the Magistrates, to hear what they had to say for the late Tumult; which indeed was not owing to them, but to the *Hocus* of the Clergy and seditious Nobles, who practised upon the well-meaning People, making them believe, they were fighting the Battles of the LORD: So true is the Maxim.

*Fallere Plebem finge Deum.*

Sir Alexander Home Provost, Rodger M'Math, George Todrick, Patrick Cochran, and Alexander Hunter Baillies, with a Number of the Town Council, falling down on their Knees before the King, presented the following Offers.

'That for pacifying His Majesty's Wrath, and satisfying the Lords of Council, they ' should, upon their Oath, purge themselves of all Knowledge, or partaking in the said ' Tumult; and as they had already made a diligent Search to find out the Authors; so they ' should not cease, until they had brought the Trial to the utmost Point: Or, if his Majesty ' and Council should think fit to take the Examination, they should willingly resign their ' Place to such as his Highness would appoint, and assist him according to their Power: And

' because his Majesty had taken that Tumult to proceed from certain Sermons preach'd by
' their Ministers, they should be expell'd the City, never to return, without his Majesty's
' Warrant.' Upon which, the King was reconciled to them.

Thus the Crafts behav'd as loyally at this Juncture, as they did during the Troubles occasioned by the Earl of Bothwel, when the King was assaulted in his Palace of Holy-Rood-House, which obliged him to cry aloud from the Windows, *Treason, Treason.*

The Report of the Accident going to the City of Edinburgh, the Citizens went to Arms, and made towards the Palace to give the King Relief, who show'd himself from a Window to the People, gave them Thanks for their Readiness, and desir'd them to return to their Dwellings. As the Citizens gave repeated Instances of their Valour and Loyalty to the King, while he resided amongst us so after his Accession to the Throne of England, and when he return'd to his Native Country Scotland, and made his Entry into Edinburgh, 16. of May 1617, Joy appear'd in every one of their Countenances: they were ready to cry out in the Words of Ben-Johnston's *Magnetick Lady*,

> " Now let our longing Eyes enjoy their Feast,
> And Fill of thee, our fair shap'd God-like man.
> Thou art a Banquet unto all our Senses ;
> Thy Form doth feast our Eyes, thy Voice our Ears,
> As if we felt it ductile thro' our Blood."

This passionate Love is gracefully exprest by the famous Poet and Orator, William Drummond of Hawthornden, in his Speech to the King, in Name of the Town of Edinburgh.

' SIR, if Nature could suffer Rocks to move, and abandon their natural Places, this Town,
' founded on the Strength of Rocks, (now by the clearing Rays of your Majesty's
' Presence, taking not only Motion but Life) had, with her Castle, Temples, and Houses,
' mov'd towards You, and beseech'd You to have acknowledg'd her Your's, and her Indwellers
' Your most humble and affectionate Subjects ; and to believe, how many Souls are within her
' Circuits, so many Lives are devoted to Your sacred Person and Crown. And here, SIR, she
' offers, by me, to the Altar of Your Glory, whole Hecatombs of most hearty Desires, praying
' all things may prove prosperous to You, That every Virtue and heroick Grace which make a
' Prince eminent, may with a long and blessed Government, attend You ; Your Kingdoms
' flourishing abroad with Bays, at home with Olives. Presenting You, SIR, who art the
' strong Key of this little World of Britain, with these Keys, which cast up the Gates of her

' Affection, and design You Power to open all the Springs of the Hearts of those her most
' loyal Citizens : Yet this almost were not necessary : For as the Rose, at the fair Approach of
' the Morning Sun, displays and spreads her Purples ; so, at the very Noise of Your happy
' Return to this Your Native Country, their Hearts, if they could have shin'd through their
' Breasts, were, with Joy and fair Hopes, made spacious, nor did they ever, in all Parts, feel
' a more comfortable Heat, than the Glory of Your Presence at this Time darts upon them.

    ' The Old forget their Age, and look fresh and young, at the Appearance of so gracious a
' Prince ; the Young bear a Part in Your Welcome, desiring many Years of Life, that they
' may serve You long. All have more Joys than Tongues : For as the Words of other Nations
' far go beyond, and surpass the Affections of their Hearts ; so, in this Nation, the Affection
' of their Hearts is far above all they can express by Words. Deign then, SIR, from the
' highest of Majesty, to look down on their Lowness, and embrace it, accept the Homage of
' their humble Minds, accept their grateful Zeal ; and for Deeds, accept their great good Will,
' which they have ever carried to the high Deserts of Your Ancestors, and shall ever to your
' own, and Your Royal Race, whilst these Rocks shall be overshadowed with Buildings,
' Buildings inhabited by Men ; and while Men may be indued either with Counsel or Courage,
' or enjoy any Piece of Reason, Sense, or Life.'

    This Speech was followed by another delivered at the West Port of Edin-
burgh, when His Majesty entered, by Mr John Hay, Town-Clerk Depute.

' HOW joyful your Majesties Return (gracious and dread Sovereign) is to this your native
'      Town, from that Kingdom, due to your Sacred Person, by Royal Descent, the Counten-
' ances and Eyes of your Majesties Loyal Subjects speak for their Hearts. This is that happy
' Day of our new Birth, ever to be retain'd in fresh Memory, with Consideration of the Good-
' ness of Almighty GOD considered, with the Acknowledgment of the same, acknowledged
' with Admiration, admir'd with Love, and lov'd with Joy ; wherein our Eyes behold the
' greatest humane Felicity our Hearts could wish, which is to feed upon the Royal Counten-
' ance of our true Phœnix, the bright Star of our Northern Firmament, the Ornament of our
' Age, wherein we are refresh'd and reviv'd with the Heat, and bright Beams of our Sun, (the
' powerful Adamant of our Wealth) by whose removing from our Hemisphere, we were darkened,
' deep Sorrow and Fear possessing our Hearts, (without envying of your Majesty's Happiness
' and Felicity) our Places of Solace ever giving a new Heat to the Fever of the languishing
' Remembrance of our Happiness ; the very Hills and Groves, accustomed of before to be
' refresh'd with the Dew of your Majesties Presence, not putting on their wonted Apparel,
' but with pale Looks representing their Miserie for the Departure of their Royal King.

    ' I most humbly beg Pardon of your most sacred Majesty, who, most unworthy, and
' ungarnish'd by Art or Nature with Rhetorical Colours, have presum'd to deliver your Sacred
' Majesty, form'd by Nature, and fram'd by Art and Education to the Perfection of all

' Eloquence, the publick Message of your Majesties loyal Subjects here conveen'd, on the
' Knees of my Heart, beseeching your Sacred Majesty, that my Obedience to myne Superior's
' Commands, may be a Sacrifice acceptable to expiate my Presumption, your Majesties wonted
' Clemency may give Strength and Vigour to my distrustful Spirits, in gracious Acceptance
' of that which shall be delivered, and pardon my Escapes. Receive then, dread Sovereign,
' from your Majesties faithful and loyal Subjects the Magistrates and Citizens of your
' Highness's Good Town of Edinburgh, such Welcome as is due from these, who, with thankful
' Hearts, do acknowledge the Infinite Blessings plenteously flowing to them from the Paradise
' of your Majesty's unspotted Goodness and Virtue, wishing your Majesties Eyes might pierce
' into their very Hearts, to behold the excessive Joy inwardly conceiv'd of the first Messenger.
' Your Majesties Princely Resolution to visit your Majesties Good Town, encreas'd by your
' Majesties Countenance, in prosecuting what was so happily intended, and now accomplished
' by your Majesties fortunate and safe Return, which no Tongue, how liberal soever, is capable
' to express. Who shall consider with an impartial Eye, the continual Carefulness your
' Majesty had over us from your tender Years, the settled Temper of your Majesties Govern-
' ment, wherein the nicest Eye could find no Spot ; yourself, as the Life of the Country, the
' Father of the People, instructing not so much by Precept, as Example ; your Majesty's Court
' the Marriage Place of Wisdom and Godliness, without Impiety, cannot refuse to avouch :
' But as your Prudence has won the Prize from all Kings and Emperors, that stand in the
' Degree of Comparison ; so hath your Majesty's Government been such, that every Man's Eye
' may be a Messenger to his Mind, that your Majesty stands the Quintessence of ruling Skill
' of all prosperous and peaceable Government, much wisht by our Forefathers, but most
' abundantly enjoy'd by us, praised be GOD, under your sacred Majestie. For if we shall, in
' a View, lay before us the Times bypast, even since the first Foundation of the Kingdom, and
' therein consider their Majesties most noble Progenitors, they were indeed all Princes
' renown'd for their Virtues, not inferior to any Kings or Emperors of their Time, they
' maintain'd and deliver'd their Virgine Scepters unconquer'd, from Age to Age, from the
' Foundation of the most violent Floods of conquering Swords, which overwhelm'd the rest of
' the whole Earth, and carry'd the Crowns of all other Kings of this Terrestrial Ball unto
' Thraldom ; but far short of your Majesties Nature, having plac'd in your Sacred Person
' alone, what in every one of them was excellent, the Senate-House of the Planets being, as it
' were, conveen'd at your Majesties Birth, for decreeing of all Perfections in your Royal
' Person, the Heavens and Earth witnessing your Heroical Frame, no Influence whatsoever
' being able to bring the same to a higher Degree. If we shall bring to Mind the tumultuous
' Days of your Majesties more tender Years, and therein your Majesties Prudence, Wisdom
' and Constancy, in uniting the disjointed Members of the Common Wealth, who will not,
' with the Queen of Sheba, confess he has seen more Wisdom in your Royal Person, than
' Report hath brought to foreign Ears ; and there is not of any Estate or Age within this
' Kingdom, who has not had particular Experience of the same, and sensibly felt the Fruits

2 F

'thereof ; the Fire of civil Discord, which, as a Flame, devoured us, was thereby quench'd,
'every Man possess'd his own in Peace, reaping that which he had sown, and enjoying the
'Fruits of his own Labours, your Majesties great Vigilance and Godly Zeal in propagating
'the Gospel, and defacing the Monuments of Idolatry, banishing that Roman Antichristian
'Hierarchy, and establishing our Church, repairing the Ruins thereof, protecting us from
'foreign Invasion, the rich Trophies of your Majesties Victories more powerfully atchieved
'by your Sacred Wisdom, deserves more worthily than those of the Cæsars, so much extoll'd
'by the Ancients.    All Ages shall record, and Posterity bless Almighty GOD, for giving to us
'their Fore-fathers a King, in heart upright as David, wise as Solomon, and Godly as Josias.

'And who can better witness your Majesties Royal Favour and Beneficence, than this
'your Good Town of Edinburgh, which being founded in the Days of that worthy King
'Fergus I. the first Builder of the Kingdom, and famous for her unspotted Fidelity to your
'Majesties most noble Progenitors, was by them enrich'd with many Freedoms, Priviledges
'and Dignities ; all which your Majesty not only confirm'd, but also, with Accession of many
'more enlarg'd ; beautify'd her with a new erected College, famous for Profession of all liberal
'Sciences, so that she justly doth acknowledge your Majesty the Author and Conserver of
'her Peace, her Sacred Physician, who binds up the Wounds of her distracted Common
'Wealth, the only *Magnes* of her Prosperity, and the true Fountain, from whence, under
'GOD, all her Happiness and Felicity floweth, and doth in all Humility record your Majesties
'Royal Favour extended to her at all Times.

'Neither hath the Ocean of your Majesties Virtues contain'd it self within the Precinct of
'this Isle : What Ear is so barbourous, that hath not heard of the Fame of your Majesty ?
'What foreign Prince is not indebted to your Sacred Wisdom ?   What reformed Church doth
'not bless your Majesties Birth Day, is not protected under the Wings of your Sacred
'Authority from Antichristian Locusts, whose Walls, by the Sacred Wisdom wherewith your
'Sacred Person is endow'd, hath been batter'd and shaken more than did the Goths and
'Vandals the old Frame of the same by the Sword : And for your Sacred Virtue, your
'Majesty deserves to be Monarch of the World : So for your Piety and unfeigned Zeal, in
'propagating and maintaining the Gospel does, of due, appertain to your Majestie, the Titles
'of most Christian and Catholick King.

'For all which, your Majesties most Royal Favours, having nothing to render but that
'which is due, we, your Majesties most humble Subjects, prostrate at your Sacred Feet, lay
'down our Lives, Goods, Liberties, and every Thing that is dear to us, vowing to keep to your
'Sacred Majesty, unspotted Loyalty and Subjection, and ever to be ready to consecrate and
'sacrifice our selves for Maintenance of your Royal Person and Estate, praying to the Eternal,
'our GOD, that Peace may be within your Majesties Walls, and Prosperity within your
'Palaces, length of Days to your Sacred Person ; that from your Majesties Loins may never
'be wanting one to sway the Scepter of these your Kingdoms, and that Mercy may be to your
'self and your Seed for ever.'

After the Delivery of this Speech, His Majesty went to the great Church, and there having heard Sermon from the Arch-Bishop of St. Andrews, Primate of all Scotland, proceeded on His March to His Palace of Holy Rood-House. At the Gate of the Inner Court was presented to His Royal Hands, a Book in Manuscript, of curious and learned Verses in Greek and Latin, entituled *Academiæ Edinburgensis Congratulatio*, and a Speech made in Name of that University by Mr Patrick Nisbet. Next Day, His Majesty was pleas'd to honour the University with His Presence at a Philosophical Disputation in the Oriental Languages, by the Professors of Philosophy, Mr John Adamson, Mr James Fairly, Mr Patrick Sands, Mr Andrew Young, Mr James Reid, and Mr William King. When the Exercise was over, His Majesty was pleas'd to compliment the Disputants in the following Poem, which by them was variously paraphrased in Latin.

> "As *Adam* was the first of Men, whence all beginning take,
> So *Adam-son* was President, and first Man of this Act.
> The Thesis *Fair-lie* did defend, which tho' they lies contain ;
> Yet were fair Lies, and he the same right fairly did maintain.
> The Field first entered Mr *Sands*, and there he made me see,
> That not all Sands are barren Sands, but that some fertile be.
> Then Mr *Young* most subtily the Theses did impugn,
> And kythed old in *Aristotle*, altho' his Name be *Young*.
> To him succeeded Mr *Reid*, who tho' *Red* be his Name,
> Need neither for his Dispute blush, nor of his Speech think Shame.
> Last enter'd Mr *King* the Lists, and dispute like a King,
> How Reason reigning like a Queen, should Anger underbring.
> To their deserved Praise have I thus played upon their Names,
> And wills this College hence be call'd the College of King JAMES.

Manifold Honours the King put upon this his Good Town of Edinburgh, in the Castle whereof he was born ; as appears by the Inscription yet remaining in the Room, where his mother, Queen Mary, was delivered of him, which runs thus :—

> "O JESU LORD, who crownit was with thorn,
> Preserve the Birth whais Badgie here is born,
> And grant, O LORD, that whatever of her proceed,
> May be unto they honour and Glory. Soe beid."

His Majesty, by a Charter under his great Seal, dispones to the Provost, Baillies, Town Council, and Community of the Burgh of Edinburgh, the Jurisdiction, Haven, and Harbour of Leith, and makes and constitutes them Judges amongst the Skippers, Masters and Mariners in Leith, and all other Skippers, Masters, and Sailors, as well his Subjects as Foreigners, being for the Time with their Ships, Boats, or Barks within the same Village of Leith, and Harbour of the same, in all Sea-fareing Actions and Causes whatsomever, with Power to them to make Acts and Statutes for the Increase of Sailing. And dispones to them the prime Gilt to be uplifted for sustaining of poor indigent Sea-Men within the said Village of Leith, forth of the Freight of every Tun of Goods, in manner specified in the said Charter, to be applied to the Use of the said Poor. This Charter is dated at Whitehall, 3d April 1616.

By another Charter under the great Seal, he confirms to the Magistrates, Town Council, Crafts, and Community of the said Burgh, and their Successors, all former Infeftments granted to them by his Predecessors, of the heretable Offices of Sheriff-ship, Crownry, which contains a new Gift of the Sheriff-ship and Crownry within the said Burgh, common Mills thereof, common Muir, Marish, Loch, Parts, Streets, common Ways, Passages, and Loanings, leading to and from the same; and especially the Passage leading to Leith upon both Sides of the Water thereof, and to the said Village of Leith, Haven of the samen, and within the Harbour and Village of Newhaven, and Village of Leith, Havens, Roads, Harbours, and Bulwarks thereof, and within the Lands of common Closets, Burshoilf, Passages, and other Bounds whatsoever, lying within the Liberty of the said Burgh of Edinburgh. Dated at Whitehall, 3d April 1616.

By a Gift under his Great Seal, grants to the said Provost, Baillies, and Council, the Power of having the Sword carried before them, Riding of the Marches or Bounds thereof, and of the Office of Justice of Peace, in manner therein-contain'd. Dated at Whitehall, 10th November 1609.

By another Gift, he enlarges their Powers as Justices of Peace, in which they are infeft. Dated at Hamptoun Court, 25th September 1612.

By another Gift and Infeftment, grants to them all Fines and Ammerciaments belonging to the Office of Sheriff-ship and Justiciaries of Peace. Dated at Whitehall, 17th September 1613.

By another Charter under the Great Seal, dispones to them the Custom or Excise (and to their Successors) of Four Pounds Scots, forth of every Tun of Wine to be retailed and vented in Smalls within the said Burgh, Liberties, and Jurisdiction of the same, to be uplifted by their Treasurers, Collectors, and others in their names, from the Retailers, Vinters, Tapsters, and Sellers of the same, in all Time coming. Dated at Whitehall, 10th November 1609.

By a Ratification of the said Gift, and new Disposition, he dispones the foresaid Custom and Excise of Four Pound, forth of every Tun retailed within the Village of Leith, in all Parts within the same upon the South side of the Water of Leith. Dated at Hampton, 25th September 1612.

By another under the Great Seal, Power to them and their Successors to erect a Weigh-house at the Over-Tron of the said Burgh, with divers Liberties, Duties, and Immunities therein contained. Dated at Royston, 9th December 1611.

By a Charter under his Great Seal, dispones that Part of the Lands of Highrigs, containing 10 acres of Land or thereby. Dated at Edinburgh, 30th July 1618.

By a Gift under his Great Seal, gives and grants the Jedgry of Salmon Herrings, and White Fish, packed and peill'd within the Kingdom of Scotland. Dated at Royston, 19th October 1618.

By another Gift under his Great Seal, the Power of being Overseers and Visiters of all Measurers and Sellers of Cloath, Stuffs, and Stockings made in the said Village of Leith, and Sheriffdom of Edinburgh. Dated at Whitehall, 8th March 1621.

By a Charter under his Great Seal, dated at Stirling, 14th April 1582. ratifying a Charter made by Queen Mary under her Great Seal, dated 13th March 1566, of the Lands, Tenements, Houses and Biggings, Churches, Chaplainries, Altarages, and Prebendaries, in whatsoever Churches, Chapels, or Colleges, within the Liberty of the said Burgh, founded by whatsoever Person, whereof the said Chaplain and Prebends were in Possession, with the Yards, Orchards, Annualrents, Teinds, Services, Profits, Duties, Emoluments which pertained thereto, and of all Lands which pertained to the Black Friars and Gray Friars.

By another Charter he ratifies and approves the Demission and Ratification made by John Gib, in Favours of the said Burgh of the Provostry of the Kirkfield, haill Lands and Biggings belonging to the same. And dispones the Liberty of a College, and repairing sufficient Houses for accommodating the Professors of Philosophy, Humanity and Languages, Theology, Medicine, Law, and all other Sciences; and electing sufficient Professors for teaching the said Professions; and for that Effect, disponed to them the Provostry of Kirkfield, with the Tenements, Fruits, Possessions, Rents and Duties thereof.

By another Charter under his Great Seal, 4th April 1584, considering, That the Burgh of Edinburgh had been at great Expenses in erecting the said College, and had gifted great Sums for sustaining the Professors for instructing the Youth, he disponed to the Good Town, for the Use of the said College, and for Maintenance of the Principal and Regents, the Arch-deanry of Lothian, containing the Parsonage of Curry, with the Manse, Glebe, and Kirk Lands, Teinds and Duties of the same.

By another Charter under his Great Seal, 26th May 1587, for the great Expences wared out by the Good Town, in erecting an Hospital for maintaining their Ministers, disponed to the Town the Provostry of the Trinity College, House-Rents, Kirk-Teinds, and Fruits thereto pertaining.

By another Charter under his Great Seal, 29th July 1587, Ratifies the Infeftments granted by himself and Queen Mary, his Mother, of the said Kirk-Lands, Trinity College, Provostry of Kirkfield, and Arch-deanry of Lothian, for the Use of the Ministers, College, and Poor.

By another Charter under the Great Seal, dated at Bearboar Castle, 1612, Ratifies all former Grants of the said Kirk-Lands, Provostries of Kirkfield, and Trinity-College, and Arch-deanry of Lothian, with a new Gift of the saids haill Kirk-Lands, for maintaining the Ministers, College, and Poor.

Thus did that just and gracious Prince show his Beneficence to our Metropolis, as the wise King Solomon, in his Book of Ethicks, remarks, "When the Righteous are in Authority, the City rejoyceth; but when the "Wicked bear Rule, the People mourn." And being a peaceful Prince as well as generous, he poured Oil into the Wounds of his People, and healed

the growing Contentions betwixt the Merchants and Trades, by the subsequent Decreet-Arbitral.

AT Halyruidhouse, the Twenty twa Day of Apryl, the Yeir of GOD One
thousand five hundred fourscore three Years; We Robert Fairlie of Braid,
Sir Archibald Naper of Edinbellie Knight, and James Johnstoun of Elphind-
stoun, Judges Arbitrators, chosen for the Part of Mr Michael Chisolme,
Andrew Sclater, John Adamsone, and William Fairlie Baillies of Edinburgh,
Mr John Prestoun Dean of Gild, Mungo Russel Thesaurer, John Johnstoun,
Robert Ker Younger, Henry Charters, John Morisone, William Maul, John
Harwood, John Robertsone, William Inglis, Alexander Naper, William Nesbet,
Merchants; being on the Counsel of the said Burgh, for themselves, and in
Name and Behalf, and as Commissioners for the hail Merchants Indwellers
of the said Burgh, on the ane Part, and John Cockburn of Ormestoun, Mr
Robert Pont Provost of the Trinity-Colledge, and Mr David Lindsey Minister
of Leith, Judges Arbitrators chosen for the Part of James Fergusone Bower,
John Bairnsfather Tailyeour, twa of the Crafts-men, being on the Counsel
of the said Burgh; Gilbert Prymrose Deaken of the Chirurgians, John Watt
Deaken of the Hammermen, William Hoppringle Deaken of the Tailyeours,
Edward Gilbraith Deaken of the Skinners, Edward Hairt Deaken of the
Gold-Smiths, Adam Newtoun Deaken of the Baxters, Thomas Dicksone
Deaken of the Furriers, Andrew Williamsone Deaken of the Wrights, William
Bickertoun Deaken of the Maissons, James Ker Deaken of the Fleshers,
William Weir Deaken of the Cordiners, Thomas Wright Deaken of the
Websters, William Cowtts Deaken of the Wakers, and William Somer Deaken
of the Bonnet-makers; for themselves, and in Name and behalf, and as
Commissioners for the hail Crafts-men, Indwellers of the said Brugh, on the
uther part: And the right potent and illustrious Prince, JAMES be the
Grace of GOD, King of Scots, our Soveraign Lord, Ods-man and Oversman,
commonly chosen be Advice and Consent of baith the saids Parties, anent
the removing of all Questions, Differences and Controversies, quhilks are, or hes
been betwixt the said Merchants, concerning whatsomever Cause or Occasion
whereupon Debate or Question did arise in any Time betwixt them. And

thereupon baith the saids Parties being Bund, Oblist, and Sworn, to stand, abide underly, and fulfil the Decreet-Arbitral and Deliverance of us the saids Judges and Overs-man, but Appellation, Reclamation, or Contradiction, as at length is contained in ane Submission made thereupon, baith the saids Parties Clames and Griefs given in be them, with the Answers made thereto, and their Rights, Reasons, and Alledgances being heard, seen, and considered be us, and we therewith being ryply advysit, after many sundry Conventions and Meetings, with lang Travels tane hereanent, hes all in ane Voice accordit, decernit, and concludit, upon the Heads and Articles following.

*First,* To take away all Differences quhilk hes been heretofore, concerning the Persons who had the Government of the Town, their Number, Power, or Authority, and Manner of their Election; It is finally accordit and decernit thereupon as follows:—

### MAGISTRATS.

THE Magistrats, sic as Provest, Baillies, Dean of Gild, and Thesaurer, to be in all Tymes coming of the Estait and Calling of Merchants, conforme to the Acts of Parliament; and if any Crafts-man Exerceand Merchandize, sall for his guid Qualities be promovit theirto, in that Caise he sall leive his Craft, and not occupy the same be himself nor his Servants during the Tyme of his Office, and sall not return theirto at any Tyme theireafter, quhill he obtein special Licence of the Provest, Baillies and Counsel to that Effect.

### COUNSEL.

THE Counsel to consist of Ten Merchants, to wit, The auld Provest, Four auld Baillies, Dean of Gild and Thesaurer of the nixt Year preceiding, and Three Merchants to be chosen to them, and als to consist of Eight Craftsmen theirof, Sex Deakens and Twa uther Crafts-men, makand in the hail the said Counsel Eighteen Persons, and this by the Office-men of that Year, to wit, the Provost, Baillies, Dean of Gild, and Thesaurer.

## ELECTION.

AND as to the Manner of their Election, It is first generally accordit and agriet, That na manner of Person be chosen Provost, Baillies, Dean of Gild, or Theasurer, suppose they be Burgesses of the Burgh, and able therefore, without they have been ane Year or Twa upon the Counsel of before. And anent the Counsel, the auld Maner of giving in of Tickets be the Deakens, out of the quhilk the Twa Crafts-men were Yearly chosen, to be abrogat, cease and expyre in all Tymes coming, swa that the saids Twa Crafts-men shall be chosen Yearly without any Ingiving of Tickets indifferently, of the best and worthiest of the Crafts, be the saids Provest, Baillies, Dean of Gild, Theasurer and Counsel allanerly, and nane to be on the Counsel above Twa Year together, except they be Office-men, or be Vertue of their Offices be on the Counsel. Sicklike, anent the Lytts to be Baillies, they sall not be dividet nor casten in Four Ranks, Three to every Rank, as they were wont to be ; bot to be chosen indifferently, Ane out of the Twelff Lytts, Ane uther out of Eleven Lytts, the Third out of Ten, and the Fourt out of Nyne Lytts. Anent the Deakens, That nane be electit Deaken, except he that hes been an Maister of his Craft twa Year at the least : and that nane of them be continued in their Offices of Deakenship above twa Year togidder. Last in general, That nane have Vote in Lytting, Voiting, Electing of the Provest, Baillies, Counsel, Deakens, Dean of Gild, or Theasurer, but the Persons hereafter following, in manner after specifiet.

## Election in special of DEAKENS.

AND to proceid to the said Election ; It is found guid to begin at the choosing of the Deakens of Crafts, quhilks are Fourteen in Number, to wit, Chirurgeans, Goldsymths, Skynners, Furriers, Hammermen, Wrights, Masons, Tailyeours, Baxters, Fleshers, Cordiners, Websters, Wakers, Bonnet-makers ; Swa the Deakens now present shall stand and continue quhil the third Counsel-day of before the auld Time of Election of the new Counsel, quhilk was on the Wednesday next preceding the Feast of Michaelmass ; upon the quhilk third

2 G

Counsel-day, the Provest, Baillies, and Counsel now standand, extending to Nineteen Persons, and fra thence furth Yearly, and ilk Year, the Provest, Baillies and Counsel, constitute of the said Twenty Five Persons, sall call in before them the saids Deakens of Crafts, every ane severally, and inquire their Opinion and Judgement of the best and worthiest of their Crafts; Thereafter, the saids Provest, Baillies and Counsel, shall Nominat and Lytt three Persons of the maist Discreet, Godly, and Qualified Persons of every ane of the saids Fourteen Crafts, maist expert Hand-labourers of their awen Craft, Burgesses and Freemen of the Burgh of Edinburgh, whereof the auld Deaken shall be ane, and cause deliver their Names to the Deakens, every ane according to their Craft. Quhilk Deakens, on the Morn thereafter, sall assemble and convein their Crafts, and every Craft be themselves, furth of thir Names shall elect ane Person wha sall be their Deaken for that Year; and, upon the next Counsel-day after the said Election, the auld Deakens, with some of the Masters of their Crafts, sall present the new Deakens to the Counsel, quha sall authorise them in their Offices.

### New Counsel of DEAKENS.

NEXT, To proceed to the Election of the New Counsel. The said Day of presenting of the new Deakens, the Provest, Baillies, and Counsel now standand of Nineteen Persons, and fra then furth, the said Day yearly; The Provest, Baillies and Counsell, of Twenty five Persons, sall chose furth of the saids fourteen Deakens, Sex Persons to be adjoined with the new Counsel for the Year to come, and to have special Vote in lytting and choosing of the Provest, Baillies and Counsel; and the same Day, the auld Sex Deakens quhilk was upon the Counsel the Year preceeding, to be removed, and have an farther Vote for that Year, except some of them be of the Number of the new elected Deakens.

### New Counsel of MERCHANTS and CRAFTS.

THEREAFTER, Upon the Wednesday next, preceding Michaelmas ilk Year, the Provest, Baillies, Dean of Gild, Thesaurer, and Ten Merchants of the Counsel

and the said Sex Deakens, and twa Crafts-men, and in the hail Twenty-five
Persons, and Twenty-sex Votes, be Reason of the Provest's twa Votes ordinarly
standand at all Tymes, sall conveen and choose the new Counsel, to the
Number of Eighteen Persons, to wit, the auld Provest, Baillies, Dean of Gild
and Thesaurer of that Year, and the said Sex Deacons, to make Thirteen
Persons thereof, and to them to be chosen Three Merchants, and Twa Crafts-
men, and thir Persons to be callit the New Counsel; and if any Person of the
Merchants chosen upon the New Counsel, happens to be put on the Lytte of
ane uther Ofice, and promovit thereto, an uther shall be chosen in his Room
be the saids Provest, Baillies, and Counsel.

## Lytts of MAGISTRATS.

THIRDLY, To proceid to the choosing of the Lytts to the Magistrats and Office-
men, sic as Provest, Baillies, Dean of Gild and Theasurer, upon the Friday nixt
thereafter, there sall conveen the said New Counsel of Eighteen Persons, and
the Auld Counsel constitute of Twelff Persons, viz., Ten Merchants, and Twa
Crafts-men, and in the hail Thretty Persons to the Provest's odd Vote; quhilks
Persons so solemnatly protesting before GOD, that they sall choose the Persons
whom they find maist meet, without Favour, Hatred, or any kind of Collusion;
then sall begin and choose the Lytts to the said Magistrats and Office-men, to
every ane of them three Lytts; that is to say, to the Provest, twa Lytts with
himself; to the four Baillies, every ane of them three Lytts, the auld Baillies
not beand ane, except they be new chosen thereto; to the Dean of Gild, twa
Lytts with himself; and to the Theasurer, twa Lytts with himself: Quhilks
hail Lytts sall be of the Order and Calling of Merchants, as said is.

## Election of MAGISTRATS.

FOURTHLY, To proceed to the electing and choosing of the said Magistrats and
Office-men; Upon the Tuesday nixt after Michaelmass yearly, there sall
conveen the saids Thretty Persons, of new and auld Counsel, and with them

the rest of the Deakens of Crafts quhilks are not of the Counsel, extending
to Eight Persons: the hail Persons swa conveenand, extending to Thretty-
eight Persons by the Provest's odde Vote, whereof Twenty Merchants, and
Eighteen Crafts-men; quhilks Persons sall begin at the Lytts of the Provest
and every ane in their awen Rank, give their Votes to sic as they find meet
for the weill of the Town, according to their Conscience and Knawledge, but
feid or Favour; and on whom the greatest Number of Votes sall fall, that he
be sworn, receivit and admittit Provest for that Year; and swa to proceed
throw the Lytts of the Baillies, Dean of Gild, and Thesaurer, quhilk the
said Election be compleatly endit. The saids Provest, Baillies, Dean of Gild,
Thesaurer, and Counsel, electit, as said is, makand in the hail Twenty-five
Persons; they only, and nae uthers, sall have the full Government and
Administration of the hail Common-weal of this Brugh, in all Things, as the
Provest, Baillies, and Counsel thereof, or of any uther Brugh had of before,
or may have hereafter, be the Laws or Consuetude of this Realm, Infeftments,
and Priviledges grantit to this Town be Our Sovereign Lord's maist Noble
Progenitors, exceptand always thir Causes following, in the quhilks the hail
Fourteen Deakens of Crafts sall be callit and adjoined with them, to give their
special Vote and Consultation thereinto, to wit, In Election of the Provest,
Baillies, Dean of Gild, and Thesaurer, as said is, In setting of Fews, or any
manner of Tacks, attour the yearly Rowping, on Martinmass Even, In giving
of Benefices, and uther Offices in Burgh, In granting of Extents, Contributions,
Emprimits, and sicklike bigging of common Warks, and in disponing of the
Common Good, above the Sum of Twenty Pound togidder.


## Wairning of the DEAKENS and COUNSEL.

PROVIDING nevertheless, that the Deakens not of the Counsel, or any of them,
beand personally warned to that Effect, and absenting themself, swa oft the
last Deaken, or any uther that was in Lytt with him that Yeir, shall supplie their
Room; and they beand personally warned, and absent, the rest compearand sall
have Power to proceed. If any of the Provest, Baillies, and Counsel be absent,

the rest wha are present sall choose an uther in their Room. And to avoid all Suspicioun that hes risen in Times past, through the particular Aseemblies and Conventiouns, contrair to the Acts of Parliaments, and to the Trouble of the Quyet Estait of this Brugh.

## CONVENTIOUNS.

It is agreit and concludit, that nather the Merchants amang themselfs, nather the Crafts and their Deakens, or Visitors, sall have, or make any particular or general Conventions, as Deakens with Deakens, Deakens with their Crafts, or Crafts amang themselfs, far less to make privat Laws, or Statutes, Poynd, and Distrenzie at their awen Hands for Trangressions, by the Advice and Consent of the Provest, Baillies, and Counsel.

## DEAN of GILD may conveen his COUNSEL.

EXCEPTAND always, that the Dean of Gild may assemble his Brethren and Counsel in their Gild Court, conform to their ancient Lawes of the Gildrie, and Priviledges thereof: And that any ane Craft may conveen together amang themselfs, for the choosing of their Deakens at the Tyme appointit thereto, and in manner before exprest; making of Masters and trying of their Handie-wark allanerly. And if any Brethren, or Deakens of Crafts, sall find out, or devyse any good Heids, that may tend to the Weill of their Craft, they sall propone the same to the Magistrates, wha sall set forward an Act or Statute thairupon.

## COMMISSIONERS.

*Item.* As tuitching the Commissioners in Parliament, General Counsel, and Commissioners in Conventioun of Burrows, it is thought guid be the Commissioners, that in all Tymes coming, the ane of the saids Commissioners for the Brugh of Edinburgh, sall be chosen be the said Provost and Baillies, furth of the Number and Calling of the Crafts-men, and that Person to be ane Burgess and Gild-Brother of the Brugh, of the best, expert and wise, and of Honest Conversation.

### AUDITORS.

*Item.* It is agreed, that the Auditors of all the Towns Compts sall hereafter be chosen of equal Number of Merchants and Crafts-men, be the Provest, Baillies, and Counsel.

### GILDRIE.

*Item,* Toward the long Controversies for the Gildrie, it is finally, with common Consent appointit, agreit and concludit, That als weill Crafts-men, as Merchants, sall be received and admitted Gild-Brether, and the ane not to be refuisit, or secludit therefrae mair nor the uther, they being burgesses of the Burgh, als meit and qualified thairfore; and that Gild-Brether have Liberty to use Merchandice. Their Admission, and Tryal of their Qualificatioun, to be in the Power and Hands of the Provest, Baillies, Thesaurer, and Counsel, with the Dean of Gild, and his Counsel, quhilk sall consist in equal Number of Merchants and Crafts-men, Gild-Brether, not exceiding the Number of sex Persons, by the Dean of Gild himself; and that no Person, of what Faculty soever he be, sall bruik the Benefit of an Gild-Brother, without he be receivit and admittit thereto, as said is.

### BURGESSES, CRAFTS.

*Item.* That na manner of Person be sufferit to use Merchandise, or occupy the Handie-wark of ane free Crafts-man within this Burgh, or yet to exerce the Liberty and Priviledge of the said Burgh, without he be Burgess and Freeman of the same.

### EXTENTS.

*Item.* Because the Merchants and Crafts-men of this Burgh, are now to be Incorporat in ane Society, and to make an haill Town, and an Common-weill, it is thought guid and expedient, and concludit, to abrogat the former Custome of dividing and setting of Extents, wherein the Merchants payit Four Pairts, and the Crafts the Fift Part. And therefore it is agried, that as they watch and waird together: Swa in all Extents, Emprimits, Contributions, and the like Subsidies to be imposit upon the Brugh, Merchants and Crafts-men to bear the

Burden and charge thereof indifferently overheid, according to their Ability and Substance, throw the haill Quarters of the Town, without Division of the Rolls in Merchants and Craftsmen in any Tyme coming; the Extentours sall be of equal Number of Merchants and Crafts-men, eight Persons of the ane Calling, and eight Persons of the uther, to be electit sworn and receivit be the Provest Baillies, and Counsel, out of the maist Discreit and Skilful of all the Town, void of all partial Affectioun and Hatred: And that nae Person usand the Trade of Merchant or Crafts-man, and occupyand the friedome of the Brugh, and able to pay any Extent, not beirand the Office of Provest or Baillies in the mean Time, sall be any wayis exemit frae the real and actual Payment thereof.

## COLLECTIOUN.

*Item*, As the hail Body of the Town, consistand of Merchants and Crafts-men, does beir an common Burden of Watching, Wairding, Extenting, and of the like Publick Charges, having an Commoun Good proper to nane, swa neidful it is for making an equal Unity, and charitable Concord, that there be in the hail Town but an Collectioun, and an Purse, not peculiar to any, bot common to all, of the haill Duties and Casualities, callit the Entres Silver of Prenteisses, Upsetts, Owkly Pennies, Unlaw, and sicklike, to be collected in all Tyme coming, and received baith of Merchants and Crafts-men, and put in an Common Purse, and to that Effect the Merchants to take and have Prentices, als weill as Crafts-men, and to be astrictit and obliest theirto, and na Prentice alwayes to be received of ather of them, for shorter Tyme nor the Space of fyve Yeirs compleit. And for the better Knowledge to be had heirof, and for observing an good Ordour in Collectioun of the same, that there be an commoun Book made, keipit be the commoun Clerk of this Brugh present, and to come, wherein the Names of all Prentices to Merchants, and Craftsmen, the Name of their Master, Day of their Entreis, and Space of their Penticeship, sall be insert and bookit: For the quhilk, the Clerk sall have at their Buiking of ilk Person, sex Pennies, and for the Out-draught Twelff Pennies; quhilk Buik sall be to the Prentice an sufficient Probation of his Entres, and an Charge to the Collectors of the said Dewties. If any man be an Prenteis heirafter, and not put in the said Buik, his Prenteiship sall be to him of na Effect. Alswa, be Reason every Industry is not of like Valour and Substance, it is declarit what ilk Rank or Degree of Prenteisses sall Pay, to wit, the Merchant Prenteis, and sic Kind of People as were wont to extent with them, and are not under an of the said Fourteen Crafts, to pay at his Entres the Day of his Buiking, to the said Collection Thirtie Shilling, and at his Upsett, or End of his Prenteiship fyve Pund. The Prenteis to an Skinner, Chirurgean, Gold-Smyth, Flesher, Cordiner, Tailyeour, Baxter, and Hammer-man, at their Entry and Buiking, to the said Collectioun Twenty Shilling, and for their Upsett fyve Pund: The Prenteis to an Masoun and Wright, at his Entrie thretteen Shilling four Pennies, and his Up-sett, three Pund sex Shilling eight Pennies. The Prenteis to an Webster, Waker, Bonnet-Maker, Furrier, at his Entry, ten Shilling, and for his Up-sett fyftie Shilling; and thir Dewties to be tane by their owkly Pennies, and Dewties of their Burgeships. And to cause all Persons to be mair willing to enter themselfs in Prentiship with the Burgesses and Friemen of the Brugh, this Priviledge is grantit to the saids Prenteises, That they sall pay nae mair for their Burgeship to the Dean of Gild, but fyve Punds by the Dewties foirsaids: And in Augmentatioun of the said Collectioun, when any Persons sall happen to be made Burgesses of this Brugh, wha was na Prenteis to an Merchant, or Craftsman, frie Burgess of the said Brugh, or hes not compleit his Prenteiship, sall pay to the said Collectioun, at his Admission, the double of the haill Prenteis or Entres-Silver, Up-sett and Buiking, by the Dewty paid to the Dean of Gild for his Burgeship, or Gildrie, quhilk is twenty Punds for his Burgeship, and forty Pund for his Gildrie, the Priviledge always of the Bairns of Burgesses and Gild-Brether not being prejudged heirby, quha sall pay the auld and accustomed Dewty to the Dean of Gild allanerly. Thir Dewties and Collectiouns, or Casualities of Entres-Silver, Up-setts, owkly Pennies, Un-laws, and sik-like, to be received in all Times coming, of all Merchants and Crafts-men indifferently put in the said common Purse, and imploit be the Advice and Command of the Provest, Baillies and Counsel, for Support and Relief of the failyiet and decayet Burgesses and Craftsmen, their Wyfes, Bairns, and auld Servants, and uther poor Indwellers of the Town. The Provest, Baillies, Counsel, and hail Deakens every Yeir after Electioun of the Magistrates, sall choose the Collectors of the said Dewties and Casualities, of equal Number of Merchants and Crafts-men, and to devyse and set down sic good Ordour as they sall find meet and expedient for the perfyte and readie In-bringing thereof. And last, the said Collectors sall make yeirly Compts of their Intromissioun therewith, at the Tyme of making of the Town's Compts, and sall find sufficient Cautioun at their Admissioun, for Compt, Reckoning and Payment. *Item*, It is ordained, that baith the saids Parties, Merchant and Crafts-men now present, and their Successors, sall inviolably observe, keip, and fulfill this present Appointment and Decreit Arbitral, and every Heid, Clause, and Article conteinit therein. Likeas, His Majesty, and the saids Judges, wills and ordains them, with willing Hearts, to put in Oblivion all bypast Enormities, imbrace and intertein Love and Amity, and as they are of ane City, swa to be of ane Mind ; then sall they be acceptit of GOD, stop the Mouths of them quhilk tuik Occasion be their Division to slander the Truth ; then sall they be mair able to do our Sovereign Lord acceptable Service, and have ane standing and flourishing Common-Weall. And finally, His Majesty and the saids Judges will esteem their lang Travels fruitfully bestowit.

## CERTIFICATION OF THE SETT.

ATTOUR, His Majesty and the saids Judges, Ordains the Practice and Execution of this present Appointment and Decreet to be and begin after the Day and Date hereof, and to continue, and be observit and kepit as ane perpetual Law in Tyme coming; and whasoever contraveins the samen, sall be repute and halden ane Troubler of the quiet Estate of the Common-weal, incurre the Note of Infamy, and forfault and tyne their Freedome for ever, and otherways to be persewit and punisht as seditious Persons, conform to the Laws of the Realm, with all Rigor and Extremity ; and ordains thir Presents to be Ratifiet and Approvit in his Highness next Parliament; and in the mean Tyme, the same to be Actit and Registrat in the Buiks of Counsel and Session, and to have the Strength of Acts and Decreets of the Lords thereof, and that their Authority be interponit thereto, and Letters and Executorials to pass thereupon in Form as effeirs; and for acting and registrating of the samen, Makes and constituts M$^{rs}$ John Sharp, John Prestoun, Thomas Craig, and John Skeen, our Procurators, conjunctly and severally, *in uberiore forma Promittendo de rato.* In Witness whereof, the saids Judges and Oversman, togidder with the saids Commissioners, in Token of their Consents and Acceptation of the Premisses, has subscrivit thir Presents with their Hands, Day, Year, and Place foresaids.

JAMES R. &c.

All the Charters and Donations in favours of the Town of Edinburgh, granted before and since the Union of the Two Crowns of Scotland and England, were confirmed by the succeeding Monarch CHARLES I. Whose Charter of Confirmation narrates, 'That calling to his Royal Memory, and ' perfectly understanding the many good, notable, and thankful Services ' perform'd by the Magistrates and Inhabitants of Edinburgh, the chief City ' and Burgh of the Ancient Kingdom of Scotland, not only to himself since ' his happy Accession to the Kingdom, but also to his dearest Father of ' Eternal Memory, and his other most Famous Progenitors, the particular and ' notable Expressions whereof, are contained in the ancient Infeftments ' granted to them by his Predecessors of Eternal Memory, which remain to ' Posterity as Signs of their Fidelity, and great and egregious Services done ' and performed by them, for the Good and Honour of the Kingdom: There- ' fore, confirmed,' &c. And did grant to the Magistrates of the said Town and Successors, the presenting and nominating of Ministers for serving the Cures in the haill Churches built, or to be built within the said Town, with the Right of patronage of the said haill Kirks in all Time coming. As also confirmed to them the said City, Town-Walls, Ditches, Ports, Streets, Passages, Paths, Lands, Territories, and Community of the same, with the common Lands called the Common Muir, Easter and Wester, and common Mire thereof; together with the South Loch, called the Burrow Loch, and the Loch of the said City called the North Loch, with the Lands of old called the Greenside, with the Leper-house and Yard situate on the same, arable Lands, Banks, and Marishes thereof, for the present occupied by the Lepers of the said House. And granted to the said Burgh the sole Liberty of Merchandice pertaining to a Free Royal Burgh, within the Bounds of the Sheriffdom of Edinburgh, and the Privileges of Weekly Markets every Monday, Wednesday, and Friday, or any Three Days of the Week that they shall appoint, with two Yearly Fairs, viz., Hallow-Fair and Trinity-Fair, with the haill small Customs, according to Use and Wont, especially the Sheriff Fee and Sheriff Glaves. And thereby enacted the Village of Leith into a Burgh of Barony, with Power to the Magistrates of Edinburgh to choice Baillies and Officers therein, and making laws for governing thereof. Which Charter is dated at Newmarket, 23d October 1636, and 12th Year of his Reign, before Witnesses, the most Reverend Father in Christ, and his well-beloved Counsellor, John, by the Mercy of GOD, Archbishop of St. Andrews, &c., Primate and Metropolitan of the Kingdom of Scotland, &c., his Chancellor, his well-beloved Cousin and Counsellor, James, Marquess of Hamilton, Earl of Arran and Cambridge, Lord Aven and Innerdale, &c., Thomas, Earl of Haddington, Lord Binning and Byris, Keeper of the Privy Seal; William, Earl of Stirling, Viscount of Canada, Lord Alexander of Tullibody, &c., his Secretary, his well-beloved familiar Counsellor, Sir John Hay of Barro, Clerk to his Council, Registers, and Rolls; John Hamiltoun of Orbistoun, Justice-Clerk; and John Scott of Scotstarvit, Director to his Chancellary, Knights.

These Charters shew the pious Care and Compassion of our Sovereigns for the Poor; And here, I were very unjust to our Mother City, as well as to the Memory of that Great, Good Man, GEORGE HERIOT, Burgess and Gold-smith of Edinburgh, Jeweller to the Two Renown'd Princes, JAMES VI., and this King CHARLES; if I should forget his pious Mortification to the Poor, and the magnificent Fabrick which he erected for their Hospital, Anno 1627. The Mortifications I have formerly mentioned relating to St. Eloi and St. Mungo's Altars flowed rather from Self-Interest than Charity, the Patrons believing, by their Donations, to merit Heaven, as the Charity expresses it (such is the blindness of Popery), and claimed it as purchas'd and paid for: But this Protestant Founder was a Stranger to the uncouth doctrine of Merit. He knew that Salvation is the Gift of GOD thro' CHRIST JESUS; That good Works are the Fruit and natural Result of Faith; That rich Men are the Stewards of GOD'S Goodness, the Messengers of His Favours, the Conduit-pipes of his Liberality; and, therefore, in the Statutes of the Hospital, *Caput de Fundatore Hospitali*, Statutes, That on the first Monday of June every year, Thanks be given to GOD in the Gray-Friar's Church, for the charitable Maintenance which the Poor maintained in the Hospital, receive by the Bounty of the Founder; and that the preacher exhort all Men of Ability to follow his Example, to urge the Necessity of good Works for the Testimony of their Faith; and to clear the Doctrine of our Church from the Reproaches of Adversaries, who give us out to be the Impugners of good Works.

The Fundamental Institutions of this Hospital were, at the Desire of the Founder, compil'd by the Reverend Doctor Walter Balcanquhall, Dean of Rochester, who left considerably to it himself.

If GOD Records Bezaleel and Aholiah, two Goldsmiths and Jewellers, Exod. xxxi. for their curious Workmanship in the Tabernacle, we ought certainly to Record a Goldsmith and Jeweller, who not only excell'd in Architecture, Sculpture, and Engraving; but Dedicated a Palace, and Prince's Revenues to the LORD, Psal. cxii. 9. "He hath dispersed, he hath given to the Poor, his Righteousness endureth for ever, his Horn shall be exalted with Honour."

The greatest Part of this stately Edifice is Gothick Work; but the Frontis-piece is adorn'd with stately Pillars of the Corinthian and Dorick Order, with various Groops of Figures, two of which are very curious, a Company of School Boys, in the Habits appointed by the Founder, under the Ferula of their Preceptors, with this Motto, extending to the Face of the Teachers, *Sic vos deus, ut vos eos;* and the other, the Scholars round the Table at Dinner, this Inscription above their Heads, out of the Poet Virgil, *Deus nobis hæc otia fecit.* Above this, the Arms of the Founder; within the Porch above the Entry, in a Nich, the Statute of the Patron, above his Head this Motto, alluding as well to the Building, as to the Builder: *Corporis hæc, Animi est hoc Opus Effigies.*

The Entry of the Chapel beautify'd with Pillars of the Teutonick Order, and a large Bible engraven in Stone, above which is this Inscription.

*Aurifici dederat mihi vis Divina perennem, & facere in Terris, in Cælo & Ferre*

Below an artificial Crown, which supplies the Word *Coronam*, the Sentence being design'd for an Ænigma.

Thus far have I trac'd the Loyalty of the Citizens, and shall proceed no further; but draw a Vail of Silence over the Behaviour of the City of Edinburgh, during the rest of the Reign of this unfortunate Prince. Since, the Crafts hitherto loyal, folded up their Ensign the Banner, or Blue Blanket of the Holy Ghost, when factious Sectaries were triumphant, and Majesty was in Misery, falling a Victim to the Cruelty of then Sectarians, by whose impious Hands he was brought to the Block.

## WORKS BY THE SAME AUTHOR.

RECENTLY PUBLISHED, Price 12s. 6d. (Crown 4to, 1887).

# THE GUILDRY OF EDINBURGH:

## *Is it an Incorporation?*

With INTRODUCTORY REMARKS concerning "GILDS,"
And an APPENDIX.

### BY JAMES COLSTON.

*Edinburgh: Richard Cameron, and other Booksellers.*

## *OPINIONS OF THE PRESS.*

### From the "SATURDAY REVIEW."

THE author of this volume has discussed the origin and history of several Scottish gilds or guilds; but his main object is to prove that the Guildry of Edinburgh is a corporate body. It seems that the Town-Clerk and the Town Council have persistently denied that the Edinburgh Guild has been properly incorporated, and Mr Colston is determined to show to the world that it has. As far back as 1817 this highly-interesting question occupied the attention of a Select Committee of the House of Commons for twenty-four sittings, under the chairmanship of Lord Archibald Hamilton, the second son of the ninth Duke of that name. It was made clear to the Committee that the Guildry of Edinburgh had existed as, and was really a corporation, and that the Dean of Guild and his Council had enjoyed the privilege of admitting members to the same in perpetual succession—a power of co-optation or election which of itself argued the existence of a corporate body. Unluckily the Guild was then at issue with another body— the Town Council—of which the Dean of Guild was a member. The Town Council, if we may believe the statement made by Lord Cockburn in his *Memorials of his own Time*, was a packed body, "silent, mysterious, and irresponsible." It had somehow got control of the funds. It allowed no free discussion. It was under the rule of the Dean of Guild, who paid no attention to the complaints or remonstrances of his Guild brethren, and stoutly refused to call a meeting to consider any proposals of inquiry and reform.

The tide of ill-luck still setting against the Guild, the case was given against them by the Lord Ordinary, Cringletie, who came to the conclusion that the term Guildry applied originally to the merchants of the whole kingdom, and that those of Edinburgh had never been formed into a Corporation. The judgment, which is given at length, and is termed "Copy, Note, and Interlocutor," does not appear to us lucid or conclusive; while to crown the series of mischances the case was never carried to the Inner House. Mr Colston quotes an epigram not very favourable to the judicial character of the Lord Ordinary, which may bear reproduction:—

Necessitie and Cringletie
Tally to a tittle,
Necessitie has nae law,
And Cringletie as little.

This epigram is attributed to John Clerk, known to Scotch lawyers as Lord Eldin. He was the eldest son of John Clerk of that ilk, and the brother of William Clerk, so often mentioned in Lockhart's *Life of Scott*. John Clerk, the elder, having a fervent enthusiasm for antiquities, was often played upon by his eldest son, who, having a great turn for art, used, so Lockhart tells us, "to manufacture mutilated heads, which were buried in the ground," and then, after an accidental discovery, "were received by the Laird as valuable accessories to his museum." The amusing scene in the *Antiquary*, where Edie Ochiltree ridicules the Prætorium of Oldbuck, had its origin in an incident of this kind at the residence of the Clerk family.

Several details regarding the Constitution of Scottish Guilds are likely to be more interesting to antiquaries and scholars than the question whether the judicial decision we have referred to was right or wrong. Mr Colston finds a Danish origin for the term Gilde or Gild. It means first a feast or banquet, and then, by an easy transition, a guild or corporation. Writers on this subject divide guilds into four classes—the family, the religious, the mercantile, and the trades. Scotland was behind England in date in setting up these societies ; and by common consent the first guild was established, with its statutes, at Berwick-on-Tweed. Trade by itself never became a guild in Scotland. There was always, if we can credit Mr Colston, a clear distinction between merchants and tradesmen or craftsmen. And it is easy to understand that the relative privileges of these classes led to much acrimonious discussion and to actions at law. At the peace of 1815, after Harry Dundas had ceased to rule political elections and the affairs of Scotland generally with his rod of iron, there were no less than sixty Royal burghs in Scotland, and in each of these the Town Council chose its own successors. It was owing to the aggression and usurpation of this latter body over the Guilds that the privileges of guild brethren fell into abeyance, and that the Lord Ordinary, acting on imperfect information, ruled them out of existence.

Some fifty pages of this work are taken up with the Guild disbursements from the year 1554 to the middle of the last century. Mr Colston was fully justified in printing them *in extenso*. They appear to have been copies of the original accounts which were laid before Lord Archibald Hamilton's Committee. The Dean and his colleagues discharged functions which are now divided between the Guardians of the poor and the members of divers Benevolent Societies. They relieved decayed burgesses, their wives, bairns, and servants, and "uther poor in-dwellers of the town." There are repeated entries of money, clothes and supplies bestowed on the needy and the sick. Pensions were allotted to the most deserving cases. Funeral charges were defrayed. A preacher of the gospel in the Skinner's Hall received £25 "for several great and weighty reasons" ; an expression which seems to cloak an amiable piece of mild jobbery. One Andrew Sands, who had lately captured a pirate on the high seas, was rewarded with money, and "his offences, which are great, are remitted." This was in 1574. Piracy seems to have been a common offence then, for an embassy or deputation was sent to Queen Elizabeth for remedy and relief. Betty Balingaul was given the sum of £18 on condition of her giving no more trouble to the city, and sums were advanced to various individuals to enable them to emigrate to Ireland, London, and even to Virginia. In the matter of James Foord, merchant, it was very prudently ruled that the sum of £1, 10s. sterling, to defray his expense to London, was not to be paid until he was actually going on board of his ship. The pensions of two women were not unreasonably rescinded ; of one because she married, and the other because she went into hospital. We conclude the extracts by noting the exact sum of £45, 3s. 8d. paid to the surgeons for curing the persons wounded in the "Grass Mercat" on the 14th of April 1736, at the execution of Andrew Wilson. This can only be the occasion when Jock Porteous ordered his men to fire on the mob. And in the very next year we find an entry of £3 paid to "Isoble Gordon, relict of Capt. John Porteous." Readers of Scott and of Lord Stanhope's *History of England* (vol. ii. p. 298) may remember that, in addition to the above trifling relief, the old cook—for that had been Mrs Porteous's original calling—received the sum of £2000 from a fine imposed on the good city of Edinburgh. An extract from the writings of Lord Kames on the Government of the Royal Burghs closes a volume which does credit to the research, judgment, and industry of the author.

## From the "SCOTSMAN."

THIS handsomely appointed volume contains an interesting contribution to that department of literature, the creation of quite modern times, which is made up of works investigating the origin and history of municipal institutions. Only in comparatively recent years has the development of the institutions of free government, apart from the general progress of the State, become a subject of study for others than anti-quarians. Perhaps to Dr Brentano, the learned historian of Guilds and Trade Unions, is due the acknow-ledgment, now general, that light can be shed upon the principles of self-government, and a valuable aid derived in their application to the practical problems of municipal economy from the study of past organisations of craftsmen possessing corporate privileges and peculiar rights as compared with the community at large. Be that as it may, this field of history has of late been extensively and profitably cultivated, and there can be little doubt that such publications as those of the Scottish Burgh Records Society provide material for setting the history of municipal institutions upon a broader basis of fact than that upon which it has hitherto rested. Councillor Colston's work, though similar in subject, and drawing largely upon such sources of information, is of a different kind. It is rather an argument on a set thesis than a historical essay. But the proofs adduced in the course of his discussion, and more particularly the documents printed in his copious Appendix, have a direct bearing upon the municipal history of Edin-burgh, and for this reason the book will be set upon the shelf alongside of the works belonging to the class referred to.

The author explains the nature of the work in describing the circumstances which led to its production. He says :—"The farce annually acted by the Town-Clerk of recording in the minutes of the Town Council that 'there was no incorporation of the Guildry' seemed to be so unnecessary, and so unlikely to lead to any good result, that I thought it might be interesting to the Members of the Council, and the public generally, to have placed before them information on the subject in a handy form." He accordingly addresses himself to the discussion of the question stated on his title page. But before doing so, he sketches in an introductory chapter the history of Gilds upon the Continent, and in this country, from their origin as family gilds down to the form of municipalities, which they have assumed in modern times. These preliminary observations review in broad and general terms the progress of the principles of free, popular, civic administration from the infancy of society to the present day. The work then proceeds to deal with the municipal history of this city. After discussing the evidence as to the original incorporation of the burgh, and explaining its early constitution, it goes on to consider its special subject, the position of the Guildry as a body independent of the municipality and possessing a separate identity. It is shown that the Guildry of Edinburgh originally possessed privileges and exercised functions which are usually characteristic of a corporation. The precise nature of the Guildry after the sixteenth century, however, seems to be lost in obscurity. When in the early part of this present century the question of its constitution and privileges became matter of legal judgment and inquiry by a Special Committee of Parliament, the Court decided against its right to the enjoyment of the privileges it claimed, while the Committee reported in terms inconclusive of the issue raised in these pages. Councillor Colston interprets the Committee's report as favouring the claims of the Guildry, and goes on to say :—

" We need not say that with so divergent opinions as were at that time propounded in Parliament on the one hand, and the Outer House of the Court of Session in Scotland on the other, it becomes us at once to pause and say—

Look here upon this picture and on this.

We have no hesitation whatever in accepting the former, and rejecting the latter. The former was based on a full inquiry, not only in reference to the affairs of Edinburgh and its Guildry, but also after a minute investigation into those of Aberdeen, Dundee, and Dunfermline. The latter can only be described as a hash of special historic or legal extracts, culled at random, 'fearfully and wonderfully' intermixed with a large amount of judicial imagination. It reminds us very much of the statement of the Irishman, who undertook to prove from the New Testament that suicide got encouragement from the sacred canon. When called upon for his proof, it was as follows :—(1) Have you not seen in one place that 'Judas went and hanged himself ?' and (2) Have you not seen in another place—'Go, thou, and do likewise !' Subsequent investigation into the Burgh Records has only tended to strengthen the soundness of the judgment of Committee, while the decision of Lord Cringletie has been found to be inaccurate in history, in antiquarian research, as well as in good logic and in good law."

Accordingly, Councillor Colston does not hesitate to give an affirmative answer to the question propounded by him at the outset of the discussion. Doubts will still exist, however, as to whether he has proved his case. But he has supported it by an argument forcibly stated and based upon a study of recondite authorities. Apart from his considerations on the main question, his pages contain many interesting passages of comment on the state of the Town Council at various periods of its history. In the large Appendix at the end of the work are printed the Laws of the Guild of Berwick, with a translation into English ; selections from the Guildry Records of Aberdeen ; and a long series of extracts from the accounts of the Dean of Guild of Edinburgh. These documents increase the value of the work, and will commend it to the attention of all students of municipal economy.

---

### From the "SCOTTISH LEADER."

In the preface to this volume, Mr Colston explains that he was induced to undertake the investigations, of which it embodies the result, by what he rather sharply stigmatises as "the farce annually acted by the Town-Clerk" of Edinburgh in protesting, when the Lord Dean of Guild takes his seat in the Town Council, on the ground that there is no incorporation of the Guildry," and making a record to that effect in the minutes of the Council. In one sense, no doubt, the protest is a farce, because the Lord Dean of Guild is never deterred by it from exercising all the privileges and powers of a member of the Council. But though the action of the Town-Clerk thus has no practical effect, we are not sure that there is any particular reason for desiring that it should be discontinued. It is a kind of annual memento of a municipal dispute, which is of some importance in the local annals of Edinburgh. That it is not wholly unproductive of results, Mr Colston's volume is itself a tangible proof, because without the Town-Clerk's protest we should not have had the book. Furthermore, while we think Mr Colston has at all events succeeded in amassing a strong body of testimony in support of his contention that the Guildry is not only a corporation, but was incorporated long before the Town Council itself, he also shows that there has been a difference of legal opinion on the subject, and that there is actually a judicial decision—probably not worth much, but never actually reversed—on the other side ; and since this is the case, the Town-Clerk has some show of reason for the contention that his annual protest is a matter of simple official duty.

The real question at issue, as our readers will probably be aware, is not whether the Lord Dean of Guild has a right to a seat in the Council—this he enjoys by prescription—but whether or not he has a right to take that seat without going through the form of election by the Council. In this is, of course, involved the question whether there exists an incorporation of the Guildry—a body which legally, as well as by sufferance or usage, can give to its elected head, the Lord Dean of Guild, the official status he actually enjoys ! In the researches he has made for the settlement of this point, Mr Colston has been led into a line of general inquiry as to the history and position of Guilds throughout Great Britain and Europe, of which he sums up the fruits in some " Introductory Remarks concerning Gilds." The subject is one that has engaged the attention of antiquarians and archæologists for a long time, and it cannot be affirmed that our author throws any new light upon it ; but he brings together within small compass a great number of facts collected from divers sources not ordinarily accessible, and traces very clearly the circumstances of origin of the Mercantile Gilds, the manner in which they assumed the responsibilities of municipal Government, and the rise of the Crafts' Guilds in opposition to their exclusive pretensions. He observes that " the Berwick Gild Statutes are, by common consent, admitted to be the foundation on which civic government in the Royal Burghs of Scotland mainly rested." Coming to the special subject of his work, he cites documents to show that prior to 1469 the Magistracy and Common Council of Edinburgh were practically identical with the governing body of the Gild as defined by the Berwick Statutes. In the year mentioned, however, the Scottish Parliament, " at the instance of the nobility," passed an Act practically destroying freedom of election on the part of the community, for it " provided that no officer or Council should continue longer than one year, and it further enacted that the old Council should choose the new ; and that the new and the old Council together, together with the deacons of crafts, should annually choose all officers pertaining to the town." Meantime, those engaged in the various branches of commerce and crafts in Edinburgh were incorporated by different charters, and an Act of the Scottish Parliament of 1593 confirmed the jurisdiction of the Dean of Guild ; while the Golden Charter, granted by King James VI. to the City of Edinburgh in 1603, sets forth that " we are for ever to have, enjoy, and possess, in the aforesaid town and liberties, a Mercantile Gild, with its court, council, members, jurisdictions, liberties, and privileges belonging to the same ; and in all things as freely as is granted by us and our predecessors to the aforesaid town, or to any other royal free burgh within our kingdom." This Golden Charter, as Mr Colston mentions, confirms twenty-four previous charters. Here, surely, there is a distinct incorporation of the Guildry ; and that it preceded the Town Council as the municipal authority, was formally acknowledged by that body itself in 1778, for, in an " answer " given in the course of an action in the Court of Session, it was explicitly stated that " the Town Council of Edinburgh originally consisted of the Magistrates and Merchants of the Guildry." In 1584, however, the Town Council asserted the right of electing the Dean of Guild and his court, and this was ratified by an Act of the Scottish Parliament in 1593 ; while the Council also acquired the control of the Guildry funds. For more than two hundred years everything like free municipal institutions remained extinct in Scotland, and in Edinburgh, as elsewhere, the Town Council was a self-elected close corporation. In 1817, however, the question as to whether there was not an independent incorporation of the Guildry began to be strongly agitated among the more liberal-minded of the merchant guild brethren of the city. Mr Alexander Henderson, at that time Lord Dean of Guild, made common cause with the Town Council against the agitators. Lord Archibald Hamilton's Committee of the House of Commons reported in 1819, after careful inquiry, that there was " abundant evidence of the original existence of the Guildry of Edinburgh as a corporation," and that it still possessed powers which the committee could not suppose to exist save in a corporation. But an action was raised in the Court of Session to determine the relative position of the Guildry and the corporation, and a decision was given in favour of the latter by the Lord-Ordinary (Cringletie), while the case was unfortunately never carried to the Inner House. . . . . Whether Lord Cringletie's decision was right or wrong, however, the fact remains that there is a judicial award in support of the attitude now taken up by our Town-Clerk, and none on the other side. But the Municipal Reform Act of 1833 gave back to the members of the Guildry the right to elect their own Dean—a claim of which they had been deprived since 1594 ; and thereby it practically admitted their right to be regarded as an incorporation. Mr Colston's contention is that " the Common Council and its popularly elective constitution flowed out of the *Statuta Gildæ*. For the Town Council, therefore to deny the Guildry as having a corporate existence, is like the son lawfully begotten to deny his own paternity ; " and on the whole, he seems to have fairly proved his case.

# THE
# EDINBURGH AND DISTRICT WATER SUPPLY:
## *A Historical Sketch.*

### BY JAMES COLSTON.

Printed for Private Circulation at the request of the EDINBURGH AND DISTRICT WATER TRUSTEES. (Crown 4to, 1890.)

---

### From the "SCOTSMAN," April 28, 1890.

THAN the historian of the Royal High School, no better selection could well have been made to write the history of the Edinburgh Water Supply from the earliest times to the present date. The author has long been identified with the municipal life of the city, and is thus familiar with every phase of its modern affairs ; while his interest in remoter, if perhaps more romantic, events associated with the history of Edinburgh has been shown from time to time, as the fruit of antiquarian researches, by valuable contributions to these columns. It was in the *Scotsman*, too, that the more historical portion of the present handsome volume first appeared, Councillor Colston explaining that his object in so publishing it "was to get the benefit of a wide criticism, wherein I might find information, which I did not at the time possess, for the perfecting of my work. In this I have not been disappointed." With comparatively little official data available bearing upon the earlier history of the water supply, Councillor Colston has been compelled to turn to the history of the period, as it could be gathered from the newspapers of the day, from Parliamentary papers on the subject, and from pamphlets and reports published from time to time. That he has been eminently successful in giving a "bird's-eye view" of the actual state of society and of the water supply, as he has thus been able to gather them from such sources or from the memory of persons who could recount the difficulties and hardships experienced by the householders, at a time when the supply was quite inadequate to the necessities of the population, will be frankly acknowledged by all who have the good fortune to become possessed of one of the four hundred copies to which the "impression" of this finely got-up work is limited. Water, like figures, is not a subject that lends itself to fascinating writing ; but, nevertheless, in sketching its somewhat eventful history in Edinburgh, Councillor Colston has contrived to make it alike attractive and interesting. He begins by tracing the history of the water supply from the time of public or private pump-wells ; recalling the fact, incredible though it may appear in these days, that a proposal was once actually made to have recourse to Duddingston Loch ; and mentioning that it was in 1672 the Town Council first resolved to bring into the city a good water supply from a distance. This was obtained from the Comiston springs. With the growth of the city these springs became insufficient for the requirements of the population—especially during the great drought of 1755—and the Lord Provost and Magistrates next acquired (after much legal contention) springs originating on the estate of Swanston, from which, we are told, "the water was conducted into the city by means of wooden pipes, pieces of which have of late frequently turned up in the process of excavation in several districts of Edinburgh." These wooden pipes, Councillor Colston explains, were removed in 1790, when 7-inch iron pipes took their place, and still exist. In 1789 the Bonaly springs were added to the supply, and two reservoirs were formed. But, with the introduction of the Crawley water (first mooted as the result of the alarming scarcity of water in the autumn of 1810), the Bonaly springs were abandoned, though the reservoirs were afterwards reconstructed as one reservoir, and now form part of the existing water supply. As is well known, the introduction of the Crawley water was due to the incorporation of the Edinburgh Joint-Stock Water Company. The circumstances of that Company's formation, the unlooked-for difficulties it encountered in carrying out one of the most important gravitation works of the period, and the immense relief afforded to the citizens by the introduction of this fresh supply of water, are all succinctly narrated. At the time of the introduction of the Crawley springs, it was thought the supply thus obtained would be sufficient for "several generations ;" but many years did not elapse before the cry was anew raised for more water. What followed upon this renewed agitation—how the Water Company came to be superseded by the Edinburgh and District Water Trustees; how the latter hastily and heed-lessly embarked on the St Mary's Loch project; how that scheme was defeated after one of the bitterest and keenest local and Parliamentary contests of modern times; and how the Moorfoot Water Works came into existence, is sketched with as much candour and impartiality as is almost possible by a writer of contemporary history, with which he has himself, to some extent, been prominently identified. Councillor Colston, in summing up the results of his research and labour of love, says:—

"The practical outcome of the operations of the Trustees has been that, in this year of grace, the domestic water rate is three-halfpence cheaper than it was during the Water Company's term of office, and the trade rate has been reduced one-third, while there has never been any general complaint on the part of the community, such as frequently occurred in former days—that the water supply was inadequate. The Water Trustees were at all times ready to help the neighbouring districts with a good wholesome water supply on the lowest possible terms. The Trust acted on the principle of good old George Heriot—'I distribute cheerfully.' The advantages of the increased water supply which the inhabitants of Edinburgh, Leith, and Portobello now enjoy have been shared in by nearly all the towns and villages and hamlets, as well as mansion-houses and farm-houses, in proximity to Edinburgh and the surrounding districts. . . . . Fortunately for us in the present day, it may be truly remarked that the 'lines have fallen unto us in pleasant places.' And whatever may be said of our supply of bread, we may feel the utmost confidence that at least 'Our water shall be sure.'"

Well and wisely as Councillor Colston has done his work—for he has not only written it judiciously, but printed it admirably—the value of the volume is greatly enhanced by a series of exquisite etchings and wood-engravings illustrative of the letterpress, the list of etchings including Lord Provost Boyd (in his robes of office) and other (present or late) well-known members of the Trust, together with those of deceased engineers who have had to do with the introduction of the more notable of our water schemes.

### From the "SCOTTISH LEADER," April 29, 1890.

COUNCILLOR COLSTON, like a certain well-known figure of modern comedy, "has his faults;" but never-theless he has done yeoman service for Edinburgh in more than one department, and has fully established his right to a place, and not a low place, on the roll of the city worthies. It may be doubted whether, since Mr Duncan M'Laren is dead, there is any other citizen of Edinburgh who possesses so intimate a knowledge as Mr Colston of our municipal history, or of the details of municipal business, during the past quarter of a century; and he has always displayed a commendable willingness to place his knowledge and experience at the service of his fellow-townsmen. The historical sketch of the Edinburgh and District Water Supply which he has just prepared at the request of the trustees is by no means his only contri-bution to the local annals, but it is in some respects the most important and interesting, and the hand-some volume in which it is embodied will, unless we are greatly mistaken, come in course of time to have much value in the eyes of book-collectors. Just at present, however, the worth of the work is mainly practical and utilitarian. The question of the water supply of the district, which has at brief intervals agitated the community for more than two centuries, and which has been the cause of more than one of the bitterest conflicts that ever convulsed the city, is likely before very long to come again to the front. In these circumstances it is well that the public should be furnished with the means of taking a compre-hensive view of the whole subject, and of understanding how and why there arose the dissensions—between citizens who may all be credited with a desire to promote the welfare of the whole community—which have been so costly to Edinburgh in the past. Such means are supplied in Councillor Colston's volume, for it gives a straightforward narrative of every effort made to improve the local water supply for more than four hundred years past. The tone and spirit of the book are entirely praiseworthy. The author, it is notorious, can be on occasion a keen partisan, but no trace of his partisanship is discernible in his pages, even when he is dealing with that angriest of all the water conflicts, the battle over the St Mary's Loch scheme.

From its earliest existence down to the close of the sixteenth century, Edinburgh was exclusively dependent for its water on street and private wells within the city limits, and the supply from these sources was both insufficient, as the city increased in population, and also inevitably became impure. In 1598, the Magistrates sought to relieve the dearth by bringing the waters of the South Loch—which occupied the area now covered by the East and West Meadows—to various places within the walls. But this expedient was merely temporary and wholly insufficient, and in 1621 the Town Council obtained powers from the Scots Parliament to bring in "sweet waters from the country." These powers were not, however, acted upon until 1672, when the water of the Comiston springs was introduced in leaden pipes, and conveyed to five cisterns or wells in different parts of the High Street. In the early years of the eighteenth century further works were executed for increasing the supply from Comiston, under the superintendence of a French engineer named Desagulier and a German contractor named Covey. These works were completed in 1720, and for more than forty years the inhabitants had to be content with the amount of water they provided, though it became increasingly insufficient for their requirements, and the direct supply of water into private houses by service pipes was not dreamt of till many years later. In 1760, after a good deal of litigation with Mr Trotter of Mortonhall, the proprietor, the water of the Swanston springs was brought into the city in wooden pipes, but they only went a very little way in supplementing the existing supply. In 1785 another Act of Parliament was obtained, and two reservoirs constructed at Bonaly. Afterwards they were abandoned, but subsequently converted into a single reservoir, which forms part of the existing system. Twenty years later, the water-famine had once more become of almost annual recurrence, and as the citizens placed no confidence in the unreformed and self-elected Town Council—one of the closest and most corrupt of close corporations—they formed a Joint-Stock Water Company, acquired for a substantial consideration the works and plant of the municipality, and themselves brought in the waters of the Crawley springs, which had been found after research to be the best and largest available supply within what was then considered a reasonable distance.

The benefits conferred on Edinburgh by the undertaking of the Water Company were very real and substantial, but the rapid growth of the city soon made the service inadequate to the needs of the inhabitants. Then followed a prolonged period of strife, in and out of Parliament, during which the company obtained repeated enlargements of its powers for the extension of its undertaking, and had to encounter the rivalry of dissatisfied citizens who were anxious for a still larger water supply, and also complained of the charges and policy of the company which had entire command of the field. Into the details of these struggles—minutely enough related by Councillor Colston—it is unnecessary here to enter, because the Water Company and its privileges have long been things of the past. The sweeping reform of the municipal corporations in 1835 had made the Edinburgh Town Council at last really representative of the inhabitants, and watchful over their interests; and a feeling began to manifest itself that the important function of supplying the city and district with water should be in the hands of a public body. This feeling became intensified through the failure of the company to adopt a bold and liberal policy, and the disposition it showed to rely more on the restriction of waste and the strict regulation of consumption than on the utilisation of new sources for the maintenance of an adequate service. After some preliminary sparring, a Joint Committee of the Town Councils of Edinburgh, Leith, and Portobello was formed in 1868, with a view of instituting a thorough inquiry into the whole subject. A report, prepared by Mr J. W. Stewart, C.E., on the instruction of this joint-committee, contained the first mention of St Mary's Loch as a possible source of an inexhaustible water supply. In the following year a Parliamentary struggle ended in the formation of the Edinburgh and District Water Trust, and the transfer to that body of the undertakings and powers of the Water Company; and in 1870 the Trust began their preparations for getting Parliamentary sanction to the St Mary's Loch scheme. The struggle that followed belongs to recent, if not contemporary, history. It is related by Councillor Colston with commendable impartiality; but his narrative establishes, we think, two facts—that the opposition to the scheme was based on inadequate, and to some extent on fictitious grounds, and ought not to have succeeded; and that it would have been far better for the people of Edinburgh and the surrounding district if this comprehensive project had been adopted. What is now evident is, that no more water can be obtained from the Pentlands; that the supply from the Moorfoots is also fully absorbed; and that, unless the Trust are prepared, in the face of a rapidly increasing population dependent on their under-takings, to confront the possibility of a water dearth in any dry season, they will soon be compelled to devise means for an enlargement of their system. The question which the citizens of Edinburgh will ere long have to consider is, whether they will give or refuse their sanction to a scheme that would ensure an abundant water supply to the district for many generations at least. The party who brought about the defeat of the St Mary's Loch Bill are again showing some signs of activity—doubtless moved by unwillingness to recognise, or allow the community to recognise, the magnitude of the blunder they made in 1871. They are advocating a repetition of the short-sighted policy pursued by the old Water Company in endeavouring to buttress an insufficient service by rigid economy of distribution and consumption. It is sincerely to be hoped that, when the issue is next raised, the ratepayers will not again allow themselves to be misled or befooled. Meanwhile, the study of Councillor Colston's volume may be recommended to citizens of every shade of opinion, as well as to those who have not yet formed any opinion at all. It is not, as we have said, the work of a partisan; but it brings all the essential facts of the case into reasonable compass, and presents them in a very readable form.

### From the "GLASGOW HERALD," May 10, 1890.

REQUESTED more than two years since by the District Water Trustees to write a history of the water supplies of Edinburgh, from the earliest times, ex-Bailie Colston has just sent out the result of his labours in the form of a privately printed quarto volume, not more to be commended for its outside and textual magnificence than for the completeness of its details and the orderly informing manner in which they are submitted to the reader. Fulness, if not perfection, was to be expected, since no one knows the subject better than the ex-Bailie, or took a keener interest in the somewhat bitter strife regarding the more recent supplies or proposed supplies from the Pentlands and Moorfoots, from Crosswood and St Mary's Loch. Before drawing the attention of our readers to the main contents of the book, it may be as well to state at once briefly that the duty of providing water, which was in the hands of the Corporation down to the year 1819, was then by Act of Parliament transferred to the Edinburgh Water Company, a joint-stock undertaking, which at that time received the support and co-operation of the leading citizens of Edinburgh. This continued till 1869, when a public Water Trust was created, which took over all the assets, powers, and privileges of the company. It thus came about that the primitive supply of Provost Drummond's time by men and women "caddies" gave place to something like a regular domestic indoor supply. Long as the leap is between King Hezekiah's watercourse of Gihon and the utilisation of Crawley streams, Mr Colston never flinches in his curious and often interesting history of early water supplies in eastern as well as western countries. But probably the most attractive portion for readers on of as well as within Edinburgh will be the transition period between the origin of the "caddie" and the beginning of supply by gravitation. From Mr Colston's narrative it may be readily gathered that towards the close of last century, Edinburgh, then rapidly extending in the New Town through the erection of the North Bridge, had to bear with much suffering from a deficient water supply. The chief sources were some half-a-dozen public wells—the Cross, the Netherbow or Fountain, otherwise known as The Well; Carrubber's Close, and foot of Canongate. These supplied the city from west to east. For north and south residents depended on the wells at the West Bow, the Cowgate, Potter Row, and the Calton. The supply unhappily was at all times intermittent and never abundant. When water, it is said, was expected, persons of all ages, men and women, boys and girls, had to take up their position in rotation, the rule of the water-line being that, with the exception of the water carriers or "caddies," the supply should be taken strictly in the order in which their respective vessels were placed. An array of vessels might be seen extending in a line for many hundreds of yards from the well. Domestic utensils of all kinds were in use, but the favourite was the wooden "stoup," circular, broad at the bottom, and about twenty-four inches high, a wooden handle, and girded by four iron hoops. With a pair of these and a "girr" round the person to prevent spilling, the water-carrier or domestic servant felt their outfit complete. Nor does Mr Colston fail to record that when wedding presents were not so common or costly as now, a pair of water stoups was frequently given by the groomsman to the bride, and the process of "weetting the stoups" was reckoned to be the last act performed by the bridegroom at a farewell meeting with his bachelor friends. With modern competing schemes and Parliamentary proceedings connected therewith our space will not permit us to deal, filling as they ought to do a very large portion of Mr Colston's admirable volume. But it may be worth while just mentioning that in the present year the domestic water rate levied by the Trustees is three-halfpence less than it was during the Water Company's terms of office ; the trade rate has been reduced a third, while no complaint is made of deficient supply. Mr Colston's beautiful and very deserving volume is profusely illustrated by excellent hologlyphic drawings of Corporation dignitaries, engineers, and localities associated with the Edinburgh and District Water Supply. There are also several character sketches by George Hay and the inimitable Geikie.

---

### From the "SCOTS (now NATIONAL) OBSERVER," May 17, 1890.

THE historiographer of the Edinburgh water supply traces back its annals to the time when good King Hezekiah made a pool and a conduit, and brought water straight down to the City of David. He does not appear to be aware of the circumstance that about the time when he began gathering his material some Hebrew boys, while bathing in the Pool of Siloam, discovered the inscription recording the completion of the original Jerusalem gravitation water supply. For ages after Hezekiah the duty of the local authority of providing an ample supply of wholesome water, and by consequence the practice of bathing and washing among the inhabitants, were sadly neglected, both in Jerusalem and in Edinburgh; and cleanliness was esteemed in inverse ratio to godliness. In the latter city the first awakening of the civic rulers to the need of supplementing the town wells and the South Loch from outside sources seems to have been in 1621, when the magistrates obtained from the Scottish Parliament powers to bring in sweet waters from the country, and to cast "sheuchs and ditches" for conveying it through the intervening lands; and, having got their powers, they waited for fifty-one years before beginning to put them into execution. It was a half-century in which the clash of cold steel and the babble of discordant tongues were more in the ears and thoughts of Edinburgh citizens than the murmur of cleansing waters. The one project to which it gave birth seems to have been a scheme for drawing the city water from Duddingston Loch.

The beginning of improvement may be said to date from the tapping of the Comiston sweet-water springs for the use of the town. Almost unknown to itself, Edinburgh continues to this day to refresh itself from the "Tod's Well" and the "Owl," the "Lapwing" and the "Hare" springs. The original credit of the idea belongs to "Mr John Sinclare, schoolmaster at Leith," the author of *Satan's Invisible World Discovered*, who would seem to have invoked mystical as well as mathematical knowledge in discovering the "well-spring of happiness to the good town," and in setting on foot a work which, as he truly prophesied, "will be extant among the annals and chronicles of the city, of things done from year to year to all generations, which is the glory also of succeeding magistrates." He died, "leaving nothing but an honest name." With the aid of a bribe of the best silk gown that could be bought for a Lady of Comiston, who appears to have held successive lairds in thrall, the Corporation, fifty years later, supplemented its supply from the same quarter. Covey, a German, was the contractor, and the Lord Provost and Council and prominent citizens of the day assembled at the reservoir on the Castle Hill to see him, as master of ceremonies, turn on the new supply. He opened the valve, but no water came. Mounting a fleet horse, he rode to the fountain-head, and finding there no explanation of the mystery, the unhappy man turned rein and fled to Berwick. The hydraulic science of the day had not discovered that in a pipe with undulations air accumulates, and may temporarily impede the flow of water.

Leaping with Councillor Colston another chasm of forty years, we come to 1760, and the introduction of the water from the Swanston springs in rough wooden pipes, which are still from time to time exhumed in and around the city. A hundred years ago the Bonaly springs were collected and added to the draught of cold water which the city drew from the Pentlands. For the next thirty years the national energies were absorbed in the work of foreign fighting, and sanitary progress was paralysed by the burden of taxation and the corruption of unreformed corporations. All the while the thirst of the Scottish capital and the need of purifying the local bodies, in the literal and in the figurative sense, increased with the population. In 1819, nearly two centuries after the date when the town first looked up towards the hills outside for aid, the water management was taken over from the Council by an incorporated company, which straightway set about bringing in a supply that was supposed at the time to be sufficient for an indefinite period to come, by laying hands on the abundant Crawley springs in the Glencorse valley.

This epoch may be regarded as the end of the ancient and the beginning of the modern history of the Edinburgh water supply. Though neither drought nor corruption came suddenly to an end—though both of them are still possibly liable to return—the Crawley water washed away the venerable occupation of the "water-caddie." There are old residenters who remember the water-carriers waiting with stoups and barrels in a long *queue* beside the West Bow and other public wells, and the tottering limbs and strident voices of the "caddies," male and female, as they staggered up the long stairs with the family supplies of the precious liquid. All of them went careering down the stream of time towards oblivion when the new tap was turned on behind the first fold of the Pentlands; and "stoup and gird" and bilged water-keg are as much antiquities as Hezekiah's cistern. But it is a law of modern human nature that the more water people have the more they want. The Water Company had interests of their own that did not always jump on all-fours with the interests of the public. They were tardy in meeting the demand for more to drink, in which Edinburgh was now joined by Leith and the neighbouring towns. They scoured the Pentland Hills in quest of fresh springs and drainage basins, and brought in successively the waters of Bavelaw and Listonshiels, of Harperrig and Colzium. But it was always on compulsion and in answer to loud outcry and complaint; and the ingenuity of their manager was partly expended in devising a movable "constriction" in the water pipes limiting the freedom of the flow, which some day may find its proper place among ancient instruments of torture.

With the stormy times of the formation of the Water Trust and the promotion of the St Mary's Loch scheme, Mr Colston plunges into "contemporary history;" and there comes upon his pen the stress of his self-appointed task of "holding the balance as equally as possible between contending parties"— admittedly a difficult thing when the writer himself has been in the thickest of the fray. It must be said for the Water Trust historian that his pages bear testimony of a striving to be fair, and more, perhaps, ought not to be expected of man. But in telling the story of furious battles carried from the hill-tops to the Council Chamber, from the Council Chamber to the Parliamentary Committee-rooms, and from Parliament to the law courts, there surges up now and then a certain bitter something that gives at least a colour and a flavour of its own to what might have been an insipid record of the promotion of rival water schemes. Not all the multitudinous springs of Pentland, or all the impounded waters of Moorfoot, can wash away the hankering in the minds of certain old Water Trustees to "fesh in the Loch," or can drown the mingled loathing and rage which seizes them at the mention of the redoubtable water-flea—the Daphnia Pulex—that, by devouring their scheme, saved half a million of money to the ratepayers. The progress of the city during the last thirty years in the use and enjoyment of a water supply is set forth by Councillor Colston in a table which shows that while the population provided for has increased by 123,800, the supply for domestic purposes has risen from 20·4 to 28·3 gallons per head a day, and the quantity employed for trade and sanitary purposes from 882,000 gallons to 4,600,000 gallons. The water revenue has nearly doubled, the domestic water-rate has been lowered three-halfpence per £1, and the trade rate has been reduced to one-third of what it was in 1870-71. Also the capital liabilities have been doubled. There will be water quarrels, as there have been ever since the days when the herdsmen of Gerar fought with the herdsmen of Isaac over their respective water rights; there will be blunders, and there may be "pickings" and intrigues. But the citizens, with Mr Colston's history before them, may see reason to congratulate themselves that retrospect and prospect are not worse than they are.

COLSTON AND COMPANY, PRINTERS, EDINBURGH.

THE UNIVERSITY OF MICHIGAN
GRADUATE LIBRARY

DATE DUE

Lightning Source UK Ltd.
Milton Keynes UK
06 November 2010

162493UK00001B/17/P